The New York Times

Crosswords to Keep Your Brain Young

𝔗𝔥𝔢 𝔑𝔢𝔴 𝔜𝔬𝔯𝔨 𝔗𝔦𝔪𝔢𝔰

Crosswords to Keep Your Brain Young

The 6-Step Age-Defying Program

Majid Fotuhi, M.D., Ph.D.

Foreword and Puzzles Edited by Will Shortz

St. Martin's Griffin ⚏ New York

www.stmartins.com

All of the puzzles that appear in this work were originally published in *The New York Times* from January 27, 1994, to July 2, 2004. Copyright © 1994, 1995, 1996, 1997, 1998, 1999, 2000, 2001, 2002, 2003, 2004 by The New York Times Company. All Rights Reserved. Reprinted by permission.

"Vocabulary Notes" was written by Emily Cox and Henry Rathvon.

ISBN-13: 978-0-312-37658-1
ISBN-10: 0-312-37658-8

10 9 8 7 6 5 4 3 2

I dedicate this book to my wife, Bita,
and to our two lovely daughters,
Nora and Maya.

Contents

Foreword

It's been my experience, from years of directing puzzle tournaments and meeting solvers all over the world, that puzzle people tend to be friendlier, happier and healthier than people in general.

Why this should be so, assuming I'm right, isn't clear. Do puzzles make people friendlier, happier and healthier . . . or are naturally friendly, happy, healthy people drawn to puzzles?

Not being a doctor or a psychologist, I have no way to know. But judging from this book by Dr. Majid Fotuhi, one of the world's experts on memory and mental health, I have to think that regular puzzle solving has a positive effect on the brain and one's outlook on life. And having a good brain and a positive outlook is beneficial in many ways.

Dr. Fotuhi has the credentials to write this book. He is the head of the Center for Memory and Brain Health at LifeBridge Health Brain & Spine Institute, and has faculty appointments at Harvard Medical School, Johns Hopkins University and MIT. He is the author of *The Memory Cure* and works closely with the Johns Hopkins Alzheimer's Disease Research Center.

This book contains chapters on how to improve your memory, how to understand and strengthen your brain, and how to generally lead a happier, healthier lifestyle—starting with puzzles.

To jump-start a mental regimen of puzzling, I have included 120 classic *New York Times* crosswords, ranging from easy to hard. As with all activities, it's best to start slow and easy and build up your skills. Whatever your level, do the puzzles you enjoy and skip any you don't. This is supposed to be entertainment, not school.

This book offers two brand-new puzzles about the brain and mental health (puzzles #1 and #107), constructed by Michael Shteyman, who, at age sixteen, was one of the youngest people ever to have a crossword in *The New York Times*. Michael achieved this distinction after immigrating to the United States from St. Petersburg, Russia, less than four years before, and learning

English as a second language. As I write this, he is starting his first year at the University of Maryland School of Medicine.

Michael is an excellent example of a friendly, happy, healthy person, and puzzles have had a strongly positive effect on his life. Perhaps they can make you a happier, healthier person, too.

—Will Shortz

Acknowledgments

Writing this book was one of my most exciting projects during the past four to five years. I feel passionate about educating the public on how to improve their memory and brain health. I am grateful to a dozen friends, colleagues and family members who assisted me in putting together this book and bringing me closer to my goal of helping people ease their worries about Alzheimer's and take the first steps toward a younger and stronger brain.

It was truly an honor for me to have the opportunity to work together with Mr. Will Shortz. I thank Ms. Rudy Miller, the vice president of marketing at Sinai Hospital, for putting me in contact with him and with my editor at St. Martin's Press, Ms. Meredith Mennitt. I was quite impressed by Ms. Mennitt's fund of knowledge and editorial skills as well as her respectful, thoughtful and kind remarks. It was an absolute pleasure to work with her closely, from the first day we discussed the idea for the book on the phone until the day we reviewed the final draft. I also thank Ms. Allison Levine for her critical review of the manuscript. I am fortunate to have the top literary agent in New York; I thank Ms. Anna Ghosh, from Scovil, Chichak, Galen Literary Agency, for her enthusiastic interest in promoting my work.

This book would not have been the same without the crossword puzzles created by my friend Mr. Mike Shteyman. He is a bright medical student who makes the complicated task of creating *New York Times* puzzles appear easy. I thank him for his contribution, especially since he offered to make the puzzles free of charge—"just for the love of it." I also thank my colleagues at Johns Hopkins and Sinai Hospital, especially our department chairman, Dr. Adrian Goldszmidt, and my assistant, Ms. Leslie Hubbard-Bernard.

I have a wonderful, supportive family and thank my parents along with Hamid, Maryam, Vahid, Omid and Saeed. I give my warmest thanks to my brilliant and lovely wife, Bita, for always helping me complete my ambitious projects. She is the best friend, partner and companion imaginable. Finally, I thank my two darling daughters, Nora and Maya, for whom I live.

The New York Times

Crosswords to Keep Your Brain Young

Introduction

The brain has the potential to improve every single day. This three-pound organ in your head is far more complex than today's most sophisticated computers. Yet it can actually be molded by your experiences, lifestyle and level of mental and physical activity.

Brain cells are a lot like muscle cells. Muscles grow stronger and larger with exercise. Similarly, the brain becomes stronger and larger with challenging mental activities. In both cases, the more they are used, the more powerful they get. Just as push-ups tone up biceps and triceps, doing crossword puzzles tones parts of the brain involved in memory, language and solving problems. Yes, you may think of crosswords as just a hobby you enjoy while sipping your morning coffee, but the clever wordplay, vocabulary recall and overall challenge of the *New York Times* crossword puzzle make it an ideal way to flex your mental muscles.

BUILDING A STRONGER BRAIN

Each of the 100 billion cells in the human brain has the capacity to grow new contact points with its neighbors and contribute to a more complex and richer network of interconnections. As such, the brain's capacity is endless. With training, we can learn to perform gymnastics, play the violin, fix a computer, write poetry and ride a horse. When we perform any of these activities, certain parts of our brains literally light up and become more proficient. With continued activity over time, these areas form more connections and become stronger. As the brain cells involved tone up, we find that performing the tasks we initially found challenging is now easy. This is the science behind the concept of "practice makes perfect."

Additionally, the brain has an amazing capacity to adapt and mature due to pressure from the outside world. For example, blind people capable of reading Braille have more highly developed touch sensory receptor parts in their brains than people with normal vision. You, too, can tap into this innate capacity and make your normal brain a stronger working machine.

1

TEACHING OLD DOGS NEW TRICKS

It was once assumed that learning and rapid acquisition of information was limited to children. New studies, however, indicate that indeed old dogs *can* learn new tricks. With adequate stimulation, motivation and a supportive environment, adult brains can also soak up new skills. As more and more baby boomers improve their physical fitness, they realize they can improve the fitness of their brains, too. An increasing number of people in communities across the country are attending stimulating classes and even graduate programs into their 60's and 70's. The notion that older adults need to physically slow down with age was proven wrong decades ago. Now the concept that the elderly need to slow down cognitively is also being thrown out the window. You can keep your brain young, in parallel to keeping your heart and body young, at any age.

When you go to the gym, a personal trainer designs a full-body workout for you. In this book we've prepared a full-brain workout using crosswords each step of the way. We'll focus on boosting your memory and vocabulary skills while exploring the brain's many fascinating functions and examining how stress, diet and exercise can each impact your brain's health and performance.

As you learn to appreciate your brain's boundless potential, you will make improving your brain's health a priority. By the time you finish reading this book, solving the puzzles and incorporating what you've learned into your daily life, your brain will actually become slightly larger, more powerful and healthier than it is now.

ACROSS

1 Part of Poor Richard's Almanack
6 They clear the way
12 Think over, in a way
14 Wearing white after Labor Day, e.g.
15 Rest
16 Border in the court?
17 It might help you take a turn for the better
19 "See ___ care"
20 Bill and Hillary Clinton, e.g.
21 Fast pitch
23 Place to get a C.D.
26 Gaelic tongue
29 Cinnabar, e.g.
30 Emperor under Pope Innocent III
32 Early Surrealist
35 Ten minutes in a laundry, maybe
37 Hangar site
40 Upper arm bones
44 Byron's "___ Walks in Beauty"
45 Pay (up)
47 Nutcases
48 Pilgrim to Mecca
51 Fundamental of philosophy
53 First U.S. pres. to travel in a submarine
54 "You'll have to take my word for it"
59 Informal words of concurrence
60 Attribution
62 Strife
63 A Lennon sister
64 Song from "The Music Man" with the lyric "What words could be saner or truer or plainer"

65 Word that can precede the starts of 17-, 35- and 54-Across and 16-Down

DOWN

1 Band score abbr.
2 Frying medium
3 Designate
4 U.F.O. feature, maybe
5 Minimal effort
6 Commanded
7 They are sorry
8 Yellow spring flower
9 Perspective
10 Stable places
11 Abilene-to-San Antonio dir.
13 Unlikely party animal
14 Cry of disgust
16 Low pressure area
18 Good name for a trial lawyer?
19 Abbr. on a film box
22 Tennis call
24 Columnist Maureen
25 Word repeated in a child's taunt
27 For example
28 Kind of rate in a bank: Abbr.
31 Letters on a Rémy Martin bottle
33 Jewish month
34 San ___, Italy
36 Grp. handling insurance forms
37 Wood for oars
38 "Ugh!"
39 Remedy
41 Egg-laying mammal
42 Composer of the opera "Tancredi"
43 Form of the German "to be"
46 7'6" N.B.A. star
49 Titillating
50 Kindergarten comeback
52 How most computer software is sold
55 No ___ Street
56 Kind of school
57 Salt Lake City daily, briefly, with "the"
58 Learn (of)
59 Year of an Amerigo Vespucci voyage
61 Highest tile value in Scrabble

Michael Shteyman

2

ACROSS

1 First father
5 "Voilà!"
10 Vocalized
14 Characteristic carrier
15 Pass along
16 ". . . with a banjo on my ___"
17 With 59-Across, indication of caring
19 Author Turgenev
20 ___ Deco
21 Prefix with dynamic
22 Football great Favre
23 Indication of larceny
27 Declares
29 "___ Gang"
30 Caustic chemical
31 18-wheeler
32 Test, as ore
34 Indication of detachment
41 Bing, bang or boom
42 Future attorney's hurdle: Abbr.
43 Appropriate
46 U.S. or Can. money
47 Like an oboe's sound
48 Indication of opportunity
53 Plant life
54 Quark's place
55 Place to retire
58 Jazz's Fitzgerald
59 See 17-Across
62 Like some dorms
63 Patronized, as a restaurant
64 Starting from
65 It ebbs and flows
66 Tiny poker stake
67 Having an angle

DOWN

1 Turkish title
2 Does and bucks
3 Object of loathing
4 Debussy's "La ___"
5 True's partner
6 Painter Matisse
7 Rock's ___ John
8 Stadium sound
9 Watch closely
10 Blouse accompanier
11 Show, as plans
12 With precision
13 Tamed
18 Gets some color, as they say
22 Gem mineral
24 Like the Sahara
25 ". . . off ___ the wizard"
26 1950's Communist-hunting grp.
27 Cigarette's end
28 Two-finger sign
32 Leaning
33 Sounds from a librarian
35 Delhi's land
36 It follows 11
37 Butter alternative
38 Computer company's customers
39 Father
40 Where hogs wallow
43 Have an influence on
44 Hoi ___
45 Drove (along)
47 Frolic
49 Give and take?
50 Broadway actress Uta
51 Wharton's "___ Frome"
52 Daft
56 Supply-and-demand subj.
57 Skillful
59 Perform like Salt-N-Pepa
60 Suffix with Manhattan
61 Place for beakers

by Sarah Keller

ACROSS

1 Network with an eye logo
4 Call bad names
10 High school class
14 Santa ___, Calif.
15 Twist-filled Broadway musical?
16 Vito Corleone's creator
17 Bedouin at a major waterway?
20 Not-so-secret secret language
21 Pirate rival
22 Chemical suffix
23 Cracker Jack bonus
25 Cloud's place
26 Rounded lump
29 Harshly criticize
31 Light sailboat at a hotel chain?
39 Indian prince in Mobile?
40 Tales about a 1980's singing group?
41 Actress Garr
42 ___ Flynn Boyle of "The Practice"
43 Tachometer abbr.
46 Performed
47 Magazine revenue source
49 Run for one's wife?
51 Sweetie
56 Gilda Radner character's embodiment?
59 Mideast guns
60 Paparazzo's device
61 In the past
62 Pretzel topper
63 Dissertation
64 "Help!"

DOWN

1 Andy of the comics
2 ___ B'rith
3 Turned state's evidence
4 Like some noses and numerals
5 Overjoy
6 "Veni, vidi, ___"
7 Tennis great Lendl
8 Spy novelist Deighton
9 Pitcher's stat.
10 Luxury resorts
11 Smarts
12 Arkansas's ___ Mountains
13 New Orleans sandwich
18 "Open, sesame!" speaker
19 Set down
23 Japanese floor covering
24 Missouri River city
26 Snatch
27 In ___ land
28 Neighbor of Yemen
29 Chicken
30 Missouri town where Harry Truman was born
32 Actor Aykroyd
33 Noted Italian violinmaker
34 More, in Madrid
35 Body of water between Kazakhstan and Uzbekistan
36 Hindu music form
37 Not fully shut
38 Space shuttle org.
43 Picture puzzle
44 Public square
45 Big gas brand
46 Frost relative
47 Early video game company
48 Famously temperamental singers
50 Future's opposite
51 Arrived
52 Employs
53 School orgs.
54 "Othello" villain
55 God of love
57 Play part
58 When repeated, a trombone sound

by Peter Gordon

5

ACROSS

1 Santa Anna at the Alamo, e.g.
9 "Dixie" composer
15 Judge too highly
16 Like a big grin
17 Start of a comment on a popular adage
18 Cries of pain
19 Papas on the screen
20 "The Mikado" accessories
22 "What was ___ do?"
23 To be, to Bernadette
24 Comment, part 2
27 It may be raw
29 Hind, e.g.
30 C.S.A. state
33 Response to an insult
35 Hammett pooch
39 Comment, part 3
44 Rest area sight
45 Favor one side?
46 Thus far
47 "You betcha!"
51 South Vietnam's Ngo Dinh ___
53 Comment, part 4
57 Certain column
61 Just fine
62 Regarding
63 Hand warmer?
64 Ascended
66 End of the comment
69 Not so remote
70 Bombarding
71 Take stock of
72 Brunch order

DOWN

1 Alamo defender
2 Three-time Wimbledon champ
3 Setting for a famous "Les Misérables" scene
4 Smoothed (out)
5 Seaside raptor
6 Flit about
7 Hot time in Paris
8 Arrange into new lines
9 Star of France
10 Chilled dessert
11 Soft shoe
12 Set of principles
13 Certain sorority woman
14 Iron Mike
21 Oyster's home
24 Circle overhead?
25 Norwegian king
26 Part of Q.E.D.
28 Sigmoid shape
30 They may be crunched in a gym
31 Get prone
32 Usher's offering
34 Bud
36 Short
37 Pipe joint
38 Frick collection
40 45, e.g.
41 Friend of Rover
42 Send forth
43 Bad way to go?
48 Czars' edicts
49 Stair parts
50 Young newt
52 Mark with blotches
53 Zoologist's study
54 Bounds along
55 Podded plants
56 "___ fast!"
58 Like seven Ryan games
59 Marathon, e.g.
60 Conductor Koussevitzky
63 It may be hard or soft
65 Vein find
67 Resistance unit
68 "I'm impressed!"

by Ed Early

ACROSS

1 Diagnostic data, informally
5 "Chitty Chitty Bang Bang" screenwriter
9 Office correspondence
14 Gas's partner: Abbr.
15 1958 Pulitzer winner
16 Rod Stewart's ex
17 Tropical tuber
18 Botch
19 Wrap up
20 It may allow you to make an entrance
22 Single-named supermodel
23 Woody Guthrie's "I Ain't ___ Home"
24 Football Hall-of-Famer Ford
26 Some people pass on them: Abbr.
28 Suffix with verb
29 "___ there?"
33 Update a factory
35 Pipe problem
37 Data
38 Focus of an interplanetary search
42 It may be abstract
43 Remove roughly
44 Took pains
46 In stitches
47 South-of-the-border title: Abbr.
50 Go for the bronze?
51 Some speeding vehicles' destinations, briefly
53 Drive forward
55 Ordination, e.g.
57 Comeback, maybe
61 High hat
62 December 13th, e.g.
63 Act like an ass
64 Like some skies
65 They can get rough
66 "___ cost you!"
67 Halfhearted
68 Vigorous
69 Misses

DOWN

1 "C'mon!"
2 Los ___
3 Dress down
4 Pooh-pooh
5 Ste. Jeanne ___
6 Mexican water
7 One who has it coming?
8 Tennis great who never won Wimbledon
9 Devil dog
10 Ca, Ga or Pa
11 Tubes on a plate
12 Intermittently
13 Aphid's sustenance
21 Spa handout
25 Heretofore
27 Member of the rose family
30 Revealing top
31 Dust Bowl figure
32 No quick reads
34 Feature of the Earth
35 NBC host
36 "American Gigolo" star
38 Part of V.M.I.: Abbr.
39 Stamp and sign, perhaps
40 "Louder!"
41 Cover-up in 47-Down
45 Didn't go straight
47 Ancient military hub
48 Amnesiac's lack
49 Univalent chemical groups
52 Cager's favorite sound
54 Head honcho
56 Actress Polo
58 Guess
59 Navy commando
60 "___ est percipi" (old Latin motto)
61 Yoga class need

by Elizabeth C. Gorski

7

ACROSS
1 Clipper feature
5 "Hogwash!"
10 Coventry cleaner
14 Cousin of a hawk
15 Up the ante
16 Take on
17 Improve one's golf game?
20 Marbles, so to speak
21 Jukebox favorite
22 Barely miss, as the golf cup
25 Hatcher of "Lois & Clark"
26 Grammy-winner Black
27 Meter reading
29 Son of Cain
32 Heads downtown?
34 Sticky stuff
35 Like some noodle dishes
39 Inexperienced golfers?
42 Links rarities
43 Cheer
44 Hardly cheery
45 1996 A.L. rookie of the year
47 Composer's basis
48 Bewildered
52 First name in Polish politics
54 Mach 1 breaker
55 Common fraternity activity
56 Friend of Pooh
58 Taking one's time on the green?
63 Wanton look
64 Olympics broadcaster Jim
65 Mary Kay competitor

66 Little spin
67 Edges (out)
68 Duchamp's movement

DOWN
1 Schuss, e.g.
2 Cause of inflation?
3 Midori on the ice
4 Place for a cap
5 Kind of danish
6 Many a Swift work
7 Playing golf
8 Unhealthy-looking
9 Minute
10 "Relax, bro!"
11 Language from which "thug" is derived
12 Alan of "Gattaca"
13 PlayStation button
18 Horse operas
19 "How'm I doin'?" asker
22 Arthur Murray lesson
23 Father of Esau
24 Noncommittal response
28 Takes off
30 "That's amazing!"
31 Like Vassar, now
33 Beget
35 Brit's "Baloney!"
36 Zeroes (in on)
37 First vice president
38 ___ of Langerhans (pancreas part)

40 Rebellious Turner
41 Become wizened
45 Hemingway's Barnes
46 Rasta's music
48 iPod maker
49 Made level
50 Beyond full
51 Diary bit
53 Potter's buys
56 Trillionth: Prefix
57 Warty hopper
59 Loser to J.F.K.
60 Charlottesville sch.
61 Approval of sorts
62 Genomic matter

by James Rogers

ACROSS

1 Prepares for a bout
6 Easter serving
10 A lot
14 John Lennon's last million-selling single
15 String puller
16 Bibliophile's label
17 Apologize and then some
18 Commercial prefix with bank
19 Big furniture retailer
20 Start of a quip by hockey commentator Don Cherry about his autobiography
22 Pain in the neck
23 Boy-girl
24 "___ So Easy"
26 Muckraker Tarbell
27 Settings for some TV dramas: Abbr.
28 Quip, part 2
32 Dignified
33 Federation
34 Carryall
37 Top
39 Match parts
40 Brightest star in Aquila
43 Pizazz
46 Quip, part 3
48 Top
51 Souvenir from Aruba?
52 English ___
53 "I've had enough"
55 Trash can, perhaps
57 End of the quip
60 Pickable
61 Kind of doctor
62 Countenance
63 ___ even keel
64 Farm cry
65 Upholstery fabric
66 Bump on a branch
67 Hungary's Imre
68 "+" site

DOWN

1 Bandage
2 Uproar
3 Loan payment schedules: Abbr.
4 Bombay royal
5 Ridicule
6 Life's founder
7 Sri Lanka's locale
8 ___ system
9 Connecticut city that's home to ESPN
10 Traffic chart
11 Institute of Nuclear Studies site
12 Mexican tree with large, edible seeds
13 Navigable channels
21 Series of postures, basically
25 Go after
29 Bribe
30 Dunderhead
31 Eye protector
32 Eskimo's catch
34 Not subject to change
35 "Heat" star, 1995
36 Place for shorthand
38 Play-___
41 Out of sorts
42 More than dampens
44 Author Simpson
45 How refunds may be made
47 More work
48 "Gangsta's Paradise" rapper
49 Traitor's name
50 Little one
54 It's opened with a knife
56 Island bird
58 Faction
59 Black

by David J. Kahn

8

ACROSS
1 Stationer's stock
5 Not choppy
9 F.D.R.'s Interior secretary
14 Robert ___ Prewitt ("From Here to Eternity" soldier)
15 Latin trio part
16 Banned blocks
17 Like some D.A.'s
18 Spark plug, so to speak
20 Not straight
22 Brooks
23 Game stickers?
24 Unlit?
26 Show respect, in a way
27 Some barometers
31 ___ Sea (Amu Darya's outlet)
33 Surgeon's wear
35 Down
36 Guitarist Montgomery
37 VCR speed measure: Abbr.
38 Actress Vardalos of "My Big Fat Greek Wedding"
39 Chain reaction facilitator
42 Chop order
43 Way to get one's message across
44 Wishes undone
46 Best dishes, perhaps
47 Peeved
50 ___ National Battlefield in Mississippi
53 Where someone may get a buzz
55 Elliptical comment on local customs
57 "___ Heartache" (#1 country hit for Janie Fricke)
58 Special qualities
59 Rounded end
60 One of the Waltons
61 Sleep on it
62 "It ___ so"
63 Successor of Mao

DOWN
1 Loud bursts
2 "Matter of Fact" columnist
3 Bonnie and Clyde, e.g.
4 Cast off
5 Pick from a deck
6 Billet-doux writer
7 Remote-sensing orbiter
8 Fight site: Abbr.
9 They may come off a shelf
10 Procter & Gamble brand
11 Hanged pirate
12 Modern pentathlete's need
13 Former union mems.
19 Action that may produce a reaction
21 Return addressee?
25 Baseball great Buck
28 Radio wave reflector
29 Early sixth-century year
30 Bean of "The Lord of the Rings"
31 "Stat"
32 Pro ___
34 Cottonwood's cousin
36 Things you want
40 Legendary capital of King Agamemnon
41 Mature insects
42 On-line?
45 Balzac's "___ Double Famille"
48 Biological stain
49 String sound
50 "Jabberwocky" starter
51 "No way"
52 Member of la famille
54 Mass exodus preceder?
56 N.Y. engineering sch.

by Jim Page

ACROSS

1 Theater professionals
8 Suddenly hits
15 Sign-off from there
17 Camper's supply
18 Elegant
19 Twit
20 Full-size
21 ___ monde
22 Olympian Katarina et al.
23 Info
24 Schubert's "The ___-King"
25 "Misery" Oscar winner Bates
26 Order with udon, maybe
27 Fixed beam?
29 Trinity part
30 Harbor vessel
32 Lays to rest
35 Setting for Robert Frost's "A Masque of Mercy"
39 Not used to
40 Eastern Hemisphere island visited by Magellan, 1521
41 Samuel Gompers org.
42 Sack
43 Train
44 Loaded
45 Ashcroft and Reno: Abbr.
46 Acknowledge
47 Acknowledged
48 "Time to go"
51 Phone line?
52 Grumbler
53 Captain portrayer in 1960's TV

DOWN

1 Rustles
2 Some plates
3 Delta team work
4 "The ___ Altarpiece," a painting by . . .
5 . . . Jan van ___
6 Rubbish
7 Translation aid at an opera
8 Number two
9 Former Israeli minister Moshe
10 Sore spot
11 Hart Trophy awarder: Abbr.
12 Grouper, for one
13 Bird: Prefix
14 Profit
16 Like oceanfront houses, often
22 Doesn't take off
23 1993 Sinatra CD
25 S. S. Kresge, today
26 Throw off
28 Real effort
29 Bridge support
31 Refuses to deal with
32 Giving birth
33 Part of the Cenozoic era
34 Ballroom dance
36 Like some voodoo
37 Insult or injury
38 One showing promise?
40 Daybook
43 Grammy's Best Male Jazz Vocalist of 1982–83
44 Pin
46 It may say "DINER"
47 Float's base, maybe
49 1979 nuclear accident site: Abbr.
50 Speedometer letters

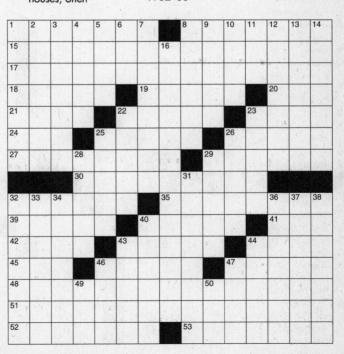

by Manny Nosowsky

ACROSS

1 Subject of a classic hoax
10 Bit of laughter
15 Wye Accord figure
16 Actor Rutger ___ of "Blade Runner"
17 Crayola color retired in 1990
18 Well
19 Like some wills
20 Dylan Thomas's home
21 One went to Washington in 2002
22 High grade
24 ___ grass
25 Some votes
26 Growing business establishment
28 Clattery transports
29 Gunk
30 Like much protective wear
31 Things to stew about
32 Crook
33 More easily attainable
36 Whup
37 Trendy
40 Flower whose blooms open in the late afternoon
42 Red-hot one?
43 Catholic title
44 Get to
45 "Good ___" (1966 Young Rascals hit)
46 Sporting equipment that's strapped to the wrist
48 Gauge
50 Klingon, e.g.

51 The Seneca Chief was the first vessel to travel its entire length
52 Gloria ___, first black president of the Girl Scouts, 1975
53 Review unfairly
54 Subdues, with "down"
55 Full of the devil

DOWN

1 Summer cooler
2 Kind of bomb
3 Bearings
4 Overseas carrier
5 Madison's mate
6 Some votes

7 Region below Hades, in Greek myth
8 Made little sounds
9 Field meeting
10 Prison in a Stephen King novella
11 Winemaking valley
12 One way to think
13 Studio product
14 Met
23 Empty boxes
26 Nation aided by the Truman Doctrine
27 John Logan's "To the Cuckoo," e.g.
29 Shade providers
31 Reason for restrictions

32 Spiny-rayed fishes popular in aquariums
33 Discarded
34 Maker of clippers and trimmers
35 Effort to convince
36 International conference site in Switzerland, 1925
37 Illegal imports
38 Copy
39 Denlike, say
41 Like some boots
42 Back biters
45 Monetary gain
47 French noodle?
49 Crescent shapes

by Patrick Berry

ACROSS

1 Party line?
9 Store sights around Christmas
15 Classified
16 Do a smith's job
17 Distribution
18 Focused
19 Night-before event
20 "Don't bother"
22 Grid positions: Abbr.
23 '54 N.L. home run leader, familiarly
24 Castigates
25 Government center
26 Bear's warning
28 Prefix with meter or sphere
29 "Don't ___ surprised"
30 Rhein showers?
32 Dope
34 American Airlines Arena players
36 Like some relationships
38 Avoid tipping
41 Early Athenian democrat
42 Suffixes with sultan
44 Yank, e.g.
46 Place to get the big picture
47 Tennyson work
48 Tribute of a kind
49 Label in a foreign-language dict.
50 Early king of Serbia
52 Ranger nickname
53 Pretentious
55 Begin to attack
57 Ultimate goal
58 1982 media debut
59 Held
60 Cast again

DOWN

1 Rapid, sweeping strokes
2 Scams
3 Jump
4 Tough
5 50's song syllable
6 "Cats" director Trevor ___
7 One of the Fords
8 Song from the Beatles' "Sgt. Pepper" album
9 Entreaties
10 Divide
11 Düsseldorf direction
12 Question to one who just got in
13 "It's worse than you thought"
14 Begins
21 Long time
25 Edinburgh's locale, in poetry
27 Ape
28 Second in a classical trio
29 Sci. course
31 "___ ne va plus" (roulette call)
33 Amerada ___ (Fortune 500 company)
35 Army of the Potomac leader
36 Nat King Cole's "___ You Love"
37 Like some desserts
39 Its motto is "In God we trust"
40 Gangster film accessories
41 Went (through)
43 Pass
45 Fly-by-night?
47 "___ you!"
50 Unique
51 Recurring marine event
52 ___ effort
54 Cap
56 Utmost

by Rich Norris

ACROSS

1 Health resorts
5 TV series with Hawkeye and Hot Lips
9 Aspirin maker
14 N.Y.S.E. listing
15 Nabisco cookie
16 Miss Doolittle of "My Fair Lady"
17 Large section in an atlas
18 Thumbtack, British-style
20 Error
22 Office message
23 Drunkard
24 Church bell spot
26 Fall in scattered drops, as rain
28 Boot camp reply
30 Not on the road
34 Sheets and pillowcases
37 Sandwich shop
39 Restaurant chain acronym
40 Immediately, after "at"
41 Job title (giving a hint to this puzzle's theme)
42 Gooey ground
43 Hearty drink made with honey
44 Center of a Christmas display
45 Hearty steak
46 Flowering shrub
48 Water at the mouth
50 One-named Irish singer
52 Avenues
56 "What's the ___?"
59 Reps.' foes
61 Bluesman ___ Wolf

62 Well-worn
65 German "a"
66 Art stand
67 Fiction teller
68 R & B/jazz singer James
69 Beach souvenir
70 Stately trees
71 Work station

DOWN

1 Rip-offs
2 Put
3 Get up
4 Seattle landmark
5 Catwalk walkers
6 The "A" in E.T.A.: Abbr.
7 Line made by a 41-Across
8 Inventor Elias and others

9 Marathon runner Joan
10 High school math: Abbr.
11 Puppy sounds
12 Operatic singer Pinza
13 Long, angry complaint
19 Damage
21 Atop
25 Duck down?
27 White-flowered plant
29 Marry again
31 Cincinnati's home
32 Time starting at dawn
33 Fencing rapier
34 ___ Linda, Calif.
35 "Il Trovatore" soprano

36 Interscholastic sports org.
38 Lecherous looks
41 Stuck around
45 Bull in a bullring
47 Ultimate purpose
49 Additional ones
51 Walk
53 Best of the best
54 Salon jobs
55 ___ preview
56 Tableland tribe
57 Iranian "king"
58 Scots Gaelic
60 Flying jib, e.g.
63 Electric fish
64 Hit head-on

by Gregory E. Paul

ONE

Jump-Start Your Memory

Memory is one of the most fascinating functions of the human brain, from children who entertain themselves with memory games and songs to adults who strive to recall the details of an increasingly complex world. A sharp memory is an immensely valuable tool. We all wish we could improve our memory.

LEARNING HOW MEMORY WORKS

You can close your eyes and remember your childhood home. You can remember your own room; you may even remember how many windows there were in your kitchen. You can remember your high school graduation and the first time you had a romantic adventure. With your eyes closed you may vividly remember the taste of your first kiss, the smell of your grandmother's cookies and how you felt the first time you walked into your freshman dorm. You can also recall major historic events such as the day Neil Armstrong walked on the moon or the events of September 11, 2001. Many of you also carry loads of not-so-essential facts and figures like the statistics of your favorite baseball or football players.

It's amazing that so much memory can be crammed into our three-pound brain and then retrieved in the blink of an eye. How we can memorize a phone number and keep it in our head for minutes (short-term memory) and how we can remember so much information from the past (long-term memory) is a puzzle that scientists around the world are struggling to solve.

A few general principles and interesting facts are emerging from the research in the field of memory. For example, we now know that different types of memory are stored in different parts of the brain. Procedural memory, such as learning how to ride a bicycle, is independent of any verbal or language skills and depends heavily on a part of the brain called the cerebellum. Declarative memory, such as learning baseball stats and historic events as well as remembering how to spell a long word or tell a story, is stored in the parts of the brain called the hippocampus and the cortex (see "Anatomy of Learning" box for details).

Emotional memory, the way we remember emotionally charged events in our life, depends heavily on parts of the brain called the limbic system. Certain high-intensity events can have a major impact on our brain and make us remember them for decades. For example, witnessing a heinous accident is something we could never forget. We all remember where we were, what we were doing, and who we were with as the Twin Towers fell on September 11, 2001. While we remember explicit details of conversations we had that day, many of us will not remember what we were doing on September 10 or September 12. Those two days lacked anything emotionally exciting for most of us, so our brains did not find the need to put details of their events in long-term storage.

Emotional memory is stronger than all other forms of memory. We can use this innate ability of the brain to our advantage by adding an emotional tone to seemingly boring details of daily routines that we wish to memorize, like remembering a list of grocery items while shopping. We will show you the tricks toward the end of this chapter.

ANATOMY OF LEARNING

Scientists now know that there are different types of memory and that each type is stored in a different area of the brain, though there is a great deal of overlap. They are now in the process of discovering the molecular intricacies of how brain cells help you remember both recent events from yesterday and distant events from 30 years ago.

A part of our brain called the hippocampus is closely associated with learning and acquiring new facts and information. The hippocampus is composed of two small, banana-shaped structures located on either side of the brain near the ears. These structures light up when you learn a new phone number or a historical fact. Your short-term memory and your ability to follow a discussion require the normal functioning of your hippocampus. This part of the brain, however, is not responsible for your ability to recall distant events like remembering the name of your high school.

Scientists believe that a large layer of cells covering the top surface of the brain is responsible for storing files from our past. This sheet of brain cells, called the cortex, is about 2.5 square feet in size, and to fit inside the brain it's folded in on itself many times.

Consider the memory of your first child's birth: the sounds in the room are stored in one corner of the cortex while the sight of baby's face is kept in a different area. The feeling you had when you held your firstborn is stored in yet a different part. Somehow these bits of information magically come together when you remember that day, and you can describe and vividly feel, hear and imagine all the details as one coherent story.

While it is apparent that different parts of the brain are responsible for storing different types of memory, two questions still plague scientists today: What is the link between the hippocampus and the cortex? Why does only some information get stored in the cortex?

The brain has a system that stores important information and simultaneously deletes unnecessary details. We do not remember who we had lunch with last month, what we wore to work three months ago, or which movie we saw last year, but we do remember the day we started our first job, our meeting with the boss last week, or (in most cases) why our spouse was mad at us last night. Animals, too, have a selective memory. Dogs know the likes and dislikes of people they live with and remember how to attract their attention in order to get better treatment.

One of the interesting new facts about the brain is its ability to store together information that has related meanings. For example, names of animals are grouped together in one corner of the brain while names of kitchen appliances are kept in a different area. The complex details behind this discovery will probably not become clear in our own lifetime. Much of how the brain works remains a mystery.

MEMORY PROBLEMS

Memory problems are commonplace. Many people complain that they cannot recall an individual's name although they can recognize his or her face. It is easier for us to recognize information from a list of possible options than to recall the full information from scratch. This could explain why many students prefer multiple-choice-test questions versus open-ended essays; with multiple-choice, they know the correct answer is there somewhere.

Most people, especially baby boomers, often complain about their memory and wonder if this signals the onset of Alzheimer's disease. More than 90 percent are worrying in vain. One easy way to distinguish between ordinary memory lapses and serious memory loss is to determine how easily a person can recall details with prompting. If you remember when given guidance, then chances are you do not have a serious memory condition. However, should you forget major events and fail to remember things even with hints and suggestions, you should visit a doctor. Your memory problems may be due to low thyroid levels, depression or stress. It's important to remember that memory loss should not be and is not synonymous with the early signs of Alzheimer's disease.

STEP 1: JUMP-START YOUR MEMORY WITH NEW TRICKS

Tricks to improving memory are easy. Anyone can memorize a list of 10 or 20 objects. Here are some helpful hints to boost your memory skills:

1. PAY ATTENTION. There is no substitute for fully focusing on information you are presented in order to remember it later. The more you pay attention, the easier it is to remember later. If I were to ask you to memorize a phone number with the promise that if you could remember it two hours later you would receive $10,000, would you listen carefully when I recite the digits? You would most likely stop your other activities, look at me and wait to hear the number.

2. USE POSITIVE REINFORCEMENT. Every time you do remember a simple fact or set of digits, give yourself a pat on the back. You need to convince yourself that your memory is indeed adequate, if not above average. Positive reinforcement allows you to get excited for the next opportunity to learn something new. For example, if you remember an acquaintance's phone number and your family members notice this outstanding performance, they will see you as a person with a strong memory. Next time an issue arises, they will look to you to recall the details. Knowing that you will be called upon, chances are you will now pay more attention to details.

3. USE YOUR IMAGINATION. If you need to memorize a list of grocery items such as eggs, milk, orange juice, newspaper, meat loaf and shaving cream, you can create a ridiculous story such as this one: Imagine walking to a store that has two huge eggs at its entrance. Vividly see the ten-foot-tall eggs on either side; the better you can imagine it, the higher the chance that you will remember it later. Then picture yourself walking to the store. You accidentally hit one of the eggs, which falls to the ground and knocks over the milk cartons in the store. Vividly picture the milk spilling across the floor, then picture yourself trying to cover and hide the milk with orange juice. Finally, picture the manager arriving and helping you soak up the mess of eggs, milk and orange juice on the ground with newspapers. Imagine the ridiculous sight of newspapers soaked with the milk and orange juice, then picture the cashier coming to your rescue with dozens of absorbent meat loaves! See yourself and the employees tossing the meat loaves on the ground to cover the milk, the orange juice and the newspapers. Finally, you decide you have had enough of this mess, so you get some shaving cream to put on the face of the cashier! The story can go on and on, and you can add at least 20 more items to your list. The funnier and more ridiculous the story, the better your chances of remembering your list. The story must be funny, unusual and dramatic so you can easily tap into your emotional memory.

4. REPEAT. If you have to memorize something, keep repeating it. You learned this at school, and it still remains a helpful way to memorize phone numbers, lists of up to five items and names.

5. MAKE ASSOCIATIONS. To remember people's names, you can make up funny stories about them; to remember what they look like, form an unusual image of them in your head. For example, if you meet someone named Armstrong, imagine that he or she actually turns into a tall person with strong, very muscular arms. The trick is to create a funny picture you can associate with the name of the person in front of you.

6. CONSOLIDATE. When you are given a long set of information, summarize it in your own head and create a brief summary of what you learned. In doing so, you consolidate information in your head as one unit and thus are more likely to remember the overall picture. For example, if someone gives you directions to get to their house, rehearse and summarize what they told you. In doing so, you are repeating information and consolidating it through summarization.

7. MAKE MNEMONICS. Medical students are able to memorize long lists by making up mnemonics. For example, you can remember a list of eggs, milk, orange juice, newspapers, meat loaf and shaving cream as "EMON-meat shaves." If you can find a funny mnemonic, your chances of remembering the list increase.

8. WRITE IT DOWN, ENVISION IT OR SAY IT OUT LOUD. Some people learn better by seeing the information and others remember by hearing it. If you are a visual learner, either write down the information on a piece of paper and look at it or close your eyes and envision the phone number, the name or other information you want to learn. If you are a person who remembers better by listening, repeat the information out loud. Hearing yourself saying it will freeze the information in your brain.

9. LEARN THINGS THE FIRST TIME AROUND. Most people have a tendency to delay memorizing things or avoid it altogether. Especially with learning concepts and instructions, it is best to pay attention and learn things correctly the first time around. Incomplete information will not carry the full picture and will be more challenging to complete later. The brain can hold on to a concept and full picture better than a fragmented list.

10. SHARE THE BURDEN. If you want to memorize names of new people at a party, try a new game. Have your spouse/partner remember first names and you remember last names; then go over the list after you leave the party. In memorizing long lists, give one half to a friend and keep the rest for yourself.

IMPROVING YOUR BRAIN'S ABILITY TO REMEMBER MORE

The parts of the brain involved in learning can be improved and made stronger with training and exercise. Just like playing piano enhances parts of the brain for music and control of finger movements, practicing to memorize longer and longer lists and recalling trivia improves your brain's ability to learn new information more easily.

CROSSWORD CHALLENGE ■

Crossword puzzles are a perfect way to help you tone up those brain cells involved in memory and recall. Each clue requires you to retrieve past knowledge. The more often you do so the faster you'll be able to spit out the answer. Here we have provided some puzzles to get you started in toning up your hippocampus and cortex. The following crosswords also offer you an additional challenge: After you've solved the puzzles you'll be quizzed about certain answers. ■

ACROSS

1 Part of Q.E.D.
5 Contradict
10 "You can say that again!"
14 Mascara site
15 Ain't correct?
16 What the fourth little piggy got
17 Take the bait
18 Construction playthings
20 Like Mickey Mouse
22 Coup ___
23 Metric measure
24 ___ Solo of "Star Wars"
25 Like some suits
31 Houston-based org.
35 Bikini, e.g.
36 Way off
37 Play starter
38 Warmed the bench
39 Author connected to this puzzle's theme
42 Sushi offering
43 Verbal assault
45 Emporium event
46 Michaels of "Saturday Night Live"
48 Literary lioness
49 Shirelles hit of 1962
51 Pathet ___
53 First U.S. color TV maker
54 Taxpayer's dread
57 Part of L.E.D.
62 Crow's-nest instruments
65 Lionel train layout, maybe
66 "Nana" star Anna

67 Fake jewelry
68 Declare "good" or "excellent," say
69 Drops off
70 Grace word
71 Snick and ___

DOWN

1 Alabama county seat named for a European island
2 Wet forecast
3 Italian wine town
4 Teen's hangout, perhaps
5 One who's up
6 Canal of song
7 Do banker's work
8 Publicity
9 When Dijon gets hot
10 Pre-cable need
11 Like some points
12 New Age singer
13 Branch headquarters?
19 Nutritional fig.
21 On ___ (doing well)
24 München mister
25 Café holder
26 Whatsoever
27 Tiny bits
28 Port near Hong Kong
29 Headed for ___ (in imminent trouble)
30 Wasn't afraid
32 Sharp-tongued
33 Pool person
34 Alvin of dance

40 Flying A competitor
41 Opt
44 Bad-mouths
47 Spellbinders
50 Pigmented eye parts
52 Part of A & P: Abbr.
54 Org.
55 Until
56 Turned blue, maybe
57 To be, to Brutus
58 1969 miracle team
59 Terrible man?
60 Hoopster Archibald
61 ___ club
63 Msg. sent to squad cars
64 Mineo of film

by Adam G. Perl

ACROSS

1 Not telling
4 Drink before bed, maybe
9 Belt clip-on
14 Part of a World Cup chant
15 Sister of Terpsichore
16 Squirreled-away item
17 Merkel of old movies
18 Irish symbol
20 Time off, briefly
22 Fuller than full
23 Bottom line
27 Something to draw from
30 ___ fille (French girl)
31 Society Islands island
34 Item in a thimblerig game
37 Fixes, in a way
39 Exorcist's quarry
40 Like a snap decision
44 Lines man?
45 "You've got a deal!"
46 Huge expanse
47 Tastelessly affected
49 Christina of "The Opposite of Sex"
52 Letters at a Nascar race
53 Commodity in the old South
58 Strand in winter, maybe
61 Grenoble's river
62 Informal discussion
67 Subj. of this puzzle's theme
68 Healing plants
69 Leave out, in speech
70 "Get comfy"
71 "Same here"
72 In shape
73 D.D.E.'s W.W. II command

DOWN

1 Opposite of celebrate
2 Carpi connectors
3 Stood for
4 It's the law
5 Palindrome center
6 Nutritional fig.
7 A.B.A. member: Abbr.
8 Impose (on)
9 Munich ___ of 1938
10 One to grow on?
11 Esther Rolle sitcom
12 Hosp. areas
13 12-Down staffers
19 Start angling
21 Basketball Hall of Fame nickname
24 Beach lapper
25 Condos, e.g.
26 Chicken breed
28 Make amends
29 Ship commanded by Pinzón
32 Hubbub
33 Confine, with "in"
34 Jrs.' exams
35 ___ Center
36 Cockpit aid
38 Baseball's Bud
41 Baloney
42 Montana's motto starter
43 1700
48 "The Grapes of Wrath" figure
50 Invented
51 T.G.I.F. part
54 Atlas feature
55 High-strung
56 Go around in circles?
57 "Cool!"
59 1963 role for Liz
60 Big name in petrol
62 "Batman" sound
63 Relative of -let
64 Highway warning
65 "Boy, am ___ trouble!"
66 Lofty lines

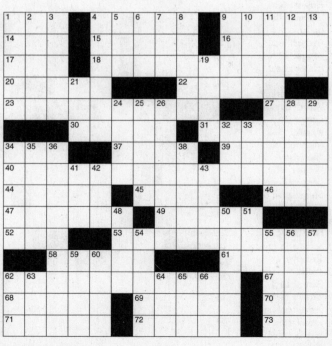

by Brendan Emmett Quigley

ACROSS

1, 5 & 10 Need for 69-, 70- and 71-Across
14 "___ off?"
15 Earthling
16 Vargas Llosa novel "___ Julia and the Scriptwriter"
17 Ye follower
18 Blue dyes
19 Atlases, e.g.: Abbr.
20 Cruelty
22 Hebrew prophet
24 Milk provider
25 P.D. alert
27 Cheated
30 Div. of a former union
31 They have big bills
34 Outside: Prefix
35 Relating to life
36 Philips product
38 Label on many an advertising photo
41 Washington State's Sea-___ Airport
42 Pantywaist
43 Adherent in Iran
44 Work boot feature
46 Clockmaker Terry
47 How some rebukes are made
49 "Life ___ cabaret"
52 Creepy-crawlies
54 38-Down was the second one
55 R.N.'s treatment
56 Rarely
59 Unconcerned retort
61 Kind of bag
63 Period
65 Surrounding light
66 Litigious one
67 "And then again . . ."
68 Desktop marker
69, 70 & 71 What the middle of this puzzle is

DOWN

1 Snares
2 Marriage byproduct
3 Yes-man, perhaps
4 "___ Sleep, for Every Favor" (old hymn)
5 It might be next to a bar of soap
6 Bit of wit
7 Provençal pal
8 "Safe" or "out"
9 Academy graduate
10 ___ Abdel Nasser
11 Unfeeling
12 Place to lay over
13 Skid row ailment
21 Like Britain's Private Eye magazine
23 Antidrug mantra
26 Fit up against
28 Split personalities?
29 Feeble-minded
32 Informal goodbyes
33 Ins have it
35 She played Maude on "Maude"
37 Limo passenger
38 See 54-Across
39 Scottie in the White House
40 Craved
45 Nearly
48 Ted Williams and others
49 Cornell's home
50 Winter Olympics event
51 Broadway opening?
53 Turns
57 Other, in España
58 "Death in Venice" author
60 Antiroyalist, in the Revolution
61 Scolding sound
62 Ja, across the Rhine
64 Vishnu, e.g.

by Patrick Merrell

Clue Quiz: What company made the first color TVs in the United States? (Hint: Puzzle 13, 53-Across)

16

ACROSS

1 Woman in a "Paint Your Wagon" song
6 They may go on park walks
11 Kind of pad
14 Like musical instruments
15 Loose on
16 Violinist Jean-___ Ponty
17 "___ Thief" (1950 movie)
18 Not separate from
20 Mountain goat's perch
21 Site of Churchill College
22 1967 Pulitzer-winning novel by Bernard Malamud
24 Radioactive isotope
25 One who suspends an action, in law
26 ___ Aigner, noted designer of shoes and handbags
27 Romantic verse starter
30 Feller
31 Hand-held entrees
32 ___ city atty.
36 Brando, notably
38 Web-surfing needs, at times
42 Ideals
43 Early 20th-century art movement
44 Marcher's instrument
46 Tough spots
48 No more
49 Essays
50 Pick up
52 Shoe spec.
53 Like typical Georgian woods
54 Council member, maybe
55 Places for sgts.
56 Popeye's creator
57 Procedures: Abbr.

DOWN

1 W.W. II area
2 Collectible for a so-called paileontologist
3 Up
4 Check on
5 Some ballet twosomes
6 Find a job for
7 Fix, as a road
8 Little bit
9 Quintessential news headline
10 Olympics no-no
11 Came home feet first, maybe
12 Overpower in battle
13 Be up to something
19 Red or white
22 Renowned 1939 film setting
23 Site of raw material?
26 Suffix with smack
28 Stinkers
29 Command level: Abbr.
32 With real effort
33 Allowances
34 Duke in "King Henry VI"
35 Skipping syllables
36 Fender benders, e.g.
37 Puts side by side
38 Household expenses
39 Lay out
40 Wears down
41 Solemnity
44 Kentucky college
45 From Nineveh: Abbr.
47 Like "War and Peace"
51 Ambulances' destinations: Abbr.

by Sherry O. Blackard

ACROSS
1 Specialty
16 Her film debut was as Woody Allen's date in "Annie Hall"
17 Food item made with olive oil and spices
18 Place for a duck
19 Give up
20 It's often left hanging
21 Japanese historical period from the 17th to 19th centuries
22 Respectful greeting
24 "Hey!"
25 Donna ___, "Don Giovanni" soprano
28 Hack, e.g.
31 Matters
34 A challenge
38 Bag holders
40 Some primetime TV
41 Ennui
43 Was goatish
44 "The wait is over!"
46 Baseball's Tony or Alejandro
47 Box without a prize
50 Sign in the heart of downtown
53 Lay low
54 Take in
56 30-day mo.
57 Tablet holder
60 1960's pop group named after a phrase from "A Midsummer Night's Dream"
64 Graph point locator
65 Welfare

DOWN
1 "Yeah, right!"
2 Observance
3 Star of "A Summer Place," 1959
4 Trio after @, perhaps
5 Novelist Louise de la Ramée's pen name
6 Delicate
7 Baseball team
8 Marked
9 Gets bigger and bigger
10 Relief pitcher?
11 Lie
12 Class leaders: Abbr.
13 Creepers
14 More than gladdens
15 Plant problem
22 Mariner's worry
23 He wed a White House widow
24 Commandment
25 Broker's file: Abbr.
26 Vessel maker of old
27 Painting type
29 Resort near Beaver Creek
30 "The Oriental Ballet" designer
32 Abrupt ending of a sort
33 Word with state or great
35 Past time
36 Prophet's wish
37 Inspector's employer: Abbr.
39 They clean locks
42 Fed. benefit source
45 Jewish calendar starter
47 Some guard dogs, for short
48 Court position
49 "A Passage to India" woman
51 Food and shelter
52 Nautical pole
54 Circular course
55 Pool site, maybe
57 "___ uncertain actor on the stage" (Shakespearean sonnet start)
58 Drilling grp.
59 Pants part
61 Sing
62 How-___
63 Dundee precip.

by Harvey Estes

Clue Quiz: Who wrote "Death in Venice"? (Hint: Puzzle 15, 58-Down)

ACROSS

1 Put off, as a motion
6 Life stories, for short
10 Poison ivy symptom
14 Trojan War epic
15 As a twosome, musically
16 Initial stake
17 "Norma Rae" director
19 London privies
20 Extra wager
21 Tennis champ Pete
23 The "L" of L.C.D.
25 "___ to break it to you, but . . ."
26 Horticulturist who developed the Shasta daisy
31 Sky color, in Paris
32 Terra ___
33 Noted French Dadaist
37 Was remunerative
41 Princess topper
43 Writer ___ Stanley Gardner
44 1965 Roger Miller hit
48 In the midst of
50 Group of three
51 A truck may go uphill in it
53 "College" member who votes for president
58 Frist's predecessor as Senate majority leader
59 It may follow grade school
61 Ending for buck
62 Tennis score after deuce

63 City in northern France
64 Cut, as wood
65 Dems.' foes
66 Cosmetician Lauder

DOWN

1 Actors Robbins and Allen
2 Jai ___
3 Nest builder
4 After midnight, say
5 Fit to be eaten
6 Drinker's total
7 Dictator Amin
8 Surpass
9 ___ good example
10 2000 Green Party candidate
11 Polar jacket

12 Summer ermine
13 Hermann who wrote "Steppenwolf"
18 ___-do-well
22 City near Fort Lauderdale
24 "-er" or "-ing," e.g.: Abbr.
26 J.F.K.'s successor
27 Ending with sched-
28 Oolong, for one
29 Coal-mining city of West Virginia
30 Hidden means of support?
34 Former N.B.A. star Danny
35 Scott Joplin piece
36 Stick out
38 Spanish gold

39 22-Down's state: Abbr.
40 Nourished
42 Mozambique's locale: Abbr.
44 Be obsequious (to)
45 Connections
46 Ring up?
47 Channel swimmer Gertrude
48 To whom Muslims pray
49 007 player Roger
52 Barely open
54 X's, in Greece
55 Lean slightly
56 Eye amorously
57 Korean leader Syngman ___
60 Light bite

by Alan Arbesfeld

ACROSS

1 Airline to Tel Aviv
5 Soothing spots
9 Pueblo dwelling
14 Broadway Auntie
15 Strait-laced
16 Like a highway
17 Some bargains
20 ___ Sark
21 Make use of
22 Trident feature
23 Sweetie
24 Top rating, perhaps
26 ___ room
28 Diamond ___
29 Not the finest dog
31 Be an agent (for)
33 Dukes and earls
35 Prefix with graphic
37 Punk's pistol
39 Overly ominous
43 Scarsdale, e.g., to New York City
44 Dummy Mortimer
46 "Honor Thy Father" author
49 Part of S.P.C.A.: Abbr.
51 Door sign
52 Maugham's "Cakes and ___"
53 Look over
55 A bartender may run one
57 42-Down scores: Abbr.
58 Ella Fitzgerald specialty
60 "Slippery" tree
62 "___ beaucoup"
64 Reelection toast?
68 Happening
69 Devil's doings
70 Starting from
71 Turn blue, maybe
72 Cincinnati team
73 TV host who wrote "Leading With My Chin"

DOWN

1 C.P.R. expert
2 Where some suits are pressed
3 Be the equivalent of
4 Hit the road
5 More agile
6 In favor
7 "Say it ___ so!"
8 Sling mud at
9 Sitcom extraterrestrial
10 Off one's trolley
11 Tip of Massachusetts
12 Songwriter Taupin
13 Classic Fords
18 Mel of the Polo Grounds
19 Willing to try
23 Patient-care grp.
25 Associate of Gandhi
27 Yale students starting in 1969
30 Not these
32 Jury's makeup
34 Pickling need
36 Helpful
38 Monastery head
40 Compliant one
41 Cry heard in a 2-Down
42 Where Giants and Titans clash
45 Skid row woe
46 Wine expert
47 Dinette set spot
48 Flipped (through)
50 Desert ruminants
54 Bugs bugged him
56 Former Tunisian ruler
59 Cousin of an Obie
61 Pull up stakes
63 "Get ___!"
65 Western native
66 Free (of)
67 Bay area airport letters

by Richard Chisholm

27

20

ACROSS
1 Followers of Tyler and Taylor
6 One-inch pencil, say
9 To boot
13 So out it's in
14 Home to José
15 Place
16 See 48-Across
17 Hurl a barb at
18 Sacred creatures of old
19 Woodworker's own tool?
22 Oxy-5 target
23 Takes off
24 Main lines
26 Boxing Day's mo.
29 Place for a ring
30 Deliver by chute
31 Son of Aphrodite
33 City north of Nancy
35 Trash hauler
38 1990's civil war site
40 Losing purposely
42 Jam producer?
43 Voice mail prompt
45 Use binoculars, say
46 P.T.A. and N.E.A., for two
48 With 16-Across, places to pull over
50 Baseball stat
51 Slain
53 Kansas motto word
55 Cellular ___
56 Apt title for this puzzle
61 Label info
63 Visitor to Cathay
64 Talks nonsense
65 Neutral shade
66 Assist, in a way
67 Concerning
68 Letter opener
69 French possessive
70 They're verboten

DOWN
1 End of shooting
2 Epitaph starter
3 Road to old Rome
4 Llano growth
5 "Already?"
6 Home builder's tool
7 Jimmy Carter's coll.
8 City on the Tigris: Var.
9 Cookbook phrase
10 Cost of a 19th-century composer's work?
11 Brown pigment
12 Gives the boot to
14 Winter Palace throne?
20 Campbell or Judd
21 1964 Anthony Quinn role
25 They may have forks
26 Fam. tree member
27 Switch add-on
28 Undistinguished poet Pound?
32 Le ___ (Buick model)
34 Photo of the Panama Canal, once?
36 Sports stuff
37 Peak near Taormina
39 Aristotle's forte
41 Bunting places
44 Wise counsels
47 Be short with
49 "Iliad" warrior
51 Gave medicine to
52 In reserve
54 ___ acid
57 Soliloquy starter
58 Flush
59 Paradoxical Greek
60 Fast fliers
62 Where It.'s at

by Michael Shteyman

28

ACROSS

1 Instant replay ruling
8 "How's it going?"
15 Stacked
16 Perk for carpoolers
17 Wait on
18 Gastronome
19 Author LeShan
20 One may be spent
22 Got the picture
23 Dr.'s professional magazine
25 Eleven-year-old, e.g.
26 Bank
27 Way around
29 Saucer contents, for short?
30 "That's too bad"
31 Strong holds
33 Fortifies
34 Diagram with signs
36 Echo chamber?
39 Bomb
43 It goes coast-to-coast
44 N.L. city: Abbr.
45 Have another go at
46 It's touched in a touchdown
47 "___ the sea and wind when both contend": "Hamlet"
49 Part of a sentence?
50 W.W. II inits.
51 After a while
53 Genetic letters
54 Jumping-off place
56 "You should listen to me"
58 Source of a lot of talk
59 Come (from)

60 Affirmative for Huckleberry Finn
61 Decided

DOWN

1 "Well done!"
2 How someone might sky-dive for the first time
3 Latino cry
4 Distant cousin
5 Bickering
6 Influence
7 Comment before "Whee!"
8 "___ the fire?"
9 Biker's invitation
10 Keen
11 Letters of concern
12 Link
13 Come apart

14 Half-pints
21 Ignores
24 Scatterbrain
26 A.F.L.-C.I.O. head John J. ___
28 Sticker
30 Face-valued
32 It never rains, but it pours
33 Dim sum sauce
35 Singers
36 Rare time in hell
37 College life
38 Façades
40 Always around
41 New Hampshire product
42 Danced wildly
44 Tabbies' world
47 Rage
48 Amiens is its capital

51 Clytemnestra's mother
52 Trim
55 Popular cooking spray
57 Social worker?

by Manny Nosowsky

ACROSS

1 Got together
9 Family member, affectionately
15 Out of the can
16 Punjab's capital
17 "Barney Miller" set
18 Slips by
19 Dark shape near Orion's Belt
21 Securer in Japanese dress
22 Pullover material
23 Whop
24 Possible sexual harassment
27 Hem but not haw
28 Forklift burden
30 1960's doo-wop group that was a one-hit wonder, with "the"
32 Makes manifest
34 Come out ahead
36 Topsoil of choice
37 San Francisco tourist attraction
41 Trembling with fear
45 Dabblers
46 Delivery person?
48 Santa ___
49 Worker with two-masters
50 Doc who might become a vet?
52 Place
53 Qualifier for an observation
58 Underworld figure
59 Concert run?
60 Mount ___, scene of the Transfiguration
61 Aviator Douglas
62 Early capital of Macedonia
63 Cold sound

DOWN

1 Superb, in British slang
2 Not nude
3 Practical jokes
4 Jobs offerings
5 City near Fort Presque Isle
6 Singer who co-starred in "Joe's Apartment"
7 Corrupting influences
8 Like most flowers
9 Friendship 7 astronaut
10 Enthusiastic write-up
11 Captain for Stubb and Fedallah
12 In self-contained units
13 Holy dignitary
14 Bagel toppers
20 Thick pin
25 August
26 Crib parts
28 Santa ___
29 Japanese noodle dish
31 Kingly honoree
33 Hotel room extra
35 Demand from the House Un-American Activities Committee
37 Paper holder
38 Under control, in a way
39 Transportation cost
40 Circular diagrams
42 Nicholas ___, who wrote "Wiseguy"
43 Popular cuisine
44 Extensive, as a celebration
47 Minuscule unit
50 It's a godsend
51 Old Mercury
54 Kind of dealer
55 Little hoppers
56 Toy label launched in 1969
57 Letters exchanged by employees?

by Patrick Berry

Clue Quiz: What was the title of Bernard Malamud's 1967 Pulitzer Prize–winning novel? (Hint: Puzzle 16, 22-Across)

30

ACROSS

1 Strike from a manuscript
5 Gomer Pyle's org.
9 Larger than extra-large
14 Summit
15 Talk show host Dr. ___
16 Maker of the Legend
17 Mailed
18 Linoleum alternative
19 Amber or umber
20 Joseph Conrad novel
23 Slightly
24 Ballgame spoiler
25 Actress Brigitte
28 Discharge a cannon
29 Make a choice
32 Once more
33 Pitchfork part
34 0 on a phone: Abbr.
35 Balance point
38 In the past
39 Examines closely
40 Carriers of heredity
41 To the ___ degree
42 Spit four-letter words
43 Run in
44 "___ la vie"
45 Matured
46 Neither liberal nor conservative
53 Love, to Pavarotti
54 Comedian Rudner
55 Concerning
56 Stubble remover
57 Yale students
58 Turkey, businesswise
59 Antagonist

60 Religious offshoot
61 Heavy book

DOWN

1 Short run
2 Fencing weapon
3 Melodious Horne
4 Obtain, as a suspect, from another state
5 Ready for the task
6 Typewriter key
7 Not at all spicy
8 Forest gaps
9 Chan of action films
10 Storrs school, for short
11 Stubborn beast
12 Warner ___
13 Paddles

21 Steak cut
22 Not as common
25 Breakfast sizzler
26 Ticket seller
27 Salad dressing style
28 Marching band instruments
29 Share one's views
30 "For ___ sake!"
31 Secret meeting
33 Where Barbies are bought
34 Checking account woe
36 Get more mileage from
37 Be of one mind
42 Crunchy vegetable
43 Horrified

44 Modern encyclopedia medium
45 Storage area
46 Colt's mother
47 One-named supermodel
48 Take a nap
49 Dossier
50 Norway's capital
51 Unit of matter
52 Chucklehead

by Stanley Newman

31

24

ACROSS
1 Speak off the cuff
6 ___ of Commons
11 Govt. property overseer
14 Hotelier Helmsley
15 ___ salts
16 Shoemaker's tool
17 Court filings
19 Microwave, slangily
20 ". . . ___ shall die"
21 Deprived
22 It may be cut in a studio
23 Ice down again
25 ___ Reader (magazine)
27 Some ugly ducklings, so to speak
33 Scottish hillside
36 Mme., in Madrid
37 Fear
38 Spirits
40 Picnic crasher
42 End of many a college major
43 Jobs of limited duration
45 Big part of a dinosaur skeleton
47 "Much" preceder
48 Some athletes in training
51 Fencing need
52 "Stop acting up!"
56 "Roseanne" star
59 Short compositions
62 By way of
63 Eggs, in bio labs
64 Common sight after a burglary
66 Clearasil target
67 "As You Like It" woman
68 Like a sumo wrestler

69 "___ on a Grecian Urn"
70 "Yum!"
71 Commend highly

DOWN
1 ___ nothing
2 Big name in tractors
3 Computer programmer's need
4 "___ New York minute"
5 Sighter of the Pacific Ocean, 1513
6 München "sir"
7 Mayberry boy
8 Beneficial
9 Convertible type
10 CPR pros

11 Surveyor's look
12 Did one-third of a triathlon
13 Gravy Train competitor
18 Passenger safety items
22 Total
24 Ornamental shrub
26 Neighborhood that overlaps part of Greenwich Village
28 Time in history
29 What a plucker may pluck
30 Black, to poets
31 Baltic capital
32 "___ who?"
33 Low pitch?
34 Baby ___
35 Song for Sills

39 "Enough!"
41 Duty
44 Popeye's son
46 Artist Max
49 Asian nut-bearing palms
50 Antique dealer's transaction
53 Turn away
54 Sign of late summer
55 Stand for something?
56 Popular clown
57 Eager
58 Appraise
60 Military group
61 6/6/1944
64 Sept. follower
65 Wane's partner

by Christina Houlihan

Clue Quiz: What city was an early capital of Macedonia? (Hint: Puzzle 22, 62-Across)

ACROSS

1 Much of the back of a baseball card
6 Mac, e.g.
10 Genesis victim
14 Piece of cave art
15 Hawaii County's seat
16 Our Gang pooch
17 Yemeni thieves' hangout?
19 Keen about
20 Jockey Turcotte
21 Wrecker's job
22 Marketing lures
24 Blond hair, hot temper, etc.
26 Pouts
27 Chaucer pilgrim
29 Nebraska river
33 Fine fiddle, for short
36 Musket attachment?
38 Obie or Edgar
39 "Indeed!"
40 Sing-along syllable
41 Racer Luyendyk
42 Strengthens, with "up"
44 Schuss or wedel
45 Dish's partner in flight
46 Disassembler
48 Dwight licked him twice
50 Flinch, say
52 Give power to
56 Greek city-state
59 On vacation
60 Galley tool
61 Eggs order
62 Why the tourist departed for Africa?
65 Actress Ward
66 P.D.Q.
67 Tore to the ground
68 Quotation attribution: Abbr.
69 Shrimpers' gear
70 John of low fame

DOWN

1 Eligible for Mensa
2 Henry VIII's house
3 Fight locale
4 Whip but good
5 Like a revealing skirt, maybe
6 Plug of tobacco
7 Suffix with fact or planet
8 Oldsmobile model
9 Get into shape
10 Actress Zadora visited Samoa's capital?
11 Out of shape
12 Kitchen annex?
13 Thirteen popes
18 Schnozzola
23 Gymnastics coach Karolyi
25 Mideast Olympic marathoner's claim?
26 African mongoose
28 Docs for dachshunds
30 Poi base
31 Rock's Cream, for instance
32 Perfect place
33 "Elephant Boy" boy
34 Some feds
35 Marsh growth
37 Fridge foray
43 "As ___ on TV!"
45 Fred played by Redd
47 Wicker material
49 Hit the road
51 X'd, as a candidate's name
53 Likker
54 Stein contents
55 Chip away at
56 ___ Nostra
57 Place for a cake
58 Move, in the realty biz
59 "So sorry!"
63 Gun moll's gun
64 ___ kwon do

by Fred Piscop

33

ACROSS

1 Pool pull-over
5 Shooters
9 It may let you see a hearing
14 Fawning target
15 Buckets
16 1939 Best Actress role
17 The "T" in Britain's ITV
18 Cause for alarm?
19 Millionairess portrayer in "The Millionairess"
20 Shoots for a salad
23 Poorest
24 Bank acct. info
25 Accident scene arrival, for short
26 Fog
30 Big name in TV journalism
34 Stadiumgoer
35 Mrs. McKinley
36 Approximate number of weeks in a Roman year
37 Rose buds?
44 Spick-and-span, now
45 Vardalos of "My Big Fat Greek Wedding"
46 Global positioning meas.
47 Checks out
52 Sacagawea, for one
55 Like some curves
56 Elated
57 Old newspaper section
58 12/25, e.g.
59 "Coriolanus" setting
60 Mix
61 Quire member
62 Ablutionary vessel
63 Sign of overexertion

DOWN

1 Colossus
2 Dance partner for Fred
3 Husband of Pocahontas
4 One on bended knee, maybe
5 Crisp fabric
6 A thief may go under one
7 Get the better of
8 Measure to take
9 North, for one
10 Really let have it
11 Separate
12 Spear carrier of myth
13 Photographer Goldin
21 Bird's perch
22 "Rubyfruit Jungle" novelist ___ Mae Brown
26 Acronym on a police jacket
27 Card game declaration
28 "The Haj" novelist
29 ESP and such
30 It may be skipped or jumped
31 Frank or Francis
32 Orange coat
33 Inits. on a toothpaste tube
34 Broadcasting overseer: Abbr.
38 Pepsi One's one
39 Up the creek
40 Neighbor of Ger.
41 No typical stock trader
42 Nothing, in Nantes
43 Fashionable pendant
47 Simmering
48 Former New York mayor
49 Orchestra seat
50 Have something at home
51 High-hat
52 Pahlavi, for one
53 Can't take
54 Mean man
55 L.S.A.T. takers

by Alan Arbesfeld

ACROSS

1 "Star Trek: Voyager" captain
8 "Look out!"
15 "You haven't started yet, have you?"
16 "Paradise City" rocker
17 Make a bad entrance?
18 Library collection
19 It may keep you on your toes
20 It gets shelved
21 Ones who are handed sentences: Abbr.
22 First Russian Literature Nobelist
24 Reparteeist
25 Per ___
27 Large red hog with drooping ears
28 Nothin'
29 One way to buy things
31 They're represented by blue
32 Skiffle instrument
33 Prince, e.g.
34 Choreographer Moiseyev
36 Starter course at a Spanish meal
41 Uppity type
42 Library science innovator
43 A head
45 U.S.A.F. E-7, e.g.
46 Like some bonds
47 Common female middle name
48 Nostalgic time
50 Señorita, say
53 Arrivals
54 Perth Amboy is at its mouth
55 Generally speaking
56 Gate-crash
57 Two fins
58 It doesn't include overtime

DOWN

1 Made a painful connection to
2 Common news source
3 Big name in ratings
4 It's known for its tight security
5 Twister's trail
6 Slaving away
7 Thirst
8 Poor soul
9 Unheard-of
10 Scottish poet ___ Ramsay
11 Psychedelic, say
12 By fair means or foul
13 Passwords' partners
14 The euro replaced it
22 Immature one
23 Altdorf is its capital
26 Going-nowhere position, in modern lingo
27 Temperature abbr.
28 Present occasion
30 1921 man-vs.-machine play
31 Burlesque accessory
33 One may bug you
34 Nearby
35 Krupa played for him
36 Gears up
37 Really move
38 Series end, in England
39 Chew the scenery
40 It's heard at some hockey games
41 Vehicle with caterpillar treads
42 Kind of colors
44 "Death of a Naturalist" poet
46 Incurred
49 Ones who make scenes?: Abbr.
50 Superboy's sweetheart
51 Newspaper section, with "the"
52 It may need air
54 Corduroy feature

by Brendan Emmett Quigley

Clue Quiz: What was the name of the dog in the Our Gang movies? (Hint: Puzzle 25, 16-Across)

TWO

Appreciate Your Brain

To make your body stronger, it would not suffice to do just push-ups or sit-ups. You would need an exercise plan to tone up your arms, legs and abdominal muscles, and at the same time improve your cardiac fitness and endurance. The same general principle applies to your brain. In order for you to have a healthier and stronger brain, you need to tone different areas using a targeted plan of action. But first you need to familiarize yourself with how the brain works.

Brain cells are called neurons. Every day, the more than 100 billion neurons in your brain work together through trillions of interconnections in order for you to perform your daily tasks. Because you can accomplish them with ease, you do not always appreciate the complexities involved. Imagine how difficult it would be if you had to build a robot to do even a miniscule fraction of your daily routines. The more you appreciate the many aspects of your brain's abilities, the better you can develop and upgrade them.

TAKING A TOUR OF YOUR BRAIN

To illustrate some of the complicated tasks your brain allows you to perform effortlessly, let us take a tour of your brain as you make your daily drive home from work. First, let us give you some anatomical landmarks. When looking at the brain, you can orient yourself using the cortex. It is the folded sheet of neurons that forms the outer layer of your brain, hiding many pairs of structures deep inside. Neurons throughout the cortex are highly interconnected and account for your cognitive abilities, such as reading, writing, solving puzzles or planning for your weekend activities. Some of the folds in the cortex are prominent and occur in roughly the same place in every brain. They are used as landmarks to subdivide the brain into four different lobes. Now let's begin the tour.

Frontal Lobes

The frontal lobes, located right behind your forehead, control your ability to organize a sequence of movements—as in the right order of steps involved in unlocking, entering and starting the car. If you were to picture your left and right brain hemispheres as two boxing gloves put side by side (in reverse order such that each thumb would face out), then the area from knuckles forward would be considered frontal lobes. Aside from planning your hand and foot movements, the billions of neurons in your frontal lobes also help you with planning your driving behavior. You choose, based on your experience in driving in your own town, to either slow down next to an aggressive driver or to challenge and move ahead of him. You may choose a different style of driving on the busy highways around Los Angeles or on the quiet streets of Beverly Hills. If you notice a truck tailgating behind you, you may decide to pull to the right and be on the safe side. You choose to stop at a stop sign or wait at the red light. All these decisions are formed and executed by your frontal lobes.

Parietal Lobes

The part of your cortex responsible for your sense of orientation in space is called the parietal lobe. The right and left parietal lobes lie behind the frontal lobes, in a space roughly between your temples and the top of your head. The parietal lobe on the right side is particularly essential for your sense of orientation while driving; it allows you to judge the distance of your car from those around you.

As you pass streets and approach your home, you follow an internal brain map of where you are in the city and where you need to be. This instinctive map is also generated by your parietal lobes. If confronted with heavy traffic, you may consider alternate routes that still end at your destination. The parietal lobes even provide you with a subconscious awareness of where you are in your neighborhood, in the city, in the country and on the planet. Parts of your parietal lobes also govern your sense of touch and appreciation of texture; if you feel your set of keys in your pocket, you can tell which key is your car key and which is your house key or your mailbox key.

Your frontal and parietal lobes work closely with each other on most tasks. The neurons in these two lobes coordinate the motions you use to buckle your seat belt without looking at your hands. Your parietal lobe provides you with a sense of the location of your hands in relation to the buckle. Your frontal lobe uses this information to move your hands with the right force and direction to line up the two ends of the buckle and fasten it. Your frontal-parietal team also coordinates your neck, head, hand, foot and eye movements, which allow you to pull out of the parking spot and navigate around the cars without hitting them (in most cases!). Amazingly, your hands on the wheel, your feet on the accelerator and brake, and your head/neck movements function seemingly as one unit.

If you were to design a robot to perform the functions described so far, you would need to build a computer at least the size of your house. However, you have only used about 10 percent of your cortex.

Temporal Lobes

As you drive, you may listen to the radio, read the signs on the streets and think about some of the conversations you had at work. You may (or may not) remember your spouse asking you to stop by the grocery store on the way home. All these tasks depend on the normal functioning of your temporal lobes. These areas (the thumbs in the boxing glove analogy) govern your sense of hearing, language comprehension and memory. Your hippocampus, the banana-shaped structure essential for learning new names, facts and directions, lies on the inner side of the temporal lobe (one in each side).

Occipital Lobes

The occipital lobes reside on the very back part of your brain and control your sense of vision. They enable you to distinguish shapes and forms in the different makes and models of cars on the road, recognize a familiar face among people crossing a street, and distinguish different colors. Your occipital lobes have direct connections with the frontal, parietal and temporal lobes, and they govern your ability to fix your eyes and read an advertisement on a bus as it moves away from you. At least a million calculations per second are needed to do this, since both you and the bus are moving at different speeds in different directions, and yet your eyes need to lock in to the beginning of the sentence and move from left to right (as if you were standing motionless in front of it).

Cerebellum

Tucked under the visual cortex in the occipital lobe, the cerebellum is a separate brain structure of two apple-size lobes, dedicated to the timing of muscles and movements. As you approach your car, the cerebellum has billions of connections with different areas of the cortex in order to monitor and control the more than one hundred different muscles involved in the sequence of motions that place you effortlessly behind the wheel. It orchestrates the exact sequence of motions so that you adjust your posture to grab the door handle and pull your body back just right to open the car door smoothly. As you negotiate your way into the car, your cerebellum works closely with the deeper brain parts for balance to ensure that you do not hit your head or bang your elbows. It takes into account the force of gravity and your body weight and shape, and establishes the exact timing and energy needed for you to push your body into the car.

Limbic Lobes

As you approach your home, you may feel happy about seeing your family, or you may worry about having arguments with them. You may anticipate the joy in hugging your children, or you may dread fixing the broken heater in the basement. All these emotions seem to be the product of activity in fragments of the cortical areas collectively called the limbic lobe. These cortical areas lie deep in the temporal lobe as well as in other areas not seen from the exposed areas of the brain.

In summary, billions of your brain cells carefully work together in an organized manner to complete the thousand ministeps involved to get you from work to home. They are not tired and they do not complain. They help you prepare dinner, interact with your family and catch up on chores around the house. Computer scientists interested in artificial intelligence can only dream of making robots capable of performing a fraction of your daily routines so effortlessly. They can send a shuttle to the moon or Mars, but they can never build a robot that can have a full-time job, drive home and cook dinner.

YOUR BRAIN IN ACTION

Please pick up a pen and draw a clock in the space below. Guess the time without looking at your watch. Draw the hands of the clock to show the time. Below the clock, write your address and phone number.

Here is a list of the many tasks your brain just performed: You were able to smoothly pick up a pen or pencil and effortlessly draw a circle. You remembered what the clock looks like and you could write the numbers inside the circle in an orderly fashion. You also were close in guessing the time. As you drew the hands of a clock, you made several decisions as to the length of each hand and where they needed to point. For example, if the time is 3:25, you know that the long hand of the clock would point to 5 (and not to both 2 and 5). You were able to write your address and phone number with dexterity. You remembered how to spell.

Each component of the functions listed above requires a sophisticated set of calculations, decisions and control. Your healthy brain allowed you to express your dexterity, sense of time, sense of space and ability to execute a predetermined plan, and also to sequence a set of letters to present factual information from memory. Though it may appear easy, drawing a clock and writing are truly difficult; they require billions of healthy neurons to work together in an organized fashion. You may take it for granted that you can perform this task in less than a minute, but patients suffering from Alzheimer's, Parkinson's or a stroke would find the same trivial drawing quite challenging.

STEP 2: APPRECIATE YOUR AMAZING BRAIN

Your cortex is far more sophisticated than the most complex computers on earth. Yet the more amazing fact about your brain is its ability to reshape and improve based on your experiences and your environment. Each inch of cortex can be trained to become even more powerful, thus enabling you to perform and function at a higher level. On a daily basis, you have the opportunity to make your brain a more sophisticated working machine.

You will learn how to achieve this goal in the coming chapters. For now, take a moment to marvel on the amazing capacities of your brain. Think of tasks you complete at work or at home. Make a list of 10 complex functions that you may have taken for granted today.

1. _____

2. _____

3. _____

4. _____

5. _____

6. _____

7. _____

8. _____

9. _____

10. _____

YOUR BRAIN IN LOVE

When you look at someone you love, the thrill occurs first in your brain, not your heart. Parts of your limbic lobe, especially segments in the temporal lobe, light up. Activity in these brain cells in turn stimulates the areas of the brain that regulate hormones. Adrenaline is released and causes your heart to beat faster. You interpret the palpitation you experience in your chest as the love deep in your heart. In reality, the heart muscles have no means to detect feeling or emotions. The aching sensation of a broken heart also originates in your brain, not in your heart.

Many of the neurons in the limbic lobe have a direct link to your hippocampus, where memories are formed. This may explain why events and experiences with a strong emotional component are remembered better. Such memories form easier and last longer because of the privileged and direct access between the hippocampus and those parts of the limbic lobe that govern feelings.

Animals use their emotional memory to survive in nature. A deer that hears gun shots or sees a sibling get wounded by a bullet will remember which areas of the forest to avoid. And a bird pleasantly surprised to find a pile of seeds in your garden will remember where to return the next day.

CROSSWORD CHALLENGE ■

As you will learn in the next chapter, you can tone and improve the function of those brain areas involved in spatial orientation. Magnetic resonance images taken of London taxi drivers' brains actually show that drivers with more experience have even larger hippocampi than those who are new at the job.

You too can learn to expand different corners of your brain involved with spatial orientation. You can try to learn more side streets and shortcuts in your own city. You can also use crossword puzzles. As you complete the next set of crossword puzzles, pay attention and memorize the words in the upper right corner of each puzzle. Visualize them well. After you finish reading the next chapter, ask yourself what the words were. You can also try to memorize the words in the center and lower left (down) corner. You will find yourself paying extra attention as you complete the next set of puzzles; this will be a perfect exercise to tone up your frontal lobes, too. You are now officially starting to stretch and expand your brain! ■

ACROSS

1 Other
5 Ping-Pong table dividers
9 Move like a lion
14 Ponce de ___
15 Mishmash
16 Send, as payment
17 "It is the ___, and Juliet is the sun!"
18 Movers' trucks
19 African antelope
20 Hot movie of 1981?
23 Poker pot starter
24 Head of a flock: Abbr.
25 Get satisfaction for
28 Siren luring sailors to shipwreck
32 Enchantress in Homer
33 Third-place finish
35 Bruin legend Bobby
36 Hot movie of 1974, with "The"?
40 Carmaker Ransom ___ Olds
41 Loony
42 ___ a million
43 Waltzing, say
46 2000 Olympics city
47 Suffix with meth-
48 Big furniture retailer
49 Hot movie of 1966?
56 Permit
57 Just minutes from now
58 Secluded valley
59 Late English princess

60 Run ___ (go wild)
61 Biblical twin who sold his birthright
62 Whom Truman defeated for president
63 Talks one's head off
64 Vermin

DOWN

1 The "E" in P.G.&E.: Abbr.
2 Wife of Jacob
3 Slugger Sammy
4 Beguile
5 "Nay"
6 Gladden
7 Pie containers
8 Nothing special
9 Lean toward
10 Experience again
11 Bradley or Sharif
12 Chianti or Chablis
13 Inc., in England
21 Actress Stevens of 60's TV
22 Displeased look
25 Performed
26 Quartet member
27 Field Marshal Rommel
28 Lane of "Superman"
29 Actress Sophia
30 Baseball Hall-of-Famer Banks
31 Twisted humor
33 Like a bug in a rug
34 Elev.

37 Word with strength or sanctum
38 Entry room
39 Imperil
44 Gangster known as Scarface
45 Sort of
46 They may raise a big stink
48 Macintosh laptop
49 Tennis champ Nastase
50 Cole ___
51 "Oho, dear chap!"
52 ___ cube (popular 60's–70's puzzle)
53 Ingrid's "Casablanca" role
54 Natty
55 Wildebeests
56 Do sums

by Sheldon Benardo

ACROSS

1 Punishment for a child, maybe
5 Ill-gotten gains
9 "The Lord of the Rings" figure
14 Notion
15 Bandleader Puente
16 Land colonized by ancient Greeks
17 Hoops contests since '38
18 "What's gotten ___ you?"
19 Zeal
20 "Just a moment . . ."
23 Pumps for info
24 Sparkler
25 Peter Graves's role on "Mission: Impossible"
28 It may be framed
29 Zealous
33 "You've got mail" co.
34 Martini's partner
36 Reason for not apologizing
37 Some training for a football team
40 100 bucks
41 Kind of checking
42 Albanian money
43 Did groundwork?
44 Ukr., once
45 Uses finger paints, say
47 Homer Simpson outburst
48 Battery liquid
49 Minivacation
57 Existence
58 Figure in academia
59 Anita who sang "And Her Tears Flowed Like Wine"
60 Range maker
61 Oklahoma city
62 French film
63 Angers
64 Jet set jets
65 Brain's site

DOWN

1 Spanish child
2 Norse deity
3 French for 65-Across
4 Land user of yore
5 Affixes with glue
6 Skid row types
7 Abbr. at the top of a memo
8 "Oh!"
9 What to do "for murder" in a Hitchcock film
10 Had on
11 Time ___ half
12 Mexican rivers
13 Subway purchase
21 Verve
22 Penthouse centerfold
25 Nicotine ___
26 "In what way?"
27 Bond on the run?
28 John Jacob ___
29 White House spokesman Fleischer
30 Home in Rome
31 Loafer
32 Office stations
35 Parasols
36 Early arrival, shortly: Var.
38 Cool, 60's-style
39 Falls
44 Ground cover
46 Big Apple mayor who asked "How'm I doin'?"
47 "At the Milliner's" painter
48 Expect
49 Ski lift
50 Prefix with sphere
51 Tabriz money
52 Feminizing suffix
53 Cravings
54 Falco of "The Sopranos"
55 Zola novel
56 Like Easter eggs

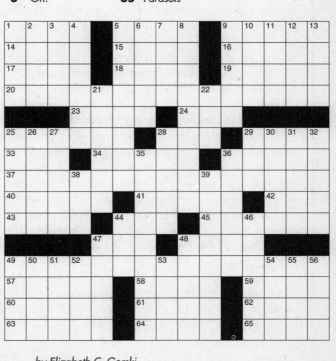

by Elizabeth C. Gorski

APPROACHES FOR DISCOVERING HOW THE BRAIN WORKS

How does your brain control so many different tasks? Neuroscientists have used at least five different approaches to study how the brain controls movements, behavior and the ability to have thoughts and feelings.

One approach is to study patients who have suffered head trauma. For example, one day in 1848 a railroad crew foreman, Phineas Gage, experienced a devastating brain injury. The thirteen-pound, one-inch-thick metal bar he was working with hit a mine and was blown upward. It penetrated his left cheek and eye and flew out through the top of his head. Amazingly, he survived. After the accident, there was a significant change in his behavior. The formerly polite and considerate man had become aggressive, rude and impulsive. He left his wife and children, and many of his friends abandoned him. When he died decades later, his physician examined his brain. He saw that Gage's frontal lobe was seriously damaged. The doctor concluded that frontal lobes must be important for behavioral control. Gage's skull now resides in Harvard Medical School's museum.

Another approach involves studying stroke victims. When a blood vessel becomes occluded, or clotted, the distant brain regions become deprived of oxygen and die. Depending on the brain area affected, different patients would exhibit different symptoms. For example, a patient with damage to the left side of the brain may lose the ability to speak but have no other apparent symptoms. Such observations have increased our understanding of how areas in the left temporal lobe control language.

Similarly, brain tumors have also revealed how the brain works. For example, a growing tumor may impair a patient's ability to navigate the drive home from work, thus suggesting that the affected area, in this case the right parietal lobe, may be important for our sense of orientation. Some surgeons electrically stimulate brain areas with hair-thin electrodes in order to ensure that only the tumor is removed and the normal healthy brain tissue remains intact. During brain stimulations, they may note, for example, that the patient's left thumb is twitching, thus revealing which part of the brain's right hemisphere controls the movement of the thumb.

In the modern era, sophisticated brain-imaging technology has shed light on the mysteries of the brain—while it is in action. Patients or research volunteers are placed inside the machine and asked to solve a puzzle, repeat a number, or think about moving their fingers (without actually moving them). The resulting images, reflecting the degree of blood flow or increased brain activity, reveal how certain areas light up during specific tasks. For example, listening to music would light up the right side of the brain, while listening to the news would light up the left side of the brain.

One of the greatest challenges for the neuroscientists now is to discover how the brain can control a diverse set of actions such as driving a car, listening to music and talking simultaneously. (This is called parallel processing.) Trillions of electrical and chemical reactions and communications among billions of cells are needed for each of these functions on a second-by-second basis, yet you can perform them all at the same time.

ACROSS

1 Airborne toy
6 "The Simpsons" storekeeper
9 Loafers holder
14 Après-ski drink
15 Zip
16 Spacious
17 Native on the Bering Sea
18 Sea lion, e.g.
20 Horseshoer's tool
21 Sports page summary
22 Purge
23 Sinuous swimmer
25 Galley tool
26 Fall off
27 Like the verb "to be"
31 Bigot
32 Society page word
33 "Step ___!"
34 Bamako's land
35 Theater receipts
37 It shouldn't be stuffed
40 Boozehound
41 Smidgens
42 Dundee denial
43 French seaport
45 Food device
47 10K, for one
48 "You stink!"
49 Triangle part: Abbr.
50 CPR giver
51 Tune player
53 Scads
57 "Come to think of it . . ."
59 A-1
60 Pitchfork wielder
61 Actor Billy ___ Williams
62 Emerson piece
63 Excellent viewing spot
64 Comics bark
65 Transmission

DOWN

1 Part of a freight train
2 ___ nut (caffeine source)
3 Boardwalk treats
4 False top
5 Chow down
6 Zoo animals
7 Naval attire
8 Commotion
9 One-named singer from Nigeria
10 Pinafore letters
11 Organ transplants, e.g.
12 "Seinfeld" pal
13 Tree of the maple family
19 Blunder
21 Meal-to-go
24 Self-interested one
26 Mural site
27 Correspondence collector
28 Antique auto
29 Like a mirror
30 Get prone
31 W.W. II U.S. admiral nicknamed "Bull"
34 Miniature auto brand
36 It may be blown
37 Life story, in brief
38 Chinese "path"
39 Filmdom's Rocky, e.g.
41 Range part
43 Classic item in size comparisons
44 Any of several Egyptian kings
45 Spanish inn
46 Meager
48 Florida N.F.L.er
51 Become soft
52 Staff leader
54 Actress Kudrow
55 Mullah ___, former Afghan leader
56 Place for playthings
58 River inlet
59 Hard throw, in baseball

by Ron O'Hair

ACROSS

1 "All I ___ Do" (Sheryl Crow song)
6 Singer in Bob Dylan's Rolling Thunder Revue
10 Clinches
14 Afghan, e.g.
15 Director Wertmuller
16 Clammy
17 Number one assistant, strictly speaking?
20 Some degree
21 Posted
22 Orwell's "Animal Farm," e.g.
23 Lbs. and ozs.
25 Pain
27 Instruction for casual dress
28 Going around a clock every minute?
31 Sheikdom of song
32 Regarded guardedly
33 Enlivens
35 Shrimp dish
41 Bric-a-___
45 Diamond situation after a single hit
46 Nonchalant gait?
51 Trap
52 Hubbubs
53 Without limit
54 Doo-wop hits, e.g.
56 Has markers out
58 Cleveland ___, O.
60 Where farm workers take a dip?
63 Indigo plant
64 Chip in
65 Place for a hawk
66 Burns and Allen: Abbr.
67 Doldrums, for one
68 "Texaco Star Theater" star

DOWN

1 Tip off
2 So to speak
3 Second half of a doubleheader
4 "No way"
5 Aardvark's prey
6 "A Streetcar Named Desire" role
7 Is of value, slangily
8 Eliminate
9 Eliminates by remote control
10 Words of agreement
11 Per ___
12 Chef Lagasse
13 Wild time
18 Cattle rancher's unit
19 Called
24 Sad sounds
26 Suffix with ethyl-
28 Weaken
29 School situated at Washington Sq.
30 Person with a practice: Abbr.
34 Alley org.
36 Bunko game
37 "The King and I" character
38 Hamburg honorific
39 Barbie feature, at times
40 Like Mahler's Symphony No. 4
42 Carrier of genetic info
43 Expand
44 Packed
46 Reading e-mail, e.g.
47 Movie technique
48 Gimcrackery
49 Take note of
50 Exploits
51 TV room features
55 Only make-believe
57 Poke holes in
59 "Peter Pan" pirate
61 Pitch ___-hitter
62 Riddle-me-___

by Manny Nosowsky

49

ACROSS

1 Old-fashioned outburst
5 ". . . to your beauteous blessings ___ curse": Shak.
9 Soul/pop singer Bryson
14 Admonition to a noisy child
17 Big bang creator
18 Places for seals
19 Mar, in a way
20 It may be spoiled
21 1988 Wimbledon champ
24 Record holders
29 Arena arrangement
30 Country name from 1971–97
31 Elimination
32 Frights to look at
33 Like some notebook paper
34 ___ James, who sang "Your Cheatin' Heart"
35 ___ diet
36 Debtor's woe
37 Grabber
38 Like belly-dancing
40 Disconcerting
41 Book before Neh.
42 1970's–80's sitcom guy, with "the"
43 Time piece?
51 Its characters are drawn
52 W.W. II hero who later had a successful career in politics

53 Final defensive effort
54 Suffix with electro-
55 Buds

DOWN

1 Spanish pronoun
2 Word with crazy or guide
3 "That's ___!"
4 Strippers
5 Temporary
6 Clear à la the Pied Piper
7 "Runaround Sue" singer
8 Winemaking region
9 Dirty
10 Chemist's extracting solvent

11 Mideast port
12 Distort
13 Mint stack
15 Some strong oxidizers
16 "___ Park" (2001 whodunit)
21 Character
22 "Cheers" role
23 Ushered in
24 Diamond stat
25 Is positioned
26 Potential water contaminator
27 Never seem to end
28 Kind of operation
30 Language related to Xhosa
33 1942 Abbott and Costello film
34 "Give this some flair!"

36 Codger
37 Hindu belief
39 Gobs
40 Go hunting
42 Side
43 Flashy car accessories
44 Without ___ (daringly)
45 "Face/Off" actress Gershon
46 Dickens orphan
47 Draining effect?
48 It may be decaffeinated
49 Hang out
50 Hydrocarbon suffixes

by Michael Shteyman

ACROSS

1 Goldsmith and others
9 Half of a 70's–80's pop duo
14 Affect
15 Widespread dissatisfaction
16 Percentage interest on a C.D., e.g.
17 Almost until
18 1978 cult film directed by David Lynch
20 Derby projection
21 Good laugh
22 Spanish constructions
24 Org. with a caduceus logo
25 Hydros : England :: ___ : U.S.
27 Lens used for close-ups
28 Fund-raising grp.
29 Alongside
33 Pitched, say
36 Answers (for)
37 Kind of affair
41 Slushy seller on "The Simpsons"
42 Christmas visitor, maybe
43 It's hard-hitting
47 Free
48 Expressions with colons
50 Casual denial
51 Picker-upper?
53 "Wings on My Feet" autobiographer
56 Woodwinds member
58 Frequent collaborator with Miles Davis
59 Conspicuous consumption?
60 Entree whose ingredients may vary greatly
61 Out of humor
62 It encourages mold growth

DOWN

1 Centers of learning in the Dark Ages
2 Show angry excitement
3 Tomoyuki ___, producer of "Godzilla"
4 Exasperates
5 "That'd be fine"
6 Disjointly
7 Away
8 Receive disdainfully
9 What I might mean?
10 ___ League
11 Diamondback reptile
12 Repairman's offering
13 Food processors
15 Have too little
19 Mosque entranceway
23 Rather, slangily
26 Bustle
30 Walking ___
31 They're flexible
32 Grimm villain
33 Like peanut gallery seats
34 Not beyond redemption
35 Painstaking
38 High man
39 Tlaloc, to the Aztecs
40 Where "Uncommon valor was a common virtue": Nimitz
44 Natural
45 Big Easy team
46 Important papers
49 New England town name that means "peace" in Hebrew
52 Skinny
54 It's sometimes called for
55 Square
57 One with a cover

by Patrick Berry

34

ACROSS
1 Noted dairy line
8 Spin
15 Forever, seemingly
16 Italian city on its own gulf
17 Freight unit
18 Passionate
19 English mathematician Lovelace
20 Wraps (up)
22 Argentine province ___ Ríos
23 Exposure
25 Professor Borg in Bergman's "Wild Strawberries"
27 Scores, in a sense
29 Certain school
30 After-tax amount
32 Relative of a weasel
34 Drive
35 & 36 Rhinologist's study
38 Referential abbr.
40 60's demonstration target
43 Uninjured
45 Knife brand
49 Be unnatural
52 Dublin's ___ O'More Bridge
53 Getting on
54 "The Time Machine" race
55 ". . . ___ but the wind": Byron
56 End of ___
58 Personification of a gentle wind, in Greek myth
60 Trading place
61 It often involves geometric patterns
63 Ignoble digs
65 "Tragedy" pop group, with "the"
66 Prayer, at times
67 Supplementary material
68 Moving aids

DOWN
1 Racers
2 Losing
3 State on the Gulf of Mexico
4 LP insert
5 A wedding requires two of them
6 Snap
7 Was connected
8 Capt.'s guess
9 Celebrity
10 Award at Cannes
11 Not the first
12 Traveling (around)
13 Duration
14 Major U.S. Spanish-language daily
21 1974 Peace Prize recipient
24 Marco Polo associate
26 Popular TV co-host
28 Spot
31 High ball
33 Common
37 With 44-Down, a 1974 Al Green hit
39 Scurry
40 Spring for refreshments
41 Saccharine
42 Wasn't liberal
44 See 37-Down
46 Wrangler
47 Promo, of a sort
48 Chesapeake Bay products
50 Tense
51 Capital near the Adriatic Sea
57 Didn't just pass
59 Some ranchers drive them: Abbr.
61 Professional org. since 1878
62 She-bear: Sp.
64 In

by Rich Norris

52

ACROSS

1 Rand McNally offering
6 Señor's emphatic yes
10 Poker stake
14 It's rubbed on a cue tip
15 Garden with forbidden fruit
16 "Gone With the Wind" plantation
17 Indoor antenna
19 Egyptian goddess
20 UFO crew
21 Charged particle
22 Sneaker
24 Swan song
25 "Jelly's Last Jam" dancer Gregory ___
26 Conductor of a sham trial
31 Ramadas and such
32 Spigot
33 Pooped out
35 "Mazel ___!"
36 Zoo bosses
39 A's opposite, in England
40 Former veep Agnew
42 Extra-wide, at the shoe store
43 Sorrows' opposites
44 Sellers in stalls
48 Mattress supports
49 Sizable sandwich
50 On the ___ (preparing for battle)
53 Poet's "eternally"
54 Mai ___ cocktail
57 Skin soother
58 Inedible mushrooms
61 The "D" in CD
62 Jane Austen classic
63 Paper size
64 Editor's "let it stand"
65 Paper purchase
66 Clear the boards

DOWN

1 Good-size field
2 "How 'bout ___?!"
3 Chem classes
4 Vatican vestment
5 Downhiller's sport
6 Witnessed
7 Actress Lupino
8 Italian film director Leone
9 On the same wavelength
10 Under debate
11 Ogden who wrote light verse
12 Duet plus one
13 Simplicity
18 So far
23 Cat chat
24 U.S.N.A. grad
25 What the starts of 17-, 26-, 44- and 58-Across all are
26 Big name in book publishing
27 Blacksmith's block
28 Sally Field's "Norma ___"
29 Gillette product
30 Deuce beaters
31 "___ show time!"
34 Football gains: Abbr.
36 Furry marsupial
37 Comics shriek
38 ___ Peanut Butter Cups
41 Look up to
43 One of the Bushes
45 Mean something
46 Where telecommuters work
47 Terrapin, e.g.
50 Rolls of bills
51 Hit the ground
52 Flower for Valentine's Day
53 Red-wrapped Dutch cheese
54 Roman robe
55 Word of woe
56 Castaway's locale
59 Doc bloc: Abbr.
60 "___ the ramparts . . ."

by Nancy Salomon and Harvey Estes

ACROSS

1 Hefty volume
5 Utah city
9 Hammett sleuth
14 About half of binary coding
15 Zilch
16 Noncitizen
17 God wounded in the Trojan War
18 Observed
19 Fox comedy series
20 "Hurry up!" to a person putting on a jacket?
23 French fine
24 "Timecop" actress
28 "Car Talk" airer
29 "Last one ___ a rotten egg!"
32 Short sock
33 Beyond tipsy
35 A Chaplin
36 "Hurry up!" to a person sharpening a pencil?
40 Affright
41 Peyote
42 Guinea pigs and kin
45 Under the weather
46 Attorneys' org.
49 Approached stealthily
51 Military commando
53 "Hurry up!" to a person assigning spies?
56 Island northwest of Oahu
59 Designer Gernreich
60 To be, in Tours
61 ___ fours (crawling)
62 Poker declaration

63 Cold-shoulder
64 Hostess Mesta
65 Singer k. d. ___
66 London gallery

DOWN

1 Without exception
2 Highway entry
3 More sheepish
4 Ruhr city
5 Tither's amount
6 Tanners catch them
7 Perfect place
8 Palindromic title
9 Far East boat
10 Hasbro division
11 Helping hand
12 L.A.P.D. investigator
13 Ltr. holder

21 Dimwit
22 Zadora of "Butterfly"
25 Baseball's Moises
26 Monthly bill, for many
27 ___ loss for words
30 Gossip topic
31 Monica of tennis
33 Suburban shopping area
34 Lucy's guy
36 PRNDL pick
37 Gutter site
38 Adding up, as interest
39 Senegal's capital
40 TV watchdog: Abbr.
43 Prima ballerina
44 Isuzu Rodeo, e.g.
46 Dame of mystery writing

47 Lebanon's capital
48 Actress Dahl
50 Danger
52 Bikini experiment, for short
54 Arizona city
55 Chief Norse god
56 Keystone lawman
57 Hydrocarbon suffix
58 Former Mideast alliance

by Myles Callum

ACROSS

1 It's a no-no
6 Up for it
10 Hook attachment
14 Shia's deity
15 Letter-shaped beam
16 Long ago
17 Colorful food fish
18 Kid around
19 Mix up
20 Deeply hurt
23 Benevolent fellow
25 Poem of exaltation
26 Quitter's cry
27 Abs strengtheners
29 Big bash
32 Partner of poivre
33 Ark complement
34 Checks for errors
36 Ramadan observance
41 Be testy with
42 Pride member
44 Little terror
47 Genesis garden
48 Attached, in a way
50 Racial equality org.
52 Whale group
53 Suffix with butyl
54 Gulliver's creator
59 Mineralogists' samples
60 Met solo
61 Game played on a wall
64 Scot's attire
65 Took a turn
66 Like leprechauns
67 To be, to Brutus
68 Scots' turndowns
69 Conical dwelling

DOWN

1 "___ Te Ching"
2 Yodeler's setting
3 Semiformal
4 Pearl Harbor site
5 "Come on, that's enough!"
6 Doll for boys
7 Help in wrongdoing
8 Kind of note
9 Art Deco notable
10 Petty officer
11 Class clown's doings
12 Yule tree hanging
13 Pulitzer winner Studs
21 N.F.L. six-pointers
22 Drink heartily
23 "I know what you're thinking" ability
24 Fish story teller
28 www addresses
29 Wordless "Ouch!"
30 Summer month, in Paris
31 Rock's ___ Lobos
34 Sherlock Holmes prop
35 Red tag event
37 Klutzy
38 ___ about (rove)
39 Excursion diversion
40 Cel character
43 S.F.-to-Spokane direction
44 Bit of humor most people can't get
45 Native New Zealanders
46 Discussion groups
48 Wrecker's job
49 "Finally finished!"
51 Social stratum
52 Jr.-year exams
55 Goldie of "Laugh-In"
56 General vicinity
57 Punch-in time for many
58 MetroCard cost
62 "The Waste Land" monogram
63 ___-crab soup

by Norma Johnson

38

ACROSS

1 No-loss, no-gain situation
5 Modeled
9 Bleed for
13 Sermon's conclusion?
14 Lost
15 Chocolate source
16 A man's "better half"
18 Ivy League school, familiarly
19 LOER-PRICED BOOK
21 Better
22 Bring action against
23 Intraoffice linkup: Abbr.
25 Walker, for short
26 Gilbert & Sullivan princess
29 It may come in buckets
32 Where water is poured on the rocks
34 1985 Literature Nobelist ___ Simon
35 SAIN LOUIS BASEBALL SQUAD
38 Fish preparer's task
39 Booze
40 Worked in a judge's office
42 Due before five?
43 Where, to Caesar
46 Morse E
47 "___ pro nobis"
49 Range rover
51 ACCOR
56 Ancient assembly area
57 Indicated
58 Early 20th-century leader
59 Like some batters
60 Immensely
61 Kind of course
62 1998 National League M.V.P.
63 Bar ___

DOWN

1 Moist towelette
2 Not out
3 Three sheets to the wind
4 Confine
5 Target of some humor in The New Yorker
6 Peak in Thessaly
7 Signs on again
8 Relax
9 Hemingway sobriquet
10 Cirrus, say
11 Ale holders
12 "Silent Night" adjective
15 62-Across, e.g.
17 Lettering liquid
20 Come again?
24 Storm heading: Abbr.
27 Castle section
28 Symbol of industry
30 Money put on a horse to finish second
31 Meticulousness
32 The cooler
33 Sighed sounds
35 Opposite of "from now on"
36 Kind of correspondence
37 Chow down
38 Alphabet trio
41 Room darkeners
43 In the habit of
44 High society
45 Chant
48 As much as you like
50 Start of a clarification
52 Stalactite producer
53 Golfer Woosnam
54 Convoy lineup
55 "A Day Without Rain" singer
56 Mont Blanc, for one

by Joe DiPietro

56

ACROSS

1. ___ d'Ouessant (westernmost point of France)
4. Greek director Angelopoulos
8. 60's TV boy
12. Piatigorsky specialty
15. Place for portraits
16. Thin haze
17. At full throttle
18. Put in ___ for
19. Friend of the powerless: Abbr.
20. Changed but not seriously
22. Stops: Abbr.
23. Win over
24. Support
26. Scientology founder ___ Hubbard
28. Battlements in Spanish castles
30. Not straight
33. Ran into
35. Pocket
36. Org. for arguers?
37. "Attention!"
40. Part of a metaphor
41. Rich boy in "Nancy"
43. Heat source
44. Particular
45. It may smooth the way
47. More than "Phooey!"
49. Strong
52. The house of Juan Carlos
56. Region NW of Genoa
57. Hurricane Carter, for one
59. End of a punch?
60. Leg up
61. Certain fur
62. It has many hitches
63. Many an old Hapsburg subject
64. Nero's land
65. Horace volume
66. Deli order
67. Travel method

DOWN

1. Start of an old boast
2. Bar wedge
3. Animal with a black stripe down its back
4. Spring event
5. 1980's Mideast envoy Philip
6. Exclusive
7. Routine
8. In some way
9. Tip to solving this puzzle (with the key parts to be said out loud)
10. Fidgety, maybe
11. Pests to Australian ranchers
13. Apt
14. Two semesters
21. ___ One (indoor kart racing)
25. Founding editor of The New Yorker
27. Just out
29. Lambaste
30. At ___ speed (quickly)
31. Like poll taxes
32. This puzzle, e.g.
34. Music, dance, painting, etc.
37. Find (out)
38. 1963 title role for Paul Newman
39. Together
42. Demographer's grouping
44. Egg on
46. Tangle
48. Famous blond bombshell
50. Move furtively
51. Hoover's predecessor?
53. Ancient marketplace
54. Actress Belafonte
55. ___ of roses
56. Prefix with phobia
58. Rock group from Akron that was a 1980 one-hit wonder

by M. Francis Vuolo

THREE

Unleash Your Brain's Full Potential

If you start playing the piano today and practice every day, the corners of your brain attuned to music appreciation and hand movement will develop and mature. By practicing, the number of contact points between brain cells, called synapses, increase dramatically. As you struggle to play the correct notes, new synapses are created. Initially, this would be at a microscopic level and could not be detected with naked eyes; however, after a few months of regular practice, your brain actually grows in size to the point that a radiologist can notice the difference when comparing the brain images before and after the training period.

BIGGER BRAINS

As early as ten years ago, neuroscientists laughed at the idea that the brain could physically expand from learning new skills. Recently, however, a group of researchers in England documented this phenomenon with brain-imaging studies. Dr. Eleanor Maguire and her colleagues obtained MRIs of London cab drivers and compared them to images of brains from people who did not drive for a living. Focusing on the areas of the hippocampus responsible for learning directions and navigation skills, they compared the difference in brain size among drivers with various years of experience. They discovered that these "map-driven" areas were larger in drivers compared to nondrivers. Moreover, experienced drivers had larger hippocampi than the newer, recreational drivers, suggesting that more training and experience results in bigger growth in the hippocampus.

Similarly, in a neuroscience research study in Germany, Dr. Arne May and her colleagues studied the brain images of a group of adults before and after teaching them how to juggle three balls in the air for one minute. After three months, the jugglers' brains had increased in size in the areas used for hand-eye coordination and motor activity. During this time, there was no change in the brain size of the control subjects who did not participate in the juggling program. For the first time, scientists provided convincing evidence that brain cells, very much like muscles, can tone and get bigger with challenging stimulation. In an extension of their study, the German team asked jugglers to stop practicing for three months; the last set of scans showed that the improved brain areas had shrunk back to their original size. Such findings support the concept of "use it or lose it" in a concrete and convincing manner and prove that mental muscles can strengthen or weaken depending on their level of stimulation.

The studies of taxi drivers and jugglers indicated that improving brain function is just as easy as improving muscle and physical fitness. The only reflection of the growth of new synapses in your brain is the ease with which you perform tasks you initially found challenging. A musician, a wine taster, a dancer, a taxi driver, and a carpenter all have the same brain anatomy, but for each, some parts are more developed and refined than others.

The challenge with exploring your full brain potential and making it a more powerful machine depends on your willingness to take on novel and challenging tasks. Like most people, you find comfort in doing what you are good at (such as cooking the same old favorite dish) and avoid things with which you are not familiar (such as trying to make a Vietnamese dish). In doing so, you are missing out on the opportunity to sharpen your senses and construct a more versatile brain. If you choose to expose yourself to new challenges, you help your brain expand and be ready for your senior years. By stretching your mental muscles you'll keep them in top form, capable of warding off the wear-and-tear that comes with age.

MOLDING THE BRAIN'S PLASTICITY

"Brain plasticity" refers to the flexibility of the brain in altering its properties, both at a microscopic and a structural level. The belief that learning new skills only affects brain development in children has now been shattered. Hundreds of scientific studies and countless common day-to-day observations have revealed the brain's ability to adapt to life's challenges under different conditions. They also highlight the importance of brain stimulation in taking advantage of plasticity.

A rough analogy between the brain and a large company may help you understand plasticity. Brain cells can be thought of as employees in a large company such as AT&T. Different personnel work in various offices, each with a specialized job. On an average day employees always leave by 4:30. With the increase in demand, employees work harder; they phone and e-mail each other more often and contact the other departments. They require more computers, fax machines and phone lines. At some point, more help is recruited, their office expands in size and they get larger desks. Similarly, brain cells each have their routine daily responsibilities in a huge network of 100 billion coworkers. With any given challenge to the brain, the particular cells involved increase their firing rates and stimulate their neighbors. Over time, more synaptic interconnections (and perhaps the birth of new cells) lead to increased brain size in selected areas.

NEUROPLASTICITY: THE BRAIN'S INNATE ABILITY TO RECOVER AND GROW

Older adults recovering from stroke demonstrate the brain's ability to overcome adversity at any age. When parts of a brain die, the adjacent areas of the brain not affected by a stroke take on more responsibilities to compensate. If patients undergo physical therapy with vigorous stimulation of the brain, they recover faster. Now that we have more appreciation of the brain's innate ability to heal itself with proper stimulation, the rehabilitation field has become the most important part of the recovery process for patients who have suffered a stroke. No medication can provide the same degree of brain repair and recovery as those nutrients and growth factors released naturally by the brain itself once it is adequately stimulated.

Another example of the brain's amazing capability to remodel itself is to observe people who become deaf or blind as adults. While no degree of change in the brain can make a blind person see again, the brain finds another clever way to overcome its loss. The parts of the brain used for processing tactile information from the fingertips or the areas that govern hearing become sharper and more sophisticated. A blind man can learn to detect the delicate shapes and figures in Braille to the point where he could enjoy reading novels again. With extreme emphasis on detecting details and variations in sounds, some blind people, such as Ray Charles or Andrea Bocelli, even become famous musicians or singers.

You can tap into your brain's innate ability to grow and strengthen, even without brain injury, trauma or loss of sight. The biochemical machinery for growth and development is already available, waiting to be switched on.

So what are you waiting for? Take a class, gain a new hobby, stimulate your senses and unleash your brain's potential.

A PERSONAL STORY OF TRIUMPH AGAINST ALL ODDS*

A friend of mine from Harvard Medical School was a radiologist involved in medical research. One day while biking downhill, he crashed into a car that had suddenly pulled in front of him. Unfortunately, he was not wearing a helmet; he flew off his bike and landed on his head, losing consciousness. An ambulance took him to the nearest hospital, and a CT scan showed more than half of his frontal lobes were lost. This part of the brain is important for planning and executing movements, decision making and abstract thinking. In his case, the left frontal lobe had turned into a mush of blood, skull pieces and dead brain tissue.

I stood at his bedside with his mother, and I remember having to tell her that her bright "star" son may not survive. She put her head on my chest and cried. He remained in the intensive care unit for several weeks, unconscious and unresponsive to his environment. He could not speak or lift his hands. However, over the subsequent months, he gradually woke up and started to move his eyes, blink and interact with people around him.

After one year, with rigorous rehabilitation, he started to walk again. His family and friends were shocked to find they could resume normal conversations with him again. After two years, he returned to work. It was amazing to see that someone with such a profound brain injury could end up returning to his full-time job of complex and challenging research. Such instances of remarkable recovery in adult brains are not uncommon. *ABC News* anchorman Bob Woodruff had a similar story of miraculous recovery after parts of his brain were blown away in Iraq.

* *Details have been changed to respect confidentiality.*

CAN YOU TEACH OLD DOGS NEW TRICKS?

In more recent years, brain researchers have debated whether the same degree of plasticity also applies to senior citizens. They accepted that middle-aged people could improve their brains, but it was uncertain if people in their 70's and 80's had the same ability. Could we really teach old dogs new tricks?

In a study published in the *Journal of the American Medical Association*, scientists reported surprisingly positive results when older adults with an average age of 73 received 90-minute training sessions for memory, problem solving and speed to perform manual movements. After only ten sessions, the majority of elderly men and women who participated showed significant improvements in their ability to solve problems, remember facts and move faster.

When they were tested five years later, they were still doing better than their counterparts who did not participate in the training program. They could complete daily routines faster, solve problems better and recall information more quickly.

In a study of elderly people in Hawaii, Dr. Jennifer Balfour and her colleagues discovered that those who participate in volunteer activities to keep their brains engaged often remained sharper for a longer period of time. In a study in New York, a team of researchers led by Dr. Yaakov Stern discovered that elderly persons who participate in brain-stimulating activity such as crossword puzzles remained sharper for a longer period of time.

So remember: No matter what your age, it's never too late to boost your brainpower!

HOW DOES THE BRAIN GROW?

How exactly does the adult brain grow when new skills are learned? Specific protein nutrients are released inside the brain when it is presented with a new challenge. The proteins, called "growth factors," help nourish the formation of new synapses. As more synapses are created, the communication between networks of brain cells improves. This allows you to learn and perform the new task more easily. When training or stimulation occurs for more than three consecutive months, there is a noticeable increase in the number of synapses, and the brain areas more closely linked to the nature of the stimulation become large enough to be detected with imaging techniques. Some scientists believe new brain cells are also created in the process of brain plasticity and growth, but the exact details remain unknown.

These new findings are providing an optimistic picture for achieving successful aging. With aging, some wear and tear in the brain results in loss of synapses. However, those who began with more synapses in their midlife have the capacity to resist and outlast any loss of synapses in late life. The term "brain reserve" implies that the more you learn throughout your life, the more brain cells and synapses you will have in reserve for your senior years. Your more powerful brain can withstand the effects of aging or even damages caused by trauma, stroke or Alzheimer's disease.

STEP 3: TEN EASY WAYS TO UPGRADE YOUR BRAIN TODAY

In previous chapters, you learned to appreciate the many functions that you can perform without thinking about it. Here are some examples of ways to improve these subconscious activities in order to make your brain stronger.

1. **Hand, eye and foot coordination:**
   - Learn how to dance. Join a class.

   - Learn a new sport or improve the one you already enjoy. Try to perfect the movements involved.

2. **Temporal orientation:**
   - Try to guess what time it is while you are waiting in line at the grocery store.

   - Guess how much time you have been driving or attending a lecture, then look at your watch to find out how close you guessed.

3. **Spatial orientation:**
   - When entering a building, try to keep track of which way is north and which way is south.

   - When driving to a new neighborhood, try to maintain your orientation as you take different turns. Try to remember the turns so that you can return using the same route.

4. **Performing simple calculations:**
   - Guess your total grocery bill while shopping.

   - Guess the discount for the various items in a department store and find out how close you were when the cashier rings up your bill.

5. **Performing a sequence of movements:**
   - Consider learning a new musical instrument.

   - Try Tai Chi or yoga.

6. **Following instructions:**
   - Try a new recipe.

   - Buy furniture that requires assembly at home.

7. **Manual dexterity:**
   - Learn to crochet or knit.

   - Take a drawing or painting lesson.

8. **Solving problems:**
   - Solve crossword puzzles.

   - Consider playing bridge or try sudoku.

9. **Recognizing faces:**
   - Look at group pictures and try to identify as many people as you can.

   - When looking at journals and newspapers, try to guess the names of well-known national or international personalities, then read the legend and find out if you guessed correctly.

10. **Decision making:**
    - Try maze puzzles, which require entering at one point and exiting at another point.

    - Try to become more decisive when exposed to various choices in your daily life; consider the pros and cons, and form a logical decision. Don't procrastinate.

These are only some suggestions. You can choose any activity or hobby you enjoy. Just remember that building brainpower is easier than toning your muscles. People who learn how to juggle or those who become more experienced cab drivers all improve brainpower without realizing it. You can do the same. Challenge your brain—start today.

LIGHT UP YOUR BRAIN

The cortex in the human brain consists of a sheath of cells. Each of the sensory signals from the eyes, nose, fingers or ears activates different areas of the cortex. The visual cortex becomes active when you see a picture of a face; the auditory cortex becomes active when you hear a name; and the somatosensory cortex becomes active when you hold a coin in your hand and feel its texture. Next to each basic cortical area exists a much larger number of cells that further process the information into integrated concepts we can understand. Such upper-managerial-level brain cells integrate the bits of information regarding sounds, light and aromas into one experience of, say, enjoying an outdoor concert.

Special imaging studies reveal how a handful of different areas light up when you read, solve a crossword puzzle or figure out mathematical questions. They show that different combinations of cortical areas become engaged in each of these tasks. However, the greatest level of activity occurs when a subject is exposed to new and different stimulations. While you learn to speak a new language with a friend, or if you try new dance steps, a firework of activity literally erupts in different corners of your brain. Just like a vigorous game of football tones up and cross-trains most of the muscles in your body, a challenging novel hobby can firm up the vast majority of your mental muscles. The more difficult a task feels to you, the more brain areas are pulled into action, the more synapses are formed, and the stronger your brain will become. In doing so, you tone up the different lobes of the cortex and can achieve lobes of steel.

Every day you have many opportunities to take advantage of the moment and light up your brain. Next time you are waiting in line or sitting in traffic, try closing your eyes and do some arithmetic (count backward from 100 by either 7 or 13). Try to think of two or three names of fruits or animals with each letter of the alphabet.

CROSSWORD CHALLENGE ■

One of the easiest and yet most efficient ways to enhance your brainpower is to improve your vocabulary. Guessing the meanings of new words, like solving puzzles, lights up both the temporal lobes and the parietal lobes. When you memorize a new term, most likely a new synapse is formed. With more and more new words, more and more synapses add up and help tone up the very parts of your brain that show shrinkage with aging.

Solving crossword puzzles is a great way to learn new words. Whenever you solve a crossword make sure you are familiar with all the words in the puzzle. Take the time to look up new words; not only will it make you a better puzzle solver but you will enjoy using more specific terms to express yourself, you can show off and impress your friends and employer, and you'll feel more confident that your brain will be more powerful as you get older.

In the following crosswords some of the most interesting, obscure and unusual vocabulary words are highlighted and explained by expert etymologists—for these notes, refer to the Vocabulary Notes section in the back of the book. ■

40

See Vocabulary Notes in the back.

ACROSS
1 Bank job
6 Forest opening
11 Fore's opposite
14 God, in Mecca
15 "Bye!"
16 ___-tzu (Taoism founder)
17 1994 Winter Olympics site
19 On the other hand
20 Bit of chicanery
21 Boxing venue
23 Buckles on
27 Chemical-free
29 Find not guilty
30 Part of U.S.S.R.
31 Butter maker
32 Archaeological find
33 Kilmer who played Batman
36 Furniture wood
37 Soup go-with
38 Clamp
39 Salt Lake City-to-Las Vegas dir.
40 Witches' assembly
41 "Beer Barrel ___"
42 Biblical passages
44 AT&T customer
45 Army outfit
47 Oriental
48 Belt features
49 "___ fair in love and war"
50 Tool for making 48-Across
51 1928 Winter Olympics site
58 Spectate
59 Grassy plain
60 Set free
61 Suffix with station
62 Aden's land
63 Discrimination

DOWN
1 "2001" computer
2 ___ Lilly & Co.
3 Down with the flu, say
4 "My gal" of song
5 At that place
6 Window pane
7 Hobbling
8 Convenience store convenience: Abbr.
9 Sandra of "Gidget"
10 Inconsistent
11 1992 Winter Olympics site
12 Animals collectively
13 General Mills cereal
18 Follow a fox, say

22 Bemoan
23 What to face
24 Partner of pains
25 1960 Winter Olympics site
26 Istanbul native
27 Actor Lloyd ___
28 Zealous
30 Tennis ace Monica
32 Shade of black
34 Prosecutor, at times
35 Memorize
37 Middling
38 Electric unit
40 In an angry way
41 Faint
43 Summer in Paris
44 Storm preceder
45 New moon or full moon, e.g.
46 Farther down

47 Friend of Dionne in pop music's Dionne & Friends
49 Elizabeth I's mother
52 Stout
53 "___ shocked ___ SHOCKED!"
54 Genetic letters
55 Part of T.G.I.F.
56 Small bird
57 Last letter

by Gregory E. Paul

41

See Vocabulary Notes in the back.

ACROSS

1 __, beta, gamma . . .
6 Like skyscrapers
10 Not fully closed
14 Lulu
15 Creme-filled cookie
16 Stubborn beast
17 With 37- and 56-Across, where "God Save the Queen" is the national anthem
20 Heavy weight
21 Dancer Charisse
22 Hoodwinks
23 No-no
26 Arcade game name
28 Improvement
30 Wharf
31 76ers' org.
34 Jawaharlal of India
35 Fourth-down option
36 Middle Brady Bunch girl
37 See 17-Across
41 Superlative suffix
42 Is sick
43 Parish priest
44 __ Speedwagon
45 Almanac datum
46 Torment a stand-up comedian
47 Egg beater
49 Abstract artist Albers
50 Forearm bones
52 It's bottled in Cannes
53 "7 Faces of Dr. __" (1964 flick)
56 See 17-Across
61 Apple or maple
62 Cry like a banshee
63 Kind of question

64 With 65-Across, miscellany, when separated by "and"
65 See 64-Across
66 Obsolete anesthetic

DOWN

1 Be adjacent to
2 Letterman rival
3 Celebrate
4 Simple shelter
5 Gobbled up
6 1964 Olympics host
7 Dry
8 Football great Dawson
9 Nautical journal
10 Love affair

11 Rolling Stones hit of 1968
12 Lotion ingredient
13 They keep track of pins
18 Pesticide brand
19 W.W. II turning point
24 Surrounding glow
25 Very dry, as Champagne
26 Some wedding guests
27 "Toodle-oo!"
28 Felix of "The Odd Couple"
29 Intrinsically
30 Colorful cover
32 Hackneyed
33 Wrestling's __ the Giant
35 Puncture

38 Sheepish sounds
39 Currier's partner
40 Heading on Santa's list
45 Ichthyologist's study
46 Daylight savings saving
48 Despises
49 Puts behind bars
50 Golden rule word
51 "__ of the Flies"
52 Novelist Bagnold
54 Game show host Robinson
55 Stink
57 Emitter of 38-Down
58 Competed in a 10K
59 Needle part
60 Tennis call

by Peter Gordon

See Vocabulary Notes in the back.

ACROSS

1 __ Mayer (wiener maker)
6 Doe's mate
10 Poker action
13 Great Plains tribe
14 San Diego baseballer
16 Holiday preceder
17 Informer
19 Nothing
20 Is in danger of sinking
21 Prophecy giver
23 U.K. news source
26 Mineral suffix
27 Mennonite group
28 Pennsylvania university
30 Like some Chinese cooking
33 Overflowing (with)
34 Rocket engine
35 Hubbub
36 Mangle
37 Nickels-and-__ (bothers with trivialities)
38 Last year's sr.
39 Misjudge
40 Military doctor
41 Unloads
42 Corrupts
44 100 centimos
45 Like a beaver
46 Minister: Abbr.
47 Letters after Q
48 "Aeneid" poet
50 Like ghost stories
52 Koch and Asner
53 Habitual boob tube watcher
58 "Do Ya" rock grp.
59 Extra
60 The "U" in U.S.S.R.
61 Ballpoint, e.g.
62 Gone across a pool
63 Barker of military orders

DOWN

1 Gives a thumbs-up
2 Dog command
3 Make dove sounds
4 Person missed by a 63-Across
5 North Carolina's capital
6 Volleyball kill
7 License plates
8 Summer cooler
9 Ones using brushes and combs
10 Substitute
11 Worse than knavery
12 Prefix with phone
15 Singer Caruso
18 Trodden track
22 __ Wednesday
23 Held responsible
24 "__ the Ides of March"
25 Committee head
27 Ancient Mexican
29 Suffix with organ or patriot
30 Games before finals
31 Modifies
32 Signals, as to an auctioneer
34 Document amendment
37 Unfolds
38 Film director Van Sant
40 Voodoo and wizardry
41 Crafty
43 Scott Joplin tune
44 Whom a copper apprehends
46 Fix, as cuffs
48 Prez's #2
49 Inactive
50 Creamy shade
51 Sicilian spouter
54 Big Detroit inits.
55 Lungful
56 Coat, informally
57 "You're Still the __" (1998 Grammy winner)

by Christina Houlihan

43

See Vocabulary Notes in the back.

ACROSS
1 Truck name
5 Unlike Charles Atlas
9 With 55-Down, Soap Box Derby home
14 Screen image
15 BB's, e.g.
16 Sawyer of TV news
17 With 32-Across, a hackneyed joke start
20 "Any __?"
21 Cool quality
22 Engraving tools
23 Hint for a hound
25 Peach or plum
27 What's hot
32 See 17-Across
36 La-di-da
37 __ synthesizer
38 Overact
40 Sharer's word
41 Let ride, at the track
43 With 59-Across, a heckler's interruption
45 Like some lingerie
46 "Nifty!"
47 Cratchit, for one
49 __ firma
54 Superskillful sort
58 Oater brawl site
59 See 43-Across
62 Raga instrument
63 Presque Isle lake
64 Mark permanently
65 Like Santa on Christmas Eve?
66 Split apart
67 Classic cars

DOWN
1 Hands, slangily
2 Have __ with (speak to)
3 Like the taste of some bad wine
4 Use a prie-dieu
5 Quipsters
6 Aussie runner
7 A Vanderbilt
8 Legit
9 Get comfortable with
10 Place for a firing
11 Gardener's tool
12 Till fillers
13 Beatty and Rorem
18 Author Jong
19 Take the cake
23 Bridge feat
24 Final exam giver?
26 Do as directed
28 Dig like a pig
29 Pin's place
30 Average guy?
31 Two capsules, say
32 Little rascals
33 Genesis skipper
34 Went like the dickens
35 Look like a wolf
36 TelePrompTer filler
39 Shipbuilder's wood
42 Tell's forte
44 Demolish
46 Infernal
48 Shipload
50 Church official
51 Delivery person's beat
52 Marciano's given name
53 Pharaohs' crosses
54 Radiator sound
55 See 9-Across
56 Dorothy's dog
57 Cross words?
58 Runners carry it
60 "__ pales in Heaven the morning star": Lowell
61 Yang's opposite

by Kelly Clark

See Vocabulary Notes in the back.

ACROSS

1 Tel __
5 Sired, biblically
10 Hits with phaser fire
14 Ankle-showing skirt
15 Play __ in (be involved with)
16 Quod __ faciendum
17 Folk singer Burl
18 Suppress
19 Indian music
20 Critique roughly and unfairly
23 Cryptologic grp.
24 "Fat chance!"
25 Increase the price of at auction
28 $$$ provider
31 Ideal for dieters
35 Web address ender
36 Destination from Dover
39 Press
40 Harbor personal motives
43 Extent
44 Covetous
45 Actress Tilly
46 Hardly modern
48 "__ Miniver"
49 "Touched by an Angel" star Della
51 Unruly head of hair
53 German name starter
54 Gulf war weapon
63 Five-star Bradley
64 Run on a bank
65 A party to
66 Like some amateurs
67 Indicator of freshness, perhaps
68 June celebrant
69 80's rock band from Australia

70 Ed Norton's workplace
71 Beatty and Buntline

DOWN

1 In the thick of
2 In __ (type of fertilization)
3 Inspiration
4 The Preserver, in Hinduism
5 "Enough, Enrico!"
6 Speedskater Heiden
7 Early Black Sea settler
8 Burn healer
9 Metric portion
10 Blastoff time
11 Resident of 55-Down

12 When repeated, a Samoan city
13 "South Park" kid
21 Org. that shelters strays
22 Feb.'s predecessor
25 "The View" co-host Joy
26 "Do __?" (words of indecision)
27 Comforter
28 It might scream after being tripped
29 Internal Revenue Service, e.g.
30 Small arachnids
32 Fiction genre
33 "__ of God" (1985 film)
34 Precarious perch

37 "The Ice Storm" director Lee
38 Outfield surface
41 Sets aside (for)
42 Spinning toys
47 "How exciting!"
50 Naval standard
52 Dads
53 "The __ of Wakefield"
54 3-D figures
55 Muscat is its capital
56 Kind of cat
57 Ending with hard or soft
58 Be wise to
59 Quiet type?
60 Concerning
61 Amount of work
62 Goes no further

by Alan J. Weiss

45

See Vocabulary Notes in the back.

ACROSS

1 High-hatter
5 "Where's __?" (1970 film)
10 Smooch
14 Lift
15 Hearing-related
16 Blunted blade
17 "I'll get __!"
18 Bundle-of-joy bringer
19 Peak near Taormina
20 Start of a quip
23 Actress __ Marie Saint
24 Part of a poker pot
25 Washington site
27 Add luster to
29 Hide-hair link
32 Brief fight
33 Hipster's eyewear
35 Military inits., 1946–92
37 Make out
38 Middle of the quip
42 Bear greeting?
45 Hirsute Himalayan
46 Least furnished
50 Habituate
53 Mouse's place
55 Buttinsky
56 Church laws
58 Southern constellation
60 Downing Street number
61 End of the quip
65 Diva's moment
66 They may be mowed down
67 Conductor Klemperer
68 City on the Aare
69 Steps over a fence
70 Yucca plant cousin
71 They often begin with "To"
72 Like many brandy casks
73 Jersey group?

DOWN

1 April forecast
2 Assyrian capital
3 Pacific battle site
4 __ noire
5 Easy stroll
6 Beat to the tape
7 Some Olympians, nowadays
8 Prefix with graph
9 Durable resin
10 Retro car
11 Raises, in a way
12 Having feelings
13 Swell place?
21 Foxy lady
22 Showy moths
26 Future fish
28 Flap
30 Honshu city
31 Cleaning need
34 Like Reynard
36 Hack
39 Big, fat mouth
40 Uxmal builder
41 Poetic preposition
42 Lush sound?
43 Never broadcast
44 Oater sound effect
47 Make a baron, say
48 Loud speaker
49 Practiced an Arthur Murray lesson
51 Mountain ashes
52 Wind dir.
54 Lollygag
57 Final authority
59 Out of bed
62 Pro __
63 Composer Satie
64 Ham's father
65 Blood-typing system

by Steven Picus

See Vocabulary Notes in the back.

ACROSS

1 The pyramids of Giza, e.g.
6 Newspaper's essay forum
10 "Invaders From __" (1953 sci-fi)
14 Jamaican witchcraft
15 Leaf opening
16 Baseball's Moisés
17 Business statistic
20 River that was notably crossed on Christmas 1776
21 Was jealous of
22 Soccer star Hamm
23 How spaghetti may be cooked
24 Teacher training institution
29 2004 Olympics site
30 "X Games" airer
31 __ choy
34 Painter Mondrian
35 Waitress at Mel's Diner
36 "__ Lisa"
37 Simile's middle
38 Freshwater duck
40 Peanut butter choice
42 Starting point of the Freedom Trail
44 Says yes to
47 Place for a stud
48 Hubbub
49 Walked through a puddle
54 Benefit of a steady job
56 "__ Tu" (1974 hit)
57 Sales rep's goal
58 "Gigi" star Leslie
59 __ terrier
60 Debate side
61 How eccentrics behave

DOWN

1 Sondheim's "Sweeney __"
2 Reed instrument
3 Whimper
4 Mexican peninsula
5 P. T. Barnum, for example
6 "Norma" and "Don Carlos"
7 Sit
8 Historical period
9 Add detail to
10 Publisher of "X-Men" comics
11 French author Robbe-Grillet
12 Man of many words?
13 Fancy leather
18 They may be polished
19 Finish with
23 Comment from Mr. Moto
24 California winegrowing county
25 __ & Carla, 60's singing duo
26 Emmy winner Perlman
27 Bumped into
28 Yo-Yo Ma's instrument
31 Prosperous time
32 Not fooled by
33 "Ain't We Got Fun" lyricist
35 Saturated substances
36 Popular tattoo
38 "Fiddler on the Roof" star
39 Officer Poncherello's portrayer
40 Like a lizard's skin
41 Fine leather
42 Addle
43 Gurkha or Sherpa
44 Farm units
45 Court employee
46 Not forthcoming
49 Uttered contemptuously
50 Roe source
51 Driven group
52 Environmental sci.
53 Fashion initials
55 Cartoon chihuahua

by Marjorie Richter

47

See Vocabulary Notes in the back.

ACROSS

1 90 degrees
5 Place for a cypress
10 Attempt
14 Be a monarch
15 Staples Center player
16 Hack
17 "Magnet and Steel" singer Walter
18 Word to a knight
19 Aspirin, e.g.
20 Reduce one's feelings of weariness?
23 Check for fit
24 Looped handle
25 Actress Campbell
28 Heavenly edible
33 Court decision
36 Play baseball with cheeses?
40 Water color
42 Seafood entree
43 Perplexity
44 Badly bruised president?
47 Rock producer Brian
48 Kind of bean
49 Over
51 Dutch export
55 Canadian peninsula
59 Master at wielding a tongue depressor?
64 Monopoly square
65 Piano specialist
66 Cut, as film
67 Pac 10 school
68 Grimalkin
69 Steam up
70 Keep at it
71 King of Judea
72 Sibyl

DOWN

1 Be constructive?
2 Foreshadow
3 Dark bluish-gray
4 Muscle/bone connector
5 Common side order
6 Put on notice
7 Japanese dog
8 Elementary particle
9 Urge
10 Dateless
11 Dial on the dash
12 Central line
13 Didn't pass
21 First-floor apartment
22 Shakespeare's foot?
26 Bud holder
27 Make an artistic impression
29 Famous holder of pairs
30 1982 Tony musical
31 Broadway brightener
32 Regarding
33 Arctic native
34 Prefix akin to iso-
35 Change colors
37 Singing syllable
38 Georgetown athlete
39 Adam's apple area?
41 Fitting
45 MGM Studios founder
46 Utah's state flower
50 Thin treats
52 Get rid of
53 Lapis lazuli
54 House of lords
56 "Sexy" Beatles girl
57 Audio attachment?
58 Any acetate, chemically
59 Food whose name means, literally, wadding
60 Hawaiian port
61 Zing
62 Attorney general from Miami
63 Stowe book
64 Water carrier

by Richard Silvestri

See Vocabulary Notes in the back.

ACROSS

1 With 5-Down, Microsoft co-founder
5 __ unto itself
9 Naval Academy newcomer
14 "The Weakest Link" host Robinson
15 __ land
16 Play against
17 Laissez-faire doctrine
20 Kay Kyser's "__ Reveille"
21 Earthshaking?
22 W.W. II vessel: Abbr.
23 "Music for Airports" composer
24 It may be bitter
25 Article in Le Monde
26 Board mem., maybe
27 1916–18 post for Calvin Coolidge: Abbr.
29 Concert array
31 It may wind up on the side of a house
32 Motor City monogram
34 1940's Giants manager
35 Belle's counterpart
36 Wet blanket
39 Housecat's perch
41 Snicker syllable
42 Piece activists?: Abbr.
43 Piece
44 What it is in Italy
46 Surround snugly
50 One that shoots the breeze?
51 Sixth-century date
52 Electric's partner

54 Margin
55 Director __ Lee
56 City near South Bend
58 Actress/singer Tatyana __
59 Minor obsession
62 Some Mideast dignitaries
63 Guesstimate words
64 German border river
65 Matisse's "La __"
66 Small dam
67 Nobelist Morrison

DOWN

1 Many a Degas
2 Consecrate
3 Open, in a way
4 Souvenir with a scent
5 See 1-Across
6 Oh-so-genteel
7 Cry after failing
8 Become friendly with
9 Tag line?
10 China's __ Piao
11 A saint he ain't
12 One of the strings
13 Bay State emblem
18 Invariably
19 Nascar sponsor
28 Challenging tests
30 Depression, with "the"
31 Letter-shaped girder
33 Murderous Moor
36 Begin impetuously
37 "That's nothing new to me"
38 Magic word
39 Overnight guest's spot
40 Beach in a 1964 hit song
45 1999 U.S. Open champ
47 1972 Oscar refuser
48 Soprano Farrell
49 Composer Shostakovich
51 Doltish
53 Shady plot
57 Now's partner
60 C.P.A. hirer
61 Word in a denial

by Brendan Emmett Quigley

75

49

See Vocabulary Notes in the back.

ACROSS

1. "An instructor of great sagacity": Emerson
5. Radar unit?
9. Rectory
14. Dog dish filler
15. Shivering fit
16. Something to shoot for
17. Sidesplitter
18. Self-titled CB comedy
19. __ Kea
20. Men went to the moon in it
23. Sounds of pain
24. Sugar suffix
25. What "V" means to a string player
28. "That __ lie!"
29. Dish manufacturer
32. Our planet, grandly
35. Adriatic port
36. Yucatán natives
37. Capo __ capi (big boss, in 35-Across)
38. Dried out
39. Reps.
40. Billboard line
42. Formerly
43. Cereal plant portion
44. Nets
45. One of Mickey's exes
46. City southwest of Bogotá
48. It began with the Big Bang
55. Spill source, perhaps
56. Info
57. Interlace
59. Voters' surprise
60. Sicilian smoker
61. De Valera's land
62. Peter and Paul
63. Owner's acquisition
64. Mythological ferry locale

DOWN

1. Outlying
2. "A Chapter on Ears" essayist
3. Each
4. Old newspaper part
5. "Tamburlaine the Great" playwright
6. Words with Reason or Aquarius
7. Areas within areas
8. Bunch
9. Brunch drink
10. Saw
11. Prefix with -algia
12. Arab capital
13. Biblical kingdom
21. Roller-coaster features
22. Beginning, in Hebrew
25. What a meter might measure
26. Plant: Suffix
27. Bent
28. Suffix with arthr-
29. Peace agreement signer of 9/13/93
30. Salad green
31. Planes need permission to enter it
32. One on a mission, maybe
33. Shevat follower
34. Abbr. after an officer's name
35. Pioneer in quantum theory
38. Get a bad mark on?
40. W.W. II server
41. Landing place on a roof
43. Turns inside out
45. Arabic for "commander"
46. Franklin is on it
47. Compensate (for)
48. Enter la-la land
49. Sirloin parts
50. Mrs. Victor Laszlo
51. Modern newspaper part
52. Little strings?
53. Knot or watt
54. Boglike
58. Cowboy's moniker

by Bruce F. Adams

See Vocabulary Notes in the back.

ACROSS

1 Was a crew member
6 Tooth site
10 Pack it in
14 Projection, maybe
15 Ruler with a throne
16 Ruin
17 Popular gift
20 Tofu base
21 Time and time again?
22 Rebounds
23 New Mexico tourist site
24 Delighted
25 Like a 17-Across, often
29 Arrest
32 Doesn't let the issue die
33 Like some love
34 Where the heart is
35 In districts
36 Elevator part
37 Not too hot
38 German river
39 "I'm __ in Love" (1975 hit)
40 European satellite launcher
41 Ayres of "Don't Bet on Love"
42 It may lead to romance
44 Decision makers
45 Manhandles
46 Willows
49 Love story?
50 Wane
53 Romantic time
56 Bank transaction
57 Scanned
58 Scarlett's love
59 Has
60 Desires
61 Feeling

DOWN

1 Barbecue entree
2 1847 novel about a mutiny
3 Like some floors
4 It may be massaged
5 Beat
6 Same old stuff
7 Biblical prophet
8 Attack word
9 Go
10 Almost a liter
11 "Do __ others . . ."
12 As previously mentioned
13 Start of a football game
18 Religious symbol
19 Touch down
23 More devoted
24 Nautical yard
25 Eye shade
26 Wear away
27 Running mate of '68
28 Noted violin-maker
29 Like some stock
30 Kind of acid
31 Moisten, in a way
34 Kings and queens want them
36 Fake
37 Eskimos, e.g.
39 Place for plants
40 Mongol, e.g.
42 Weightlifter's lift
43 Robots, for short
44 Casual attire
46 City ESE of Bergen
47 Put away
48 Catcher Rodriguez
49 Cartoonist Drake
50 Place of bliss
51 Loony
52 A computer processes it
54 Born
55 "__ Loves You"

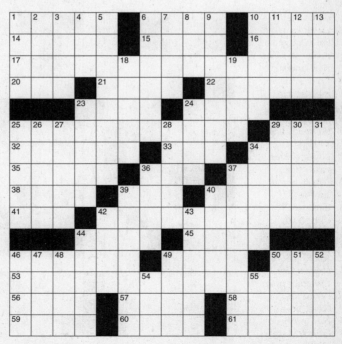

by Janet R. Bender

See Vocabulary Notes in the back.

ACROSS

1 Natl. Hot Dog Mo.
4 House of Commons members: Abbr.
7 Charged
12 "Season of Glass" artist
13 Where football's Pro Bowl is played
15 California wine town
16 Start of a quip by Alfred E. Neuman
18 Clowns
19 Quip, part 2
21 "Tristram Shandy" author
22 Half of a half-and-half
23 Poetic preposition
24 ___ room
25 Fruit in a mixed drink
27 Highlander
28 Common place for a sprain
31 Titanic
33 Quip, part 3
35 Railroad support
37 Wrung out
41 Rust sprinkled with white
42 "Deutschland ___ Alles"
43 Greenwich Village sch.
44 Three months from 1-Across: Abbr.
45 Mexico City Olympics prize
46 Degraded
49 Quip, part 4
53 Star in Aquila
54 End of the quip
56 Old Spanish coins
57 Statistics calculation
58 Elton's john
59 Eastwood's "Rawhide" role
60 Human Genome Project topic
61 Laboriously make

DOWN

1 Old Testament book
2 Like leftovers
3 Décolletage
4 Fool
5 Dolley Madison's maiden name
6 Pump, e.g.
7 Roulette bet
8 Not pro
9 Beaujolais ___
10 Current units
11 Fez attachment
14 Cesar Chavez's org.
15 Hanks's "Bosom Buddies" co-star
17 Historic Scottish county
20 Queen Victoria's royal house
21 Sp. woman's title
25 Natural fuel source
26 Film not made by a Hollywood studio
27 Attendee
29 City on the Rhone
30 Daughter of Hyperion
32 Year that Chaucer died
34 Some sharks
35 Part of the inner ear
36 Knocking sound
38 Trendy
39 Simple fastener
40 Turkey
41 Traffic circle
45 Tony's cousins
46 Dam that formed Lake Nasser
47 Safari head
48 Luxury car standard feature
50 Yarn that is spun
51 Deep Blue maker
52 Poverty
55 Adversary

by Peter Gordon

See Vocabulary Notes in the back.

ACROSS

1 Loudspeaker sound (and a letter bank for 60-Across)
6 Planets and such
10 Steamy
14 Howled
15 Raise a stink
16 Isaac's firstborn
17 See 71-Across
19 Hoosegow
20 Freshwater duck
21 Sporty Fords
23 What's more
27 Going strong
29 Became an issue
30 See 13-Down
33 Neigh-sayer
34 Educator Horace
35 Company with a dog in its logo
38 Applicable
41 Do away with
43 __ Moines
44 Harmony
46 They have long tails
47 See 50-Down
50 Many states have them
53 Mrs. Chaplin
54 "__ Breckinridge"
55 Present from birth
57 Knock for a loop
59 Dutch cheese
60 See 1-Across
66 Queue
67 French cheese
68 Singer Abdul
69 Monopoly card
70 Sound
71 Ludicrous (and a letter bank for 17-Across)

DOWN

1 London's __ 1 or __ 2
2 "Love Story" composer Francis
3 "The Fountainhead" author Rand
4 VCR button
5 Touch up
6 More than fancy
7 Seeing things as they are
8 "Wanna __?"
9 "Saturday Night Live" staple
10 It's often burning
11 Jeff Bagwell, notably
12 Hotel staff
13 Derby prize (and a letter bank for 30-Across)
18 Getting warm
22 Without exception
23 Orchard pest
24 Sierra __
25 Lord's workers
26 Approximately
28 Ruler until 1917
31 Hang tough
32 Popular card game
35 Rootin'-tootin'
36 More adorable
37 Out of it
39 Dancer Charisse
40 Opposite of ecto-
42 Abound
45 Pen up
47 Made to take the fall
48 Main course
49 Spread (on)
50 Football locale (and a letter bank for 47-Across)
51 Actress MacDowell
52 Mindless
56 Goes back out
58 Vintner's valley
61 Pitcher's stat.
62 Skedaddled
63 Track feature
64 Ivy Leaguer
65 __ Leman

by Greg Staples

53

See Vocabulary Notes in the back.

ACROSS

1 Sachet scent
6 Resting place
10 Harbinger
14 Pitcher Hideki __
15 Epps of "The Mod Squad," 1999
16 De __ (from the start)
17 Top of the military?
18 They may make great comebacks
20 Aylesbury actress?
22 Majors on TV
23 Vacation time in Valois
24 Nutritional stat
25 With 61-Across, river of Québec
26 Snake's sound
27 Michelangelo sculpture
29 Snorkeling areas
31 Dust collector?
32 Court fig.
34 Oversupply
35 Corinth cartoon character?
39 Implored
40 Arles assent
41 10th, 20th, 30th, etc., in N.Y.C.
42 West Wing workers
44 Spud
46 Self-titled 2001 #1 album
49 Loan-making org.
50 Is down with
52 A.C. stat
53 Muffin material
54 Pamplona playwright?
58 __ Day (religious observance)
59 Publisher __ Nast
60 Essential
61 See 25-Across
62 "Lou Grant" star
63 Bookie's concern
64 First to vote
65 Converges on

DOWN

1 Puts down
2 Dunne and Ryan
3 Certain soft drink buys
4 1960's–70's steelworkers' chief
5 Attractive one
6 Long-tailed finch
7 Pass over
8 Sports car since 1926
9 Challah, e.g.
10 Storybook beginning
11 In a sulky way
12 Busy
13 Most curious
19 Fruit spray
21 Ripped
28 Sly's "Rocky" co-star
30 Inflatable things
31 Eliot's "Adam __"
33 Idiot boxes
35 Saw
36 Embarrassed
37 Upstage
38 Ancient Italian
39 Pal
43 Clamber up
45 Steakhouse orders
46 Title girl in a 1983 Kool & the Gang hit
47 Storage room
48 Frisky critters
51 Analyze
55 Beatty and Rorem
56 "The Best Little Whorehouse in Texas" woman
57 Thoroughly wet, with "down"

by Elizabeth C. Gorski

See Vocabulary Notes in the back.

ACROSS

1 Sends packing
5 ___ shop
9 It holds its weight
14 Fawned-over figure
15 Extended periods
16 Acrylic fiber
17 Captain played in film by James Mason
18 Circus team
20 Baloney
22 Syndicate heads
23 Harry the hubby
24 Onetime cosmonaut's insignia
25 Clockmaker Thomas
26 Ozone layer, e.g.
30 It may be broken by a maverick
32 They're unlikely to be realized
34 Charlottesville sch.
35 Dig a heap
36 8 on a phone
37 Flank alternative
40 Thin streak
41 One hitting the tab key, maybe
42 Matching
44 Freesia's family
45 Sequined
48 Plankton, in part
50 Man of steel?
51 Agenda
53 Gilbert of "Roseanne"
54 Act introducer
55 Port captured by Allied forces in 1942

56 Latin 101 word
57 Philanthropists' concerns
58 Rose in a field
59 Pain in the neck

DOWN

1 Breeze
2 Designer Simpson
3 Gray area
4 Trudged through mud
5 Posses, possibly
6 Unleash
7 Seniors' grp.
8 Telekinesis, e.g.
9 Comforter
10 Undermine
11 On top of that
12 Things to draw
13 Lt. j.g.'s inferior
19 Klutzy
21 Lunar calendar observance
24 Enfant ___ (beloved child)
26 Wild animal trail
27 Singles may play it
28 Feathered runners
29 Short answer
30 La Scala music director beginning 1986
31 Roaster
33 Dogs it
38 Lowered oneself
39 Brings to a boil

40 McIntosh alternative
43 Washed-out
45 Time's 1977 Man of the Year
46 Turkish bread
47 Source of some swelling
48 [sigh]
49 Some ectozoa
50 Heart
51 See 52-Down
52 With 51-Down, a hit list?

by Sherry O. Blackard

55

See Vocabulary Notes in the back.

ACROSS

1 Liquor-laced dessert
9 Mad as hops
14 Oafish
16 Like a member of the fold
17 Mollusk gatherer
18 Like some classic films, now
19 What fans do
20 Radical
22 Moist
24 Brat Pack member
26 Harvard hater?
27 Still not there
29 Rip off
33 South-of-the border bad guy
36 Imposing estate
37 Places where students may face hurdles
39 Combined
40 They're revolting
41 Wasteful things?
43 Eye
44 Valueless
45 March event, maybe
47 Humans, e.g.
48 "The Mambo Kings" star, 1992
51 Math constitutes half of it: Abbr.
53 Market town
54 Like Miss Muffet, ultimately
59 Wife or daughter of Victor Hugo
60 Ex-president's income, in part
61 Don Juan
62 Historical figure in "Henry VI, Part II"

DOWN

1 "My country" follower
2 Fortune shelfmate
3 1954 suspense classic
4 Fusion
5 Dramatic opening?
6 "__ Shoes" (old spiritual)
7 See 15-Down
8 "__ Vie" (Maupassant novel)
9 W.W. II training center near Boston
10 Without exception
11 Need for some games
12 Coined word?
13 Journalist Hamill
15 With 7-Down, it's seen on some trunks
21 Deleted
22 Ruins
23 The Lily Maid of Astolat
24 It may be picked up or let off
25 Mythological hero with "douze travaux"
27 Silver-mounted figure
28 H.S. class
30 Disaffecting people
31 Divine
32 Bug
34 Avoid having to wait for a table, maybe
35 Film shot in stages?
38 Racket
42 New craft of '68
46 TV host turned New Ager
47 Kind of screen
48 Cry of French 40-Across
49 Schweppes product
50 Feeder filler
51 Limo destination, perhaps
52 Heat-cracked
55 Yellow pages listings: Abbr.
56 "I'll take that as __"
57 Disapproving cry
58 Cause of some unwanted expansion

by Gilbert H. Ludwig

82

See Vocabulary Notes in the back.

ACROSS

1 Start of a
Vol. 1 heading
4 Expected
much from
15 Eliminate as
excessive
16 Exclamation after
completing an
explanation
17 Big belly
18 Statements
from states
19 "The Vulture"
star Tamiroff
21 It may make a
wave: Abbr.
22 Pioneer bop
vibist Jackson
23 Shooter holder
27 Stroke with
a high stick
28 Yet to be
delivered
29 Horse show
directive
30 They may claim
to know stars
33 Favorable
times, for short
34 It may be played
on a mark
35 "All the King's
Men" actress
38 Some story
collectors
40 Ranger's
knowledge
43 Interlocks with
44 No regal
residence
45 Country music?
47 Bionomics: Abbr.
48 Clue collector,
slangily
49 "___ again . . ."
50 Accustoms to
indoor living
55 ___ Mae, "Ghost"
role for which
Whoopi won
an Oscar
56 Supplementary
57 Potted
58 Man in the street
59 Like some
courses: Abbr.

DOWN

1 "Author!
Author!" star
2 Dropped off
briefly
3 Ideals
4 You can
bank on it
5 Refrain syllable
6 Understanding
7 Tree heath
8 Dashboard
control
9 They're needed
for bills
10 Article in El Sol
11 Has more
troops than
12 Believer in
wu-wei
13 Words before
the consequences
14 Produce
progressive
irritation
20 Parcel
24 Oxygen carrier
25 Things to follow
26 Benefits
27 Italian town
where Napoleon
defeated the
Austrians
29 Good binder
31 Grp. concerned
with slicing and
chipping
32 Book collection
35 Do spadework?
36 Landed
37 Whip's place
38 Kind of rating
39 Rental for
a round
40 Historical
novel of 1984
41 Like Watteau's art
42 Guarantee
45 Lima's land,
to the French
46 Biting
48 Cookbook abbr.
51 Firm member:
Abbr.
52 Trouble
53 Chiang ___-shek
54 2002 Olympics
host: Abbr.

by Frank Longo

57

See Vocabulary Notes in the back.

ACROSS

1 Isn't clueless
9 Tricks
15 Exactly right
16 Cover
17 Hotel posting
18 Not so cool
19 Bank check?
20 Ghost, e.g.
22 Hydrocarbon suffix
23 Maria Luisa, for one
24 Missile feature
25 Range
27 Doozy
29 Amazon Basin creature
30 Mobile-to-Huntsville dir.
32 Kind of wheel
33 Learning ctr.
34 Most tender
38 Play stopper
40 "___ out?"
41 1968 battle period
43 Mach 1 breaker
44 Super ending
45 Berg's "Der Wein," e.g.
47 Old Ottoman title
51 Home financer since '34
52 Ocean phenomenon
54 Head shop?
55 1996 A.L. Rookie of the Year
59 Heels
60 "Twelfth Night" countess
61 Insignificant
63 More confusing
64 TV character first seen on "Cavalcade of Stars"
65 Is repulsive, in a way
66 Still

DOWN

1 Big numbers
2 Smear
3 Old railroad employee
4 Getting hardly any laughs
5 Lapse
6 Visibly shocked
7 Bit of custom work
8 Rib connection
9 Part of a Spanish play
10 Card, for one
11 Half a tea service tool
12 "No kidding!"
13 Kind of agent
14 Victor Herbert operetta, with "The"
21 Four-time Emmy-winning drama
23 Baseballer Sandberg
26 Tire-maker Michelin
28 Short pans
29 Noodles
31 Spanish form of "to be"
34 Lordships
35 Running
36 Certify
37 Clipped
39 1960's adventure series
42 Goes quietly
46 "Origins of Totalitarianism" author
48 Where Cleomenes ruled
49 1611 mutiny victim
50 Cutting out
53 Bowl
56 Damnable
57 German city on the Baltic
58 Rattles
59 Some humor
62 Monopolize

by Rich Norris

See Vocabulary Notes in the back.

ACROSS

1 "Our Town" family
6 Words of woe
10 Blows away
14 __ prix (at all costs): Fr.
15 Bullfighter Belmonte
16 Stag
17 Way out West, once
19 Indian's home
20 One having a fling?
21 What a belt might ensure
23 Ionian festival honoring Apollo
25 Carves
26 Z3 or X5
28 Holds close to one's heart?
30 Breach of security
32 Source
36 Turned a greedy eye toward
38 Voter's choice
39 Dendrologists' study
40 Stark dose of reality
43 Needle
44 Fated never to meet?
46 Street caution
47 Like a pariah
50 Celebrities, sometimes
52 Like knights
54 Rear end muscles
57 Cosmonaut Makarov
58 Oh-so-superior
60 Friends and neighbors
61 Requiem Mass word
62 Brace, in a way
63 League division
64 1955 Disney title character
65 Extra

DOWN

1 It may get agitated
2 Words heard in the Senate
3 Coney Island attraction
4 40-Across producer?
5 "The Crisis" essayist
6 Spanish eye
7 Grp. that questioned Alger Hiss
8 Cunning and deceptive one
9 Elevate
10 A question of aesthetics
11 Refreshment site
12 Dash off
13 Doesn't dash off
18 Inhibit
22 Hunt à la hounds
24 Trick shout
26 Ruin big-time
27 Start of something big?
29 Kind of pain
31 Side order?
33 Paper dispenser
34 Furnish with a lining
35 "Salus populi suprema lex __" (Missouri's motto)
37 An Allman brother
41 Come out on top
42 Place to perch
45 Nabokov novel
47 Fire sign
48 "As You Like It" daughter
49 "The Country Girl" playwright
51 Accompanied a madrigal, maybe
53 1-Down unit
55 It may follow something
56 Runners' place
59 "Oy __!"

by Dana Motley

85

59

See Vocabulary Notes in the back.

ACROSS

1 Hist. majors get them
4 Quacks
10 Fondlings
14 Swear words?
15 Noted fossil site
16 Corn product
17 With 58-Across, a hearty order
19 Ancient royal residence
20 "Bye Bye Birdie" girl or song
21 More substantial
23 "Top o' the mornin' to ye," for example
26 Present, e.g.
27 Put back
28 Accompanier of 17-/58-Across
31 Mends
34 Put to sleep, maybe
35 Occasion pertinent to this puzzle
40 Subject of Caesar's writing
41 Old camp
43 It might wash down 17-/58-Across
48 Enjoined
49 Starting now
50 Like leprechaun and four-leaf clover decorations
53 Dates
56 Washington, D.C., once
57 Drive (around)
58 See 17-Across
62 Bad thing to blow
63 Vagabond
64 Source of knocking

65 Cries from the stands
66 Keyboard instrument
67 Head shape

DOWN

1 Capped pen
2 Tempest in a teapot
3 Most miserable
4 Bygone Crayola shade
5 Angle producers
6 "The Sound of Music" figure
7 Suffix with strict
8 Hold
9 Office feature, sometimes
10 Ceramist

11 Sir Galahad's mother
12 Mother ___
13 Hit high C's, say
18 Warning on an airplane wing
22 Optimally
23 1949 armistice locale: Abbr.
24 Itinerary: Abbr.
25 They may be suspended from art class
29 "ER" character
30 Vessels also called broadhorns
32 Liszt's son-in-law
33 Bayonet
36 Partner of rosemary, in Shakespeare

37 Tops, in slang
38 N.F.L. Hall-of-Famer elected to the Minnesota Supreme Court
39 Word usually said in triplicate
42 Set
43 Depressed area
44 Add dirt to
45 Concert request
46 Étude places
47 Correct, as a computer image
51 Not out of it
52 Thick-soled shoe
54 Draws off
55 Back-talker
59 Seventh-century date
60 Booking
61 Coll. major

by Verna Suit

FOUR

Be Happier, Be Smarter

You are well aware that high levels of stress damage every organ in your body. Individuals who are overly anxious and stressed are more likely to experience hypertension, heart attacks, strokes, gastric ulcers, headaches and impotence. They often age prematurely. But did you know that chronic stress directly damages the brain, specifically your hippocampus?

When exposed to overwhelming circumstances, your brain puts your body in overdrive. The part of your brain that regulates hormones, called the hypothalamus, sets off the release of cortisol from your adrenal gland. This stress hormone increases blood circulation to your muscles, heart and lungs. If you were a deer running away from a fast-pawed predator, the increased blood circulation would allow you to run faster and with heightened attention in order to escape from the dangerous situation. Cortisol, the mediator of your fight-or-flight system, is beneficial to your survival and helps you cope with unexpected extra demands in your day-to-day life. However, over the long term, it becomes toxic to the brain by harming the hippocampus, the very part of your brain crucial for remembering phone numbers, names and places. As the hippocampus decays, it results in serious problems with learning and memory.

Scientists have discovered that cortisol has a particular attraction for the cells in the hippocampus, more than any other region in the brain. Chronic stress from working too hard, family issues or social problems can directly lead to shrinkage of the hippocampus, causing memory loss and cognitive decline with aging. As expected, people suffering from depression and who have high cortisol levels have smaller hippocampi on either side of their brains. According to studies by Dr. David Bennett at the Rush Institute in Chicago, they are up to seven times more likely to lose their mental agility and develop Alzheimer's later in life.

HOW DOES STRESS KILL NEURONS IN THE HIPPOCAMPUS?

The hippocampus is the most unique part of the brain. Not only is it the most sensitive to a drop in oxygen levels, but it is also the first part of the brain to shrink with advanced age, thus explaining why memory lapses are more common in senior citizens. Discovering why the hippocampus is so fragile and prone to damage will be a Nobel Prize–worthy accomplishment, as it will offer a chance to prevent and cure Alzheimer's disease.

How and why does chronic stress damage the hippocampus? Dr. Robert Sapolsky at Stanford University has studied this issue for more than 20 years. In the 1980's, he traveled to Africa and observed monkeys in their natural environment. He noticed that some monkeys were relaxed and content while others appeared stressed and anxious. He measured blood cortisol levels in the two groups of monkeys. Not surprisingly, cortisol levels were much higher in the stressed monkeys as compared to their relaxed and calm siblings living in the identical environment. He then compared their brains and discovered the hippocampus was much smaller in the anxious animals. In another study with rats, Dr. Sapolsky discovered that even an infusion of cortisol can kill cells in the hippocampus, ruling out other mediators of stress as the culprits.

Dr. Sapolsky believes that there are individual differences in how monkeys and humans respond to the same perceived threat, and that changing the perception of circumstances can limit cortisol surges. With an optimistic outlook and a positive attitude, seeing the glass half full, you can limit the amount of cortisol surges and prolong the health of your hippocampus.

STRESS AND THE REST OF YOUR BRAIN

People who feel stressed on their jobs for decades suffer consequences that go beyond cortisol killing cells in the hippocampus. Many of them also experience high blood pressure, which harms the brain in the long run, rendering them more vulnerable to stroke and Alzheimer's disease in their 70's and 80's.

In addition to cortisol, another hormone released with each stressful response is adrenaline. The "adrenaline rush" refers to the spikes in your blood pressure that deliver a more rapid supply of oxygen and nutrients to the muscles, the lungs and the brain. Occasional surges in adrenaline do not harm the body or the brain. However, chronic release of adrenaline leads to hypertension, defined as blood pressure above 140/90 (normal pressure is 120/80).

In a study concerning hypertension in the workplace, scientists led by Dr. Robert Rose from the University of Texas Medical Branch discovered that most air traffic controllers experienced spikes of high blood pressure every time the number of arriving flights greatly increased. When these employees were contacted 20 years later, 68 percent of those with initial higher stress responses had developed hypertension, requiring them to take multiple medications in their later years.

THE SILENT KILLER

High blood pressure acts as the silent killer in your brain. It leads to a hardening of the blood vessels in the brain, just as it does in the heart, kidneys, lungs and skin. Less blood flow through narrowed arteries limits the amount of oxygen and nutrients, which are needed for highly active brain cells. Over time, islands of brain tissue gradually deteriorate and die. These are called "silent infarcts" or "mini-strokes" because they usually do not cause sudden weakness in one side of the body or the inability to speak, which are characteristic of common large strokes. These dead pieces of brain, each measuring almost the size of a grain of rice or a bean, accumulate over decades and eventually interrupt the communication between different brain areas. As a result, thinking, walking, eating and even talking become slower and more laborious.

A brain littered with dozens or thousands of ministrokes is frail and shows cognitive deficits. Dr. David Snowdon studied nearly 700 nuns for decades and discovered that most of those who did not have signs of ministrokes in their brain remained sharp until the last days of their lives, even if their brains were loaded with the signs or "footsteps" of Alzheimer's disease.

For the first time, he raised the possibility that one can have Alzheimer's problems in the brain without any apparent symptoms of dementia, if the brain has been kept healthy and free of vascular risk factors otherwise.

Narrowing of the arteries in the heart can be a problem for the brain, too. A failing heart can no longer provide an adequate amount of blood through the hardened vessels in the neck and the brain. This results in an increase in the number and size of ministrokes. Patients with heart attacks or congestive heart failure often complain about difficulty with concentration and learning. They may not realize the real source of the problem may be the heart, not the brain.

Years of anger and frustration over minor matters at home or in the workplace take a toll on your heart and your brain. The good news is that you can control and limit the release of harmful hormones through lifestyle modifications and reducing stress. Try not to stress the smaller matters in life or it will only lead to matters that are truly stressful.

If possible, measure your blood pressure periodically at work and at home. If it is elevated, make a concentrated effort to correct it. Sometimes just eating a heart-healthy diet, losing a few pounds, walking for 45 minutes a day and reducing stress can bring your blood pressure down to the normal 120/80 range.

Sometimes you need to add prescription medications. Take high blood pressure very seriously. Consult your doctor.

ARE YOU SLEEPING WELL?

Another way stress harms brain health is by interfering with healthy sleep patterns. General anxiety is a main cause for sleeplessness and insomnia, which affects 26 percent of Americans. In a study of patients with generalized anxiety disorder, 47 percent had difficulty falling asleep, 63 percent had difficulty maintaining sleep, and 56 percent awoke early in the morning. Once stress was eliminated, 86 percent of the individuals enjoyed a full night of restful sleep. Chronic insomnia and sleep-deprivation leads to hypertension, depression and further release of harmful stress hormones.

The link between sleeping problems and stress is a two-way connection. Stress and anxiety interfere with adequate sleep. Lack of sleep and fatigue diminishes your ability to cope with your routine responsibilities and you may become more irritable and stressed. Therefore, you need to recognize the factors beyond depression and anxiety that interfere with your ability to achieve adequate sleep.

Some other common culprits are obstructive sleep apnea, chronic lower back pain, frequent bathroom use during the night, or restless leg syndrome (an urge to move your legs throughout the night). Like most, you may not have the time to discuss such problems with your physician. Many people feel they need to accept such medical issues as a normal part of life. Fortunately, simple interventions and proper medications can successfully improve these conditions. When your sleep improves, you can cope with stress more effectively, feel more in control and maintain healthier levels of blood pressure.

A STORY OF PERSONAL TRIUMPH OVER DEATH

Mr. Jackson was a 49-year-old taxi driver with a Type A personality. One day when arguing with a customer, he developed sudden chest pain. An ambulance brought him to Johns Hopkins Hospital, where he was immediately diagnosed with a heart attack. Luckily, he arrived just in time and received proper treatment that saved his life. He was brought to the critical care unit for close monitoring and treatment. This is where I met Mr. Jackson.

He appeared very angry with the food at our hospital and was yelling at nurses for giving him warm Pepsi. After becoming calmer, he mentioned that for many years he had constant fatigue throughout the day, headaches, lack of energy and memory problems. He often felt frustrated and furious at people. He repeated several times, "People are so stupid these days." He weighed 310 pounds,

---

and despite multiple attempts he was unable to lose any weight. His irritability at work also affected his relationship with his wife and they were considering divorce.

After several days of close treatment at the intensive care unit, Mr. Jackson was transferred to the rehabilitation unit and was sent home two weeks later. When I saw him in my outpatient clinic, I reviewed his risk factors for developing another heart attack, which included high blood pressure, high cholesterol, significant obesity and smoking. Because of his obesity, he also snored at night and had obstructive sleep apnea. Scared of a second heart attack, he was willing to consider lifestyle changes to improve his cardiovascular function.

We began addressing each of his risk factors individually. His blood pressure was controlled with medications and he agreed to cut back on his high-fat diet and eat more fruits and vegetables. A sleep study confirmed his sleep apnea, and he began wearing an oxygen mask at night and taking a medication called Provigil. He soon felt he had significantly more energy during the day. I encouraged him to lose two pounds every week. After six months, he lost only 10 pounds but felt much more confident. The positive comments he received from his family encouraged him to further change his lifestyle.

He enrolled in yoga lessons and felt more relaxed and less angry at work. His marriage also benefited when he started taking walks with his wife after dinner every day. Ten years later, he has now lost more than 110 pounds, is pleased about the way he looks and feels, has stopped taking blood pressure medications and continues to enjoy yoga. He successfully changed the course of his destiny from almost dying to enjoying a confident, healthy and fulfilling life with family and friends. His heart attack turned out to be a blessing in disguise.

STEP 4: *CONQUERING STRESS*

Strategies to mitigate anxiety are easy. Here are some suggestions:

1. MAINTAIN A POSITIVE ATTITUDE. Perceive problems and conflicts more as opportunities and challenges than as obstacles. When stuck in a traffic jam, remain calm; listen to music, take notes for your future activities, return some phone calls, organize the rest of your day or tease your brain with mental gymnastics. Those who constantly honk their horns and turn red with anger may cut in front of other cars but do not necessarily reach their destination much sooner. They do, however, put needless stress on their hearts and their brains. Choose to see the world in a positive way and enjoy life as much as possible.

2. GET ORGANIZED AND MANAGE YOUR TIME. At the beginning of the year, set overall goals for each month. At the beginning of each week, set goals for each day. And every morning, make a list of the top three most important items that absolutely have to get done. Throughout the day, you have options to engage in various activities. Remember to set priorities. Avoid procrastination and focus on your high-priority list. Delayed gratification, a sense of getting the tough things done first and then enjoying less work later, brings inner peace.

3. MEASURE YOUR BLOOD PRESSURE. Small blood pressure machines are inexpensive and readily available in most pharmacies. If your job stresses you on a daily basis and spikes your blood pressure to 186/100 or higher, you need to see a physician promptly. Your goal for blood pressure should be 120/80 or less. Use your blood pressure numbers as a biofeedback system, reminding yourself to calm down. Remember that your hippocampus suffers from high levels of cortisol. Relax and recall that your brain health in the future is far more important than getting frustrated over minor matters at work.

4. TRY RELAXATION TECHNIQUES. Dr. Herbert Benson, one of the pioneers in the field of stress and the brain, believes meditation can help you achieve emotional stability and inner peace. Performing these relaxation techniques once or twice per day, for 10 to 20 minutes each time, helps you achieve a sense of deep tranquility.

5. GET CHECKED. Low or high thyroid levels, anemia, B12 deficiency, tension headaches, or obstructive sleep apnea can all affect your energy level and coping mechanism, thus rendering you more irritable and stressed. All these conditions can be easily and successfully treated.

MEDITATIONS TO SOOTHE THE SOUL

One form of meditation promoted by the Benson-Henry Institute involves the following steps:

1. Find a quiet place where you can relax without interruptions for 10 to 20 minutes.
2. Take your shoes and socks off, if possible.
3. Choose a mantra; it could be a simple word, sound or prayer such as "love," "bambule," "peace," "salaam" or "the Lord is my shepherd."
4. Sit comfortably and close your eyes.
5. Relax your foot muscles, then your knees, then your abdominal muscles, your neck muscles and your facial muscles. Let go.
6. Breathe slowly and naturally. Calmly repeat your mantra in your head as you inhale and exhale.
7. As thoughts interrupt your repetitions, gently put them aside and return to your mantra.
8. Calmly continue to breathe in and out while repeating your mantra, for 10 to 20 minutes.
9. As you prepare to end the session, stop your repetitions and allow the flow of thoughts to return to your mind.
10. Remain seated, open your eyes, wait for a minute and then leave.

Other relaxation techniques also involve breathing, letting go of your muscles and distracting your mind from your daily thoughts to calming words or images.

Progressive muscle relaxation:

1. Lie down or sit quietly in a room.
2. Close your eyes and take a few deep breaths.
3. Tense the muscles of your face as if you are grimacing; squeeze your eyes shut and clench your teeth. After approximately 10 seconds, relax your facial muscles and feel the relief from tension.
4. Tense your neck and shoulder muscles for approximately 10 seconds and relax again.

5. Repeat this tension and relaxation technique in your right arm, then your left arm, your right foot and your left foot. Then slowly open your eyes.
6. Place your hand on your abdomen.
7. Inhale slowly while you count from 1 to 10, then exhale as you count from 1 to 10.
8. Repeat these slow inhalations and exhalations, with your eyes closed, for 10 to 20 minutes.
9. Rest for a few minutes before you leave.

6. CONSIDER YOGA OR TAI CHI. These amazingly relaxing exercises require slow movements of your arms and legs. They have been used in eastern countries for more than 2,000 years. You can begin by taking classes. Once you learn the moves and the maneuvers, you can incorporate 20-minute sessions in your daily routines.

7. MINGLE WITH PEOPLE. Socializing, especially with those you love and admire, has relaxing and calming effects on your nervous system. The exact mechanism for this common observation has not been identified. Attending theater, concerts, church, synagogue or sporting events can also be quite relaxing, as you feel detached from the stressful world around you for a few hours.

FRIENDS AND FUN KEEP YOUR MIND SHARP

At least three different studies in Europe and the United States have highlighted the importance of social leisure activities toward helping to maintain brain health and cognitive agility. Dr. Laura Fratiglioni, from the Karolinska Institute in Sweden, has monitored the social environment of more than 1,000 individuals in a Stockholm neighborhood for many years. Since 1987, the 1,375 elderly living in this area have reported their levels of engagements in volunteer work, traveling, attending group meetings, joining organizations or going to theaters and concerts. In this population, Dr. Fratiglioni has noted that those with a rich social network cut their risks of developing dementia by half, while those who have a lonely lifestyle double their risk of developing Alzheimer's disease.

The exact biochemical reason to explain better brain function with increasing social activities remains controversial. One possible explanation is the fact that when you are in a large group,

94

your brain constantly gets activated and stimulated. You need to re-call names of people around you and refresh your memory about their occupations, their family circumstances, and their likes and dislikes. Through conversations, you engage and update your knowledge of the current affairs nationally and around the world. You also need to be aware of body language among those present and be cognizant of the things you say or do. Release of certain brain nutrients and endorphins, the "feel-good chemical messengers," may explain why you enjoy the company of people around you. Interestingly, levels of the healing protein in the brain, called brain-derived neurotrophic factor (BDNF), seems to be lower in people with isolated lifestyles and major depression. BDNF levels may increase with social activities that involve physical and mental stimulations such as a group walk after dinner, card games, or a family weekend getaway.

8. TAKE A DANCE CLASS; MIX UP FUN WITH EXERCISE. As you learn to follow a sequence of steps, your mind is engaged and your brain is busy focusing on you and your partner. Merged in your attention to maintain balance and learn new dance steps, your mind relaxes and at least for a few minutes your worries do not occupy your brain. You also get your exercise without realizing it.

9. BEWARE OF DEPRESSION. Most people with depression do not seek medical attention. They believe that their irritability, lack of interest in daily routines, difficulty with concentration, changes in appetite and a sense of helplessness are due to their own failures. These feelings, however, are indications of a chemical imbalance in the brain and can respond favorably to treatment with antidepressants. Mild depression can improve with lifestyle modifications such as setting priorities, getting organized, reducing responsibilities, participating in social activities or taking yoga classes. Those with more severe depression need to see a physician promptly.

10. BE HAPPY. In any work environment, some people create a positive and friendly atmosphere around them, while others create a zone of hostility and negative feelings. You can choose to have a kind attitude toward your coworkers and family members even though you may be engaged and busy with a dozen different responsibilities. You can change. You can be more reasonable in expectations from yourself and those around you. By being fair and respectful of others, you gain their trust and appreciation. In doing so, you reduce the level of anxiety and stress not only for yourself but for those around you.

In summary, stress is an inherent physiological mechanism through which we can run faster, jump higher and escape life-threatening environments. While helpful in the short-term, stress and anxiety are strong triggers of damage to the brain and more specifically to the hippocampus. This banana-shaped brain structure already is prone to shrinkage with aging. Adding the threat of cortisol toxicity on a regular basis would make it decay even further and can render you more vulnerable to diseases such as heart attacks and Alzheimer's. Stay calm, smile and make pampering your hippocampus a high priority!

THE HUMOR CURE: LAUGH TO DISSOLVE YOUR STRESS

You can counter the high cortisol levels produced in your brain in response to stress by finding ways to stimulate the release of endorphins in your brain. Endorphins provide the joy you experience after an evening of chatting with your friends at a party and laughing at jokes. They govern your sense of satisfaction with life and mental relaxation after you watch a comedy or after you play with your children. You can choose to have more endorphin-stimulating moments by seeing the funny side of life more often. Instead of complaining bitterly about the economy or politics, you can tell jokes about the president. They both convey the same message, but jokes take away the heavy and negative perspective.

In addition to dissolving stress and boosting your mental health, laughter has been shown to lower blood pressure, improve your infection-fighting immune cells, reduce cravings and enhance your ability to cope with pain. According to a study at the University of Maryland, people with heart disease are 40 percent less likely to laugh in a variety of situations. If you get angry easily, you can try to incorporate more humor in your daily conversations. Humor will help you to replace distressing emotions with pleasurable feelings. You cannot feel furious, anxious, or resentful and experience humor at the same time. To laugh or not to laugh; it is your choice.

Children laugh 300 to 400 times a day while adults laugh only 17 to 30 times a day. It is easy to double how many times you laugh every day. You can pepper your days with humor in more than 100 different ways. You can read the cartoon section of your newspaper, laugh at your misunderstandings with people, observe and smile at the absurd situations around you, find delight and amusement in ordinary things, take 5- to 10-minute humor breaks and read jokes, keep a humor notebook, spend time with fun people and avoid getting too serious. To both sharpen your brain and have fun at the same time, you can enjoy completing fun crossword puzzles. Here are some of the "funnest" *New York Times* puzzles to get you started.

60

ACROSS

1 Jacuzzis
5 Box office hit
10 Man in a garden
14 Boston's Faneuil ___
15 Busch Gardens site
16 Singer Horne
17 One of the Guthries
18 Swiss mountains, to the French
19 City blight
20 What the photographer-turned-policeman said
23 Indian carving
24 Model Macpherson
25 Compadre of Fidel
27 Years at the Sorbonne
28 Cool ___ cucumber
31 Main course
33 Kind of shelter
36 P.B.A. Hall-of-Famer Anthony
37 What the sculptor-turned-policeman said
40 Man-eating giant
42 Bloodhounds' trails
43 Kind of scream
46 Weep
47 Berne's river
50 Notebook divider
51 Santa ___, Calif.
54 Way to the altar
56 What the manicurist-turned-policeman said
60 "___ Karenina"
61 Tricks
62 Tibetan priest
63 Compote fruit
64 Awaken, as feelings
65 Drei minus zwei
66 Actress Raines
67 Prevent
68 Skirt feature

DOWN

1 California peak
2 "9 to 5" actress
3 Metes out
4 Schussing site
5 Twinkler
6 Its capital is Bamako
7 Plentiful
8 Be in a bee
9 Harass
10 Too
11 Bill Clinton, e.g.
12 Second helping
13 Oui or Us, e.g.
21 Muscat resident
22 Biddy
26 Conger
29 Start of a cheer
30 "Lucky Jim" author
32 Miss Trueheart
33 "Excuse me"
34 Nile viper
35 Neighbor of Cambodia
37 Court of justice
38 Halloween cry
39 Population classification
40 Choose
41 Small anchor
44 Suffix with honor
45 Came into view
47 Lace into
48 Diploma holders
49 Banquet
52 Debonair
53 Underworld talk
55 Waits at the stoplight
57 Scarlett's home
58 Quarterback's command
59 Pete Sampras, in a way
60 Huxley's "___ and Essence"

by Randall J. Hartman

61

ACROSS
1 Minnesota ___
5 Neighbor of Cameroon
9 ___ Alpha Epsilon fraternity
14 1997 Peter Fonda role
15 Despise
16 Subsequently
17 Start of a quip about weight loss
20 Minnesotan
21 "Heavens!"
22 Soissons saison
23 Kind of code or drive
25 Classic TV brand
26 Where St. Pete is
29 Mover and shaker
31 Household name
33 Scarlett's first love
35 Ants, in dialect
38 Make fun of
39 Middle of the quip
41 In the lead
43 Kissy-kiss
44 Popular carpet style
46 Nearly worthless coin
47 Biblical country
51 "Evita" character
52 Ump
54 Kind of particle
56 Comic Philips
57 Trap
59 Michael of Disney
61 End of the quip
65 Spanish port from which Columbus sailed, 1493

66 Window part
67 Robt. ___
68 "Voilà!"
69 Actress Lamarr
70 Feel sorry for

DOWN
1 Wasn't 100% honest
2 Former San Francisco Mayor Joseph
3 Crow's home
4 Clockmaker Thomas
5 J.F.K. appeal
6 Laugh sound
7 "Up and ___!"
8 Put off
9 Like some humor
10 Uncertain

11 Car that's "really lookin' fine," in a 1960's song
12 Danny's "Lethal" co-star
13 Biblical boat
18 "___ who?"
19 Killer whale
24 Wharves
26 Criticism
27 "___ Miz"
28 Yachtie's "yes"
30 Curative center
32 Flower holders?
34 Actress Anne
36 Update
37 Posture problem
39 "As you ___"
40 Swatter's target
41 Agatha Christie's "The ___ Murders"

42 Laugh sound
45 Bring up
48 Mt. McKinley's Indian name
49 Bad place to find shells
50 Newsman Safer
53 Unwilted
55 "Richard ___"
57 Ado
58 Singer Adams
60 Dance instructor's call
61 Deed
62 "Uh-uh!"
63 Presidential inits.
64 Archaic

by Stephanie Spadaccini

98

ACROSS

1 Prisoner's protest
5 Béarnaise, e.g.
10 Athlete
14 "__ Angel" (Mae West film)
15 Increased
16 Well-ventilated
17 Incredible to behold
19 The world, to Mr. Magoo
20 Clambake item
21 Put in rollers
23 Caribbean, e.g.
24 Ornamental bowl
25 "Give it __!"
27 Upholstery flaw
29 "__ takers?"
30 Like a horror flick
35 Modeling wood
36 Whipped cream amount
37 Friend in war
40 Coffee break time, maybe
42 "Betsy's Wedding" director
43 Scarcity
45 Bedtime story?
47 Totally awesome
49 "Spy vs. Spy" magazine
52 E. Lansing campus
53 Peace alliance since '48
54 Rest room sign
56 When doubled, a dance
58 PC key
60 "West Side Story" tune
62 Scouting outing
64 Result of 17-, 30- and 47-Across?
66 Not bumpy
67 Battery terminal
68 Skier's way up
69 Abysmal test score
70 Marciano or Graziano
71 Hankerings

DOWN

1 Baja bash
2 "The Joy Luck Club" author
3 Grumpy companion
4 November birthstone
5 Building manager, briefly
6 Evaluate
7 Classic A.P. rival
8 Bleep out
9 Nose (out)
10 The "one" in a one-two
11 Exxon Valdez mishap
12 Rock's Mötley __
13 Actress Sedgwick
18 Nebraska city
22 Small combo
26 Old-timer
28 Koran religion
31 Notwithstanding that, in short
32 Commercial makers
33 Tacit assent
34 Grad sch. application info
35 "Mr. Tambourine Man" group, with "the"
37 Modifying wd.
38 Grassy area
39 Senator or representative
41 Haitian leader
44 In alignment
46 Winery process
48 Pennsylvania's __ Mountains
49 Longtime Zimbabwean leader
50 Sub sinker
51 Dissuades
55 Really neat
56 French restaurant name starter
57 Drone's home
59 Thick slice
61 Lulu
63 Rock producer Brian
65 Fenway squad, for short

by Alan Arbesfeld

99

63

ACROSS

1 One of Franklin's two certainties
6 Spielberg blockbuster
10 Library item
14 ___ Detoo of "Star Wars"
15 The Fed's Greenspan
16 Rich vein
17 Sports car at a deli?
19 Sportswear brand
20 Bake sale grp.
21 Amigo
22 People after whom things are named
24 Extremely
26 Lowly foot soldier, slangily
27 Muslim in Russia
29 Bewilder
33 Bell or shell preceder
36 Take ___ (try some)
38 "To your health!"
39 Elvis's middle name
40 Unseen title character in a Beckett play
42 "Gladiator" setting
43 Get through to
45 Arctic ice
46 Tabloid tidbit
47 Feeling of pity
49 Midway alternative
51 Building add-on
53 Pirate's supporter
57 Something to turn over on January 1
60 Alley ___
61 Buckeyes' sch.
62 European automaker

63 Pancake-eating senator at a deli?
66 Singer McEntire
67 Hand over (to)
68 Cathedral features
69 Netting
70 Co. medical offerings
71 2001 and 2010

DOWN

1 Extinguishes
2 Lord Byron's Muse
3 It may come out smelling like a rose
4 From A ___
5 Big to-do
6 One corner of a Monopoly board

7 Miss. neighbor
8 Addition to a concentrate
9 Grab quickly
10 Onslaught of crepe orders at a deli?
11 Leaking
12 1960's baseball Hall-of-Famer Blue Moon ___
13 Some sneakers
18 Company with a "lonely repairman"
23 Burden
25 What an English student wore to a deli?
26 Traffic problems at a deli?
28 Beginning on
30 ___ suiter

31 Liberace fabric
32 K-6, as a sch.
33 Canvas cover
34 Length × width, for a rectangle
35 Part of a suit
37 Literary bear
41 Place to put bags?
44 Sharpen
48 Grab quickly
50 Slo-mo footage, perhaps
52 Violinist Zimbalist
54 "___ luck!"
55 Glacial ridge
56 Conjecture
57 Bell curve peak
58 Fencing blade
59 Spider's work
60 Bills not stocked in A.T.M.'s
64 Tokyo of old
65 Mimic

by Peter Abide

ACROSS

1 Use a postscript
4 Turkish Empire founder
9 Sail extender
14 Place to do some gamboling
15 ___ Island
16 See 31-Down
17 Campus climber
18 Workaholic's memoir?
20 Greet the villain
21 Land of 47-Down
22 Sites for rites
23 Exaggerate
25 Soft cheese
26 Gaunt
27 Hardly boisterous
28 Nourished
31 Marine ___
33 Essential
35 Ancient theaters
36 Man of the casa
37 1982 sci-fi flick
38 Cargo quantities
40 "Don't You Know" singer
41 Where Mindy honeymooned
42 Fine things?
43 ___ Alto
44 Pituitary hormone
45 In 25 words or less
48 "My pleasure!"
51 Unfruitful
52 Drone, e.g.
53 Seasoning specialist's memoir?
55 Muldaur's "___ Woman"
56 Tombstone brothers
57 Former S.A.G. president

58 50 degrees, say: Abbr.
59 Chew the scenery
60 Cooper role
61 Fleur-de- ___

DOWN

1 Way out
2 English cattle breed
3 Escaped con's memoir?
4 City liberated by Joan of Arc
5 Unlikely nickname in the N.B.A.
6 Three-reeler, e.g.
7 Mideast's Gulf of ___
8 Classical start
9 Military movements
10 Chatter
11 First name in country music
12 "___ out?"
13 Crewmen
19 Dell dweller
24 Yankee junkball pitcher
25 Crunchy salad toppers
27 Watches
28 Clinton chef's memoir?
29 Passion personified
30 Unit of force
31 With 16-Across, where the Pistons used to play
32 Skunk's defense
33 Not o'er

34 Inscribed pillar
36 Somewhat
39 What some folks can't tolerate
40 1984 Super Bowl champs
43 Did comparison shopping
44 Skillful
45 Pickle juice
46 Longtime SAC chief
47 "The Winding Stair" poet
48 Exuberance
49 Actor Neeson
50 70's do
51 Church part
54 Woeful

by Alfio Micci

101

ACROSS

1 Mayberry toper
5 C sharp
10 Sound astonished
14 Job for a body shop
15 Baghdad native
16 "Takin' __ the Streets" (Doobie Brothers hit)
17 Newswoman Klensch
18 Kind of calendar
19 Enthusiasm
20 Beginning of a prayer
23 Author Bennett
24 Popeye's Olive
25 Schlemiel
26 Walrus hunter
28 Yankee legend Rizzuto
31 Pub. workers
32 Collar stain
33 Butts of jokes
36 Middle of the prayer
41 Suffer sans air conditioning
42 __ Honor
43 Sch. for ministers
46 Fateful day
47 Davis of Hollywood
48 Hunger (for)
50 __ minérale
52 Agony
53 End of the prayer
58 Clunker
59 Language of 380 million
60 Sports figure
62 After-lunch sandwich
63 Just kidding around
64 Clears
65 Easter preparation
66 Quits
67 Not just a trip across town

DOWN

1 Words of praise
2 Fib
3 Mouthing off
4 Night light
5 Totally uncool
6 Bell or whistle
7 Pool demarcation
8 Marine shade
9 Q followers?
10 Thingamajig
11 Loose
12 Slew a vampire, perhaps
13 Raft steerers
21 Part of an e-mail address
22 1990's sitcom
23 Injure
27 Bad reviews
28 Ship refueling places
29 Water (down)
30 Composer Stravinsky
33 Scurried
34 Prefix with -photo
35 Eye sore
37 Knicks center who was the 1986 Rookie of the Year
38 Deep trouble
39 Mechanize
40 It has a bark but no bite
43 $, #, % or &
44 Pooh's grumpy pal
45 Maniacs
47 Clear tables
49 Martian explorer, e.g.
50 Come out in the long run
51 Actor Claude
54 "What's __ ?"
55 Clue
56 Dope
57 Ain't correct?
61 Condescending cluck

by Nancy Salomon and Harvey Estes

ACROSS

1 Insecticide target
6 New Year's popper
10 Truck stop order
14 "Time in a Bottle" singer
15 Bit attachment
16 Where Lima is
17 With 38- and 62-Across, why the maharishi refused Novocain
19 Place to play blackjack
20 Become balanced
21 Pull out
23 "__ magnifique!"
25 Goes underground
26 Screech
30 Broadcast
33 Endless years
34 Hardly important
35 Check cashers' cards
38 See 17-Across
42 "My boy"
43 Good going down
44 Legal rights org.
45 Like Vikings
46 Gentle breeze
48 Command to Rover
51 Lead singer for the Belmonts
53 Dispute
56 Horned thing?
61 Lots of laughs
62 See 17-Across
64 __ Royale National Park
65 Spread served in bars
66 "The Faerie Queene" division
67 Orchard item
68 Grab (onto)
69 John of rock

DOWN

1 Pine (for)
2 Before: Abbr.
3 Sewing machine inventor
4 ". . . __ do better!"
5 Indicate
6 Aegean vacation locale
7 Multivolume ref. work
8 Initiation procedure
9 Fort __ (gold repository)
10 Abominable
11 Coming up
12 Subsequently
13 Heckling sounds
18 Izmir inhabitant
22 Start of many limericks
24 Like Mother Cabrini
26 Srs.' worry
27 Lifesaver, e.g.
28 Horse of a certain color
29 Caravansary
31 500 spot
32 Fishing need
34 Snafu
35 Restless desire
36 Emmy-winning Tyne
37 Insulting remark
39 Tend, as a fire
40 Sleeper or smoker
41 Velvet pile
45 Run off at the mouth
46 Suffix on era names
47 Intertwine
48 Money substitute
49 Modeling asset
50 Bomber name
52 Challenge for a nonnative speaker
54 E.P.A. concern
55 Confess
57 And others, for short
58 Make change?
59 Marquand sleuth
60 In a while
63 "Gloria in excelsis __"

by Richard Silvestri

67

ACROSS

1 "__ magic!"
4 Give a hand
8 About 60% of the world's population
14 Place for a tack
15 Busy place
16 __ in (cozy in bed)
17 Eden exile
18 Black cat, say
19 Mountain nymphs
20 Start of a wife's lament
23 Poles, e.g.
24 Society page word
25 Egyptian cobra
28 Lament, part 2
33 Sherpa sighting, maybe
34 Brazilian port
35 One of the "north 40"
39 Slowly, on a score
42 Off the mark
43 Pickler's need
45 Snack favorite
47 Lament, part 3
53 See 60-Down
54 Chaplin title
55 Louganis feats
57 End of the lament
61 "Hogan's Heroes" setting
64 Inventor's start
65 Start of many an ode's title
66 Pull in
67 Sweetums
68 "For shame!"
69 Portable homes
70 Spanish compass point
71 Printemps follower

DOWN

1 Checkout count
2 Copenhagen park
3 Plaything for two
4 Linguist Noam
5 Car with a bar, perhaps
6 State confidently
7 Brown rival
8 Yom Kippur observer
9 Walter Reed, e.g.
10 Ensures, slangily
11 Alias letters
12 Composer Rorem
13 60's college org.
21 New Deal org.
22 Having one sharp
25 Broadway opening?
26 Cousin of a herring
27 W.W. II journalist Ernie
29 Grig, when grown
30 Western tribesman
31 Burgundy grape
32 Detroit grp.
35 "Waterloo" band
36 Central point
37 Wedding, e.g.
38 Brian of the early Roxy Music
40 Robert Morse title role on Broadway
41 Anthem contraction
44 Put in shackles
46 "Most likely . . ."
48 Long fights
49 Met display
50 Have a bug
51 Actress Mimieux
52 Show to the door
56 Outpouring
57 Court foe of Bjorn
58 Camouflage
59 Dangerous time
60 With 53-Across, a cleaver
61 Posed
62 Cremona crowd?
63 Dadaism founder

by Richard Hughes

ACROSS

1 Beckoned
5 Arroyo
9 Edith Evans, e.g.
13 Travel writer Thollander
14 Arrangement containers
15 Enthralled
16 Start of a quip
19 "___ was saying . . ."
20 "Women Who Run With the Wolves" author
21 Appearance
22 Stipple
23 Rent out
24 Quip, part 2
33 Punts, e.g.
34 Out of place
35 "Bleak House" girl
36 Moons
37 TV adjusters
38 Court score
39 1959 Kingston Trio hit
40 ___ nous
41 In reserve
42 Quip, part 3
45 Stable particle
46 Super Bowl QB Dawson
47 "Kenilworth" novelist
50 "Luck and Pluck" writer
53 As well
56 End of the quip
59 A Guthrie
60 Marshal
61 Other
62 Jim Morrison, e.g.
63 Nanny, perhaps
64 Home bodies?

DOWN

1 Kind of star
2 Comments to a doctor
3 Half of sechs
4 High ways?
5 Bulb measure
6 Court V.I.P. Arthur
7 Tunisian rulers, once
8 Theory
9 Lennon's last home, with "The"
10 Exchange premium
11 One of Chaucer's travelers
12 Hash-house order
14 Horizon, maybe
17 Persian cries
18 Bright-eyed and bushy-tailed
22 Silent-spring causers
23 More than snips
24 Frightful force
25 It comes from the heart
26 Capital on the Bou Regreg river
27 Reach in total
28 Vast, in the past
29 Name on a pencil
30 Point of greatest despair
31 Order
32 Decreases
37 Puzzle
38 Betimes
40 Woman with a lyre
41 "Siegfried," e.g.
43 Lusting after
44 Thomas Gray piece
47 A herring
48 Mackerellike fish
49 Ibsen's home
50 Farming prefix
51 Turkish money
52 Backbiter?
53 Prefix with -port or -play
54 Drying oven
55 Hugo works
57 Piano tune
58 Up on

by Betty Jorgensen

105

69

ACROSS

1 New York stadium name
5 Classic toothpaste
10 Vacation spot
14 Fish for
15 Chopper blade
16 Pad sitter
17 With 27- and 47-Across, a philosophy prof's remark
20 Part of many addresses
21 Brenner Pass's region
22 Try to open a jar, say
23 Old Mideast union: Abbr.
25 With 56-Across, three-time Masters winner
27 See 17-Across
36 "___ I known!"
37 Restrain
38 Knot
39 "Where Do ___?" ("Hair" piece)
40 "The Sopranos" weapon: Var.
42 Legal scholar's deg.
43 Keep an ___ the ground
45 Mötley ___
46 It comes at a premium
47 See 17-Across
51 Repeated cry to a vampire
52 Wasn't brave
53 Pvt.'s goal?
56 See 25-Across
60 Merry dos
64 Wiseacre's reply to the prof
67 Russian poet Akhmatova
68 Bursts (with)
69 Israel
70 Crayolalike
71 Like ___ (with equal probability)
72 Masculine side

DOWN

1 Stamp on an order
2 Bell-shaped lily
3 Caraway, e.g.
4 Barely make
5 Ruffle
6 Publicize
7 Suspect's demand: Abbr.
8 King Hussein's queen
9 Melodically
10 Leonard Bernstein's "___ Love"
11 Hotel freebie
12 Resting place
13 Drain sight
18 Quiz
19 Part of a contract
24 Singer McEntire
26 January holiday inits.
27 Swindler
28 Helmeted comics character
29 Love
30 Buster?
31 Eye site
32 Atwitter
33 City invaded by Tamerlane, 1398
34 "The Hobbit" character
35 ___ a high note
40 Order in a kids' card game
41 Sympathy evoker
44 Poet Hughes
48 Opera's Scotto
49 Slumps
50 Very stylish
53 Mouthful
54 Three-time Gold Glove winner Tony
55 Wildcat
57 When people take tours in Tours?
58 Gulf port
59 Major- ___
61 Film princess
62 Soon
63 It has bars
65 Knack
66 "C' ___ la vie!"

by Jim Page

ACROSS

1 "Peanuts" boy
6 Exile of 1979
10 Carry on, as a campaign
14 Take for one's own
15 Shells, e.g.
16 Allege as fact
17 With one's fingers in a lake?
20 Grand larceny, e.g.
21 "___ Darlin'" (jazz standard)
22 Sugary drink
23 "Relax, private!"
26 Longed (for)
28 Adorns unnecessarily
31 Toiletries holder
33 Brouhaha
34 A.T.M. necessity
35 Wagnerian heroine
39 With one's fingers in a skyscraper?
43 Like last year's styles
44 Part of U.C.L.A.
45 KLM competitor
46 Echo, e.g.
48 An ex of Xavier
50 Bob Cousy's team, for short
53 Duds
55 "Bravo!"
56 Wax producer
58 Latino lady
62 With one's fingers in a socket?
66 Bering Sea island
67 At no time, to poets
68 Ceramists' needs
69 Element #10

70 City to which Helen was abducted
71 Kind of shooting

DOWN

1 Joke response, informally
2 ___ fixe (obsession)
3 December air
4 Send to a mainframe
5 Is miserly
6 Decline in value
7 Seagoing inits.
8 Evil repeller
9 Pueblo dweller
10 Kind of chest or paint
11 For the birds?
12 Hollow rock
13 Blew it
18 "The Science Guy" on TV
19 Ciudad Juárez neighbor
24 Similar
25 Marathoner's shirt
27 Borodin's prince
28 Meower, in Madrid
29 Matinee hero
30 Blaring
32 0's and 1's, to a programmer
34 Absolute worst, with "the"
36 One of the Simpsons
37 Cherished
38 Sinclair rival
40 Cyberspace conversation
41 Grimm youngster
42 Launderer's step
47 ___ Brothers
48 Haunted house sounds
49 Playwright Ibsen
50 "Over There" composer
51 Make jubilant
52 Slowly, on a score
54 Approximation suffix
57 "___ Too Proud to Beg" (1966 hit)
59 Look at flirtatiously
60 Tennis's Lacoste
61 Like some profs.
63 Pester for payment
64 Prefix with logical
65 Have a bawl

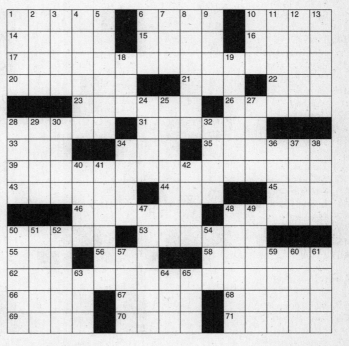

by Fred Piscop

ACROSS

1 Labor Day and many other fed. holidays
5 Canterbury can
9 "Auld Lang __"
13 Eastern nurse
14 Slow, on a score
15 Where homeys hang
16 Lamb's meat made of building blocks?
18 Got on in years
19 Six Flags New England locale
20 Utah state flower
22 For most movie audiences
24 __ y Plata (Montana's motto)
25 Decision regarding a Belafonte song?
31 Picture holder
34 1989 Oscar winner Jessica
35 Susan of "The Partridge Family"
36 Guilty one, in copspeak
37 Lion tamers' needs
38 Wine label info
39 Sister of Zsa Zsa
40 Sound on the hour
41 Totaled, costwise
42 Place for assenting Brits?
45 Ltd., here
46 Foxhole occupant
50 Guaranteed to work
55 Sen. Feinstein
56 Airline since 1948
57 Beatle's maxim?
59 Add fringe to
60 Subordinate Clauses?
61 Oozy ground
62 Hammer or sickle
63 Roy Rogers's real surname
64 Rose part

DOWN

1 Of the cheek
2 Alpha's opposite
3 Bother persistently
4 Made the scene
5 Comprehend
6 Black or red insects
7 Platte River Indian
8 A million to one, say
9 Haifa hello
10 One who sits cross-legged, maybe
11 Christmas
12 Water awhirl
14 Like inferior gravy
17 Sir's mate
21 Unrestrained revelry
23 Like some romances
26 "I love," to Yvette
27 Sets free
28 Genesis garden
29 "Cool!"
30 Newbie
31 Mimic
32 First name in jeans
33 Toot one's own horn
37 "So?"
38 Sail supports
40 Boxes: Abbr.
41 Kindled anew
43 Campus Jewish organization
44 Fusses
47 Mukluks wearer
48 __ nous
49 Shorten again, perhaps
50 Pedal pushers
51 Designer Gucci
52 Othello's ensign
53 Plug up
54 A deadly sin
58 "How about that!"

by Kelly Clark

108

ACROSS

1 Magic practicer
7 What "Bethesda" means
13 Shout of praise
15 Goblet
16 With 37- and 38-Across, a musing
18 Lap dogs
19 Eastern "way"
20 Community spirit
21 "Brian's Song" or "Roots"
24 Big inits. in bowling
27 Historian Durant
28 ___-Bo exercise
31 Person with a stick
34 Beautyrest company
37 & 38 See 16-Across
39 They may get quarters downtown
41 Speech impediment?
42 Govt. medical agency
43 Kind of center
45 Sound after a puncture
46 1958 Edna Ferber novel
50 St. Teresa's town
53 Year in the Amazon
54 "___ the loneliest number"
58 16-, 37- and 38-Across, e.g.
61 Olympic Airways founder
62 Troublemaker
63 Tenant
64 Gauge

DOWN

1 U.P.S., say
2 British vice admiral in the American Revolution
3 "Dilbert" intern
4 Like a lion
5 "___ It Goes" (Ellerbee book)
6 San Antonio-to-Ft. Worth dir.
7 "Evita" role
8 Women's group
9 Prince Valiant's wife
10 Kind of helmet
11 Off-the-wall reply
12 Bottom of the barrel
14 Conductor Toscanini
15 Washing dishes, taking out the garbage, etc.
17 Dry wash
22 Actress Tia
23 "Arabian Nights" hero
24 Mideast capital
25 New Zealander
26 Dogs do it
28 Geometrical solid
29 "___ Ghost" (Michael Ondaatje novel)
30 Parts of car test courses
32 ___ Na Na
33 Film director Kotcheff
35 Computer unit, for short
36 Fold, spindle or mutilate
40 Poppy parts
41 Rubber
44 Mandlikova of tennis
46 "___ My Sugar in Salt Lake City" (1943 hit)
47 Grounds
48 Hooded covers
49 Organic compounds
50 Get an ___ effort
51 Turbine part
52 One-named supermodel
55 Iroquoian Indian
56 Union agreements?
57 I.R.S. ID's
59 Military address
60 Word with black or green

by Dave and Diane Epperson

ACROSS

1 Siamese and Persian
5 Creator of Rabbit and Piglet
10 Soak up some sun
14 Touched down
15 10 on a scale 1 to 10
16 Minute ___
17 Look on tiptoe, say
18 Burglar deterrent
19 Russia's ___ Mountains
20 Ivy preferred by vegetarians?
23 Used car caveat
24 Cuddly bear
25 Rapscallion
28 West Pointer
31 Chit
32 Goalie's spot
35 Crunchy sandwich
39 Ivy found in Haiti?
42 Jab back and forth
43 Unperturbed
44 Mine find
45 Arson evidence
47 Harsh criticism, so to speak
49 Screening device
52 Riverbank component
54 Ivy that belongs in a museum?
60 One who's in it for himself
61 Paris landmark, with "L"
62 It's rough on roaches
64 Moments, informally
65 Fix, as a computer program
66 Microwave
67 Pot component
68 Speechify
69 Hodgepodge

DOWN

1 Insignia site
2 Actor McCowen
3 Wedding cake feature
4 Flow
5 Don Shula's team
6 Runs with no effect
7 Kind of balloon
8 D.E.A. agent
9 Ticklish one
10 Clairol choice
11 Broadcast
12 Almost boil
13 Relative of jade or emerald
21 Org. to adopt a puppy from
22 Road with a no.
25 Tastes
26 Farm combine?
27 A movie star may carry one
28 Jokesters
29 Atlas section
30 Ding
33 Send by FedEx, e.g.
34 Swordplay
36 Teensy bit
37 Business org.
38 Change for a five
40 Cross
41 Instrument played while seated
46 Prepared
48 Reversals
49 The March King
50 "Hedda Gabler" playwright
51 Button on James Bond's dashboard?
52 Swagger
53 General perception
55 Dumbbell
56 Impersonator
57 First name in country
58 Without slack
59 Go on a nature walk
63 Kind of line

by Mark Gottlieb

ACROSS

1 Make fat
5 Teaser
10 Survivalist's stockpile
14 Needle case
15 "They Died With Their Boots On," e.g.
16 Bad news for a bookie
17 It may be hit with a hammer
18 Cheesy part of the neck?
20 Kind of nerve
22 Ballpark figure
23 Tennis call
24 Cheesy 60's TV show?
28 Frito-Lay's parent
31 Longtime Delaware Senator
32 Put away
33 Not be a polite winner
35 Eerie sightings
39 Cheesy 1977 comedy?
44 Coupling
45 Element found in Geiger counters
46 Word with snake or quake
47 Writer on music David ___
51 View
53 Cheesy TV private eye?
57 "Wheel of Fortune" purchase
58 Ballpark figure
59 Lowest deck
63 Cheesy gabber?
67 "Hawaii Five-O" locale
68 Item designed to be blown up?
69 Jungle vine
70 Tito's family name

71 Bones, zoologically
72 Like happy diners
73 Exxon, once

DOWN

1 Kind of blocks
2 On
3 Shrimp
4 Fingers
5 "Ulalume" poet
6 Dosage unit at a reactor
7 Northern Japanese city
8 Initiate
9 "Twelfth Night" lover
10 Dadaism founder
11 Common bedroom furniture material
12 Track athlete
13 Dramatist Clifford
19 Secy.
21 City north of Sacramento
25 Hosiery shade
26 Kind of ring or swing
27 Racketeer
28 Ruefulness
29 Feature of an empty house
30 Furtive look
34 Pallid
36 Denizens of the 46-Across
37 It comes in black and white
38 Part of a deck chair
40 Will of "The Waltons"

41 Complaint
42 "Space cadet"
43 Año starter
48 Not an iron
49 Peers
50 Beaverlike fur
52 Photographer's light
53 "Thriller" singer, in tabloids
54 "It's ___ Kiss" (1964 hit)
55 Track events
56 Convocation of witches
60 Cousin of Sven
61 Cries of surprise
62 Corleone's creator
64 Narcs' employer: Abbr.
65 Half and half
66 Crossed through

by Mark Elliot Skolsky

ACROSS
1 Ship's complement
5 Atlas feature
10 Call's mate
14 Lifesaver
15 Yankees manager Joe
16 Nobelist Wiesel
17 Tech sch. grad
18 Beginning of a quote by W. C. Fields
20 Paparazzo's purchase
22 Place for the undecided
23 Hawaii County's seat
24 Military assaults
26 Quote, part 2
30 Napoleon, notably
31 Debatable
32 It'll take your breath away
35 Easy stride
36 Settle, in a way
38 L.B.J. in-law
39 Coast Guard off.
40 Outstanding
41 Cliffside dwelling
42 Quote, part 3
45 Got bored stiff
46 Bond foe
50 Galloping
51 Astronomer Copernicus
55 End of the quote
58 It towers over Taormina
59 It may be belted
60 Asian capital
61 Actor ___ Patrick Harris
62 ___'acte
63 Midway alternative
64 Kind of case

DOWN
1 Word in French restaurant names
2 Betting setting
3 Thus
4 Unwelcome sight on an apple
5 ". . . is fear ___"
6 "Later!"
7 Sp. ladies
8 Go off
9 Holiday in 60-Across
10 Feature of a miter joint
11 Film role for Kate Nelligan
12 "Odyssey" enchantress
13 Conservative Alan
19 Note in the C minor scale
21 Long sentence
24 Ancient colonnade
25 Mariner's cry
26 Typographer's strike
27 Neurotransmission site
28 Sounds in pounds
29 Drive forward
32 Five-time Wimbledon champ
33 Big Apple award
34 "Not on ___!"
36 1960 Olympics site
37 An OK city
38 Like perfume
40 Half of a 45
41 Part of A.D.
43 Slate.com employee
44 Comics character with an "R" on his sweater
45 Pen
46 Like many kitchens
47 Nautical direction
48 Barks hold it
51 Notable caravel
52 Suit to ___
53 Colleges, to Aussies
54 It may be shaken
56 Sorority chapter
57 Baby's cry

by Jon Delfin

112

ACROSS

1 Targets for snakes
6 Arena shouts
10 Sec
14 Dumpy digs
15 It may be outstanding
16 Chanteuse Adams
17 Capital of Guam, old-style
18 Finito
19 Finito
20 Either way, the letter carrier's work not appreciated
23 Pickled delicacy
24 Clavell's "___-Pan"
25 Rather's network
28 Prefix with sweet
31 Zero in acting
36 Zuñi's cousin
38 Protuberance
40 "M" star
41 Either way, Cupid recognized my pain
44 Nosy Parker
45 Time for eggnog
46 The gamut
47 Court battle?
49 Sine language?
51 Mexican Mrs.
52 Estuary
54 Aurora's counterpart
56 Either way, country star shunned hip-hop
65 Jerusalem's Mosque of ___
66 Hoopster Bryant
67 Like some accents
68 Act the expectant father
69 Hibernia
70 Warren of "Dillinger"
71 Charon's river
72 Take five
73 60's poster genre

DOWN

1 It may have a dimple
2 Stadium section
3 Caplet shape
4 Wish granter
5 Breaks one's back
6 Household spray target
7 Tax
8 Critic Roger
9 Place to fish
10 Skywalker, e.g.
11 Elvis, once
12 Dandy
13 Satellite transmission
21 "Maria ___" (hit of 1941)
22 Early strings
25 Highboy or lowboy
26 Shouldered
27 Three wood
29 Like a neat yard
30 Blockhead
32 Cub with a club
33 Brings (out)
34 Overthrow, e.g.
35 First name in daytime talk
37 "The Heat ___"
39 It may have a fat lip
42 Veep before Gerald
43 1979 sci-fi thriller
48 Tricky pitch
50 Baby talk
53 Really dig
55 Holster part
56 Daddy-o
57 Part of a Latin trio
58 Risqué
59 Natural history museum display
60 Nile bird
61 Mar, in a way
62 Pro ___
63 Maintain
64 Dennis, to Mr. Wilson

by Randall J. Hartman

ACROSS

1 Diplomat Deane
6 Lancia competitor, for short
10 Tee off
14 Prepared to be dubbed
15 Cash in Qom
16 1950's British P.M.
17 Advice to a driver, part 1
20 Hardly genteel
21 Court feat
22 Hardly genteel
23 Literary monogram
24 __ Park (Manhattan neighborhood)
27 Barcelona title
29 One-in-a-million
30 Botanist Gray
33 Advice, part 2
37 Clear of the sea bottom
40 Moulin Rouge performance
41 Advice, part 3
45 Buck's mate
46 Long story
47 Reasons to cram
51 Garden ornamentals
54 Beer may be on it
55 Waters on stage
58 Polo Grounds legend
59 "Dumb" comics girl
60 End of the advice
64 Director Rohmer
65 Tech support caller
66 Actress Anne
67 "Why not?!"
68 Nuclear fuel holders
69 Mountain nymph

DOWN

1 Evades
2 Imbue (with)
3 Dutch cheese
4 Lotion ingredient
5 1950's–70's senator Symington, for short
6 Small toucan
7 One of the front four
8 500-pound, say
9 Apiece, in scores
10 Put in hot oil again
11 Brainchild
12 "Why not?!"
13 Son of Seth
18 "This means __!"
19 Watchdog agcy. beginning 1887
24 Some shorthand
25 Pitching stat
26 React violently, in a way
28 Final notice
30 Sector boundary
31 Rwy. stop
32 Writer Rand
34 Write for another
35 Clotho and others
36 Jet black
37 Tag on
38 A suitor may pitch it
39 Suffix with ethyl
42 Mer contents
43 Disregarded
44 Skier's leggings
48 A.S.A.P.
49 First first lady
50 Neutered
51 British coppers
52 Bridge guru Culbertson
53 J.D. holder: Abbr.
55 Farm females
56 Like some traffic
57 One who's got it coming
59 Shy creature
61 Start of many a Catholic church name
62 G.I. entertainer
63 Telephone interrogatory

by Ed Early

ACROSS

1 Hardly a close contest
5 Marching band section
10 À la mode
14 Biblical preposition
15 Still
16 It may be minced
17 The latest
18 "The Prince of Tides" star
19 __ Minor
20 Aim
22 Underwater worker
24 Picket sign for a Cape Canaveral technician?
27 "Peer Gynt" character
28 Prudential competitor
32 Madame Bovary
36 Frightening word
37 Golden __
38 Get fatter faster?
41 Foul (up)
42 Major club
43 Nudge
44 Candied
45 Levelheaded
47 Farm animal's anatomical pronouncement?
53 Colorful playing marble
56 Reduced
57 Baseball manager Felipe
58 Yale of Yale University
61 Gung-ho
62 Use a spoon, in a way
63 Country album?
64 Clique
65 Mender's target

66 Airbase near Lubbock
67 Sommer in the movies

DOWN

1 Dustup
2 Bridge bid, briefly
3 Calendar run
4 Toughie
5 Explosive situation
6 Certain numero
7 __ canto
8 Calculating
9 Back
10 Paid reluctantly
11 Disservice
12 Lead-in to shame or boy
13 "The Chinese Parrot" hero

21 Cook's hair wear
23 City due west of Daytona Beach
25 Spoils
26 Song whose title translates as "Farewell to Thee"
29 First baseman Martinez
30 Where to go for the jugular
31 King Arthur of the courts
32 Goes back to sea?
33 Catty remark
34 Like a parent who can't bear you?
35 Idle
37 Welcoming party

39 Obligation at some churches
40 Its cap. is Quito
45 Slim and trim
46 One of the 12 tribes of Israel
48 Per annum
49 Utility bill basis
50 Like some ships at sea
51 Sound at a toast
52 Equivocate
53 Long green
54 Kind of sax
55 Hard work
59 __ de la Réunion
60 Is down with

by Manny Nosowsky

115

ACROSS

1 It can be poisonous
6 Flight fleet
10 One with idyll musings?
14 "Cosmicomics" author Calvino
15 A few words in passing?
16 1952 Olympics venue
17 Whence Sir Walter Scott's Fair Maid
18 Zola novel
19 Warbler
20 Stoppard play that made money abroad?
23 Letters for Old MacDonald
24 Mimosa-family tree
25 Cukor film that made money abroad?
29 Encouragement for Escamillo
30 Three-time Masters champ
31 Part of I.R.T.
35 Biblical verb
37 Indian attire
39 Central point
40 On a 42-Across
42 Knockabout, e.g.
44 Just out
45 Rolling Stones hit that made money abroad?
48 Acid neutralizer
51 Written commentary
52 Comedienne who made money abroad?
56 Give obligingly
57 Den din
58 Much-misunderstood writing

61 S-shaped molding
62 Tilted position
63 Follow
64 Microsoft product
65 Countercurrent
66 Swedish imports

DOWN

1 Very small serving
2 Indian tongue
3 Strict sergeants, say
4 Tennis great Gibson
5 Fortune sharers, perhaps
6 Mitchell with a guitar
7 Where bidders wait online
8 "Waterworld" actress Majorino
9 P.O.W.'s place
10 Indian confederacy founder
11 Courtier in "Hamlet"
12 Nicholas Gage novel
13 Friendly Islands
21 Some horses
22 N.E.A. member: Abbr.
23 Gulf of Aqaba port
25 Qatar's capital
26 Pick on
27 Country rocker Steve
28 No exemplar of erudition

32 Spread on Lake Tahoe
33 Head sets?
34 Moist
36 Announced
38 Boating locale
41 Annual song title starter
43 State symbols of Indiana
46 Run through
47 Clavicle connectors
48 Visibly happy
49 "Hasta ___!"
50 Seven-time N.L. home run champ
53 It may be hogged
54 "We the Living" author
55 So-o-o-o SoHo
59 Gist
60 Survey choice

by Alan Arbesfeld

FIVE

Best Diet to Rejuvenate Your Brain

If you are middle-aged and wondering why your memory is not as sharp as in the past, you may find the answer in your refrigerator or on this week's grocery list. While the link between diet and heart health is common knowledge, many are unaware that dietary factors have a powerful influence on the brain.

FOOD FOR THOUGHT

During the past ten years more than 100 studies have highlighted how diet can either expedite the road to dementia or enhance memory and clarity of thoughts. For example, in one study in Finland, Dr. Miia Kivipelto and her team followed 1,500 participants in a 25-year-long study and found that those with high cholesterol were 2.6 times more likely to develop Alzheimer's disease. Dr. Kristine Yaffe from the University of California discovered a 1.7 times higher risk of cognitive decline among the 1,037 post-menopausal women in her study who had elevated levels of bad LDL cholesterol. From these studies, it is evident that what you put in your mouth on a regular basis today can affect your brain cognition and memory much later in life.

LEADING CAUSES OF AGING IN THE BRAIN

To find ways to keep your brain young and healthy we must first examine the three problems that lead to aging in the brain.

1. Inflammation. The same inflammatory processes occurring because of the wear-and-tear of aging in your joints and skin, which leads to arthritis and wrinkles, also occur in the brain. The inflammatory response consists of releasing highly reactive oxygen molecules, called "free radicals." The free radicals aggressively bond to most molecules in their vicinity in attempt to destroy them. Some believe that the by-products of long-term brain cell activities may be triggering the age-related inflammation in the brain. Scientists have measured the levels of different molecules in cascades of inflammation to determine that older adults with more cognitive deficits have higher levels of inflammation.

2. Atherosclerosis, the clogging of arteries and blood vessels, can limit blood flow to the brain over several decades. Foods high in cholesterol, fats, salt or triglycerides contribute to hypertension and subsequent atherosclerosis in the brain. Blood vessels narrowed by atherosclerosis become less flexible and less efficient in allowing a smooth and easy flow of oxygen and nutrients to brain cells. Hardening of the blood vessels in the heart leads to chest pain and heart attacks; hardening of the blood vessels in the brain leads to a lack of energy, depression, memory loss and dementia. By lessening your intake of these unhealthy foods, you can keep your blood vessels young and thus allow more nutrients to reach your heart and your brain.

3. Amyloid buildup. Unlike inflammation and atherosclerosis, the third problem harming your brain with aging is unique to the brain. A protein called "amyloid," naturally present in synapses, clumps up and turns into hard plaques. With aging, and to a more severe degree in Alzheimer's disease, amyloid protein fragments accumulate rapidly and cannot be successfully cleared from the brain. As a result, they pile on top of each other, form toxic gumlike balls, and kill thousands of surrounding neurons. These proteins trigger a vicious inflammatory response, thus further complicating the problem and extending the scope of the mess into the brain.

FIGHTING INFLAMMATION

Combating inflammation in the brain must be your first priority. A diet rich in antioxidant vitamins is essential in protecting the brain against the consequences of inflammation. Fruits and vegetables are an ideal source of antioxidant vitamins. Dr. James Joseph, of the Human Nutrition Research Center for Aging at Tufts University, believes purple-colored fruits such as blueberries, cranberries and concord grapes are particularly beneficial. Other fruits and vegetables high in antioxidants include blackberries, plums, avocados, oranges, cherries, red apples, spinach, brussels sprouts, broccoli, beets, kale and red bell peppers.

However, for those who cannot eat four or five servings of fruits and vegetables on a daily basis, supplements of the antioxidant vitamins are a reasonable substitute. Many different large-scale studies in Europe and the United States have revealed an association between antioxidant vitamin E and better brain function in the elderly. For example, Dr. Martha Clare Morris from the Rush Institute of Healthy Aging noted that among the 815 participants in her study, vitamin E users were 70 percent less likely to develop Alzheimer's disease than those who did not take the supplement. In another study of approximately 5,000 individuals in Utah, Dr. Peter Zandi and his colleagues at Johns Hopkins, Duke University and the University of Utah reported a 68 percent reduction in Alzheimer's disease among participants who consumed vitamin E plus vitamin C on a regular basis.

CHEERS!

Not only can an apple a day keep the doctor away, but so can a glass of wine each evening. Drinking one or two glasses of wine may have some anti-inflammatory action in the brain and heart. A dozen researchers, including the group led by Dr. Monique Breteler in the Netherlands, have provided convincing evidence for the protective role of alcohol, especially red wine, for better cognitive longevity. Those with religious, medical or personal reasons to avoid alcohol may find grape juice a comparable alternative. Some researchers believe grapes and wines have similar benefits in fighting inflammation.

COMBATING ATHEROSCLEROSIS

Atherosclerosis is a major contributor to memory loss and mental decline. To combat it you'll need to eat foods low in cholesterol, low in salt and high in fibers. When confronted with a choice of fatty foods such as greasy hamburgers or a bowl of soup, you need to think twice before biting into the sandwich. Your lifestyle choices concerning food determine your chance of staying mentally sharp or declining into mental dullness. You need to act smart, give up your old habits and start choosing soups, salads and vegetable servings more often. You can still enjoy hamburgers or whichever vice you prefer, but no more than once a month.

COMBATING AMYLOID BUILDUP: A SPICY SURPRISE TO FIGHT ALZHEIMER'S

The curcumin spice that gives curry chicken its yellow color has also been a surprise in the field of nutrition and brain health. Some scientists believe the much lower incidence of Alzheimer's disease in India, 25 percent of that in the United States, may be in part due to widespread use of this herb in India. Curcumin, a natural remedy used for the past 5,000 years, appears to serve both as an anti-inflammatory agent as well as an anti-amyloid agent.

Even mice engineered to develop Alzheimer's disease show fewer amyloid plaques if their diet is supplemented with curcumin. A clinical trial for treatment of early Alzheimer's disease with curcumin is now underway in California. This powerful and natural compound has benefits for all other bodily organs faced with inflammation. While you can choose to cook with curry spice or take curcumin supplements, in India they also rub the herb on inflamed joint areas to treat arthritis.

THE BEST BRAIN FOOD

Omega-3 fatty acids, such as docosahexaenoic acid (DHA) found in seafood, are the best brain food. Up to 60 percent of the brain consists of these polyunsaturated fatty acids. Low levels of DHA are found in patients with depression, chronic fatigue syndrome and Alzheimer's. Adding this supplement improves mood, motivation and energy levels. By enriching DHA consumption, you enrich your energy levels, which in turn allows you to exercise and play brain games like crosswords more easily and often. DHA provides the building blocks for the formation of new synapses in the hippocampus to improve your memory and concentration. DHA not only slows the cognitive decline associated with aging and dementia but is critical for brain development and, as such, has been added to infant formulas. Rich DHA sources include salmon, sardines, bluefish and herring.

Cardiologists in Europe have discovered striking benefits of DHA in reducing the risk of irregular heart rate in patients who have suffered heart attacks. In the Italian GISSI-Prevenzione study in 2002, doctors saw 20 percent fewer deaths among the 11,000 heart attack patients who were taking DHA. European doctors prescribe DHA for all patients with heart disease, and now the American Cardiac Association also recommends DHA supplements. Knowing the protective benefits of DHA in the brain and heart provides increasing impetus for eating at least two servings of fish every week. Other good sources of omega-3 fatty acids include canola oil and walnut oil.

EAT YOUR VEGETABLES!

In a poignant study on the relation between food and the brain, Dr. Martha Clare Morris and her team from Rush University in Chicago noted a 40 percent reduction in risk of Alzheimer's disease among the 3,718 participants of their study if they ate 2–3 servings of fruits and vegetables daily. The study participants had enhanced their cognition to the point where their minds were comparable to that of an individual five years younger than themselves. Similar results were also seen by researchers at the National Institute of Milan. Elderly subjects reporting a diet filled with fruits, vegetables, nuts, fiber and fish could complete memory tests three times faster than their neighbors and siblings on a higher fat and cholesterol diet.

LARGER WAISTLINE, WEAKER MEMORY

People often cannot understand how they rapidly went from being slightly chubby and not fitting into their jeans to not quite fitting in an airplane seat. Here is the secret: Fat accumulating in your body secretes hormones that travel through your bloodstream, reaching your brain cells and signaling that you need to stop eating. One of the hormones, called "leptin," controls appetite. When you pass from being overweight to being obese, the appetite control system starts failing. The gut/brain link stops working and leptin loses its ability to inform your brain you have eaten too much. A vicious cycle ensues in which you eat more and have less awareness of overeating, allowing you to spiral out of control, then get surprised every time you stand on the bathroom scale.

A waistline of 35 inches or higher for women and 40 or higher for men is one of the diagnostic criteria for a prediabetic condition called "metabolic syndrome." Dr. Kristine Yaffe has discovered that people with metabolic syndrome are far more likely to experience cognitive impairment with aging. She and her colleagues believe that obese patients with metabolic syndrome experience an increase in the amount of inflammation in the brain, which causes damage to neurons and their synapses.

STEP 5: CHOOSING BRAIN-HEALTHY SUBSTITUTIONS FOR YOUR DIET

- Choose whole grains, such as whole wheat breads, cereals or brown rice (not regular white rice).

- Choose fresh fruits for dessert (not canned fruits, chocolate or cakes).

- Choose an apple or a pear for a snack (not a cookie).

- Choose salad as your main dish (not as a side dish).

- Choose balsamic vinegar and olive oil for salad dressing (not creamy Italian).

- Choose a whole-fruit blended smoothie (not a milkshake).

- Choose a baked potato (not french fries).

- Choose baked or broiled chicken (not fried chicken).

- Choose baked chips (not deep-fried potato chips).

- Choose mustard (not mayo).

- Choose salmon (not fried fish).

- Choose low-fat milk (not whole milk).

- Choose chocolate, ice cream or candy only for special occasions (not every day).

- Choose water, cranberry or grapefruit juice (not sweet soda).

- Choose low-sodium crackers, chips and snacks (not salty pretzels).

- Choose to give up minor gratifications with certain foods (not your long-term brain health and mental sharpness).

NOURISH YOUR BRAIN

You can choose to nourish your brain health or diminish your brain function by your everyday choices in what you take out of your refrigerator and what you put in your grocery shopping bag. Now that you know high cholesterol, fatty foods, salty pretzels and calorie-filled soft drinks can slowly eat away your brain synapses, you can choose to make smart decisions about what you eat.

Both the quantity and the quality of food affect your brain health. The extra weight you carry burdens your heart and your brain in the long term. While monitoring and avoiding brain-harming foods, make an honest and sincere effort to lose your extra pounds. You can set a reasonable goal, such as losing two pounds a week until you reach your ideal body weight. You will love the way you will look and feel, and your brain will be happier and sharper, too.

What you eat does affect your brain both in the short term and the long term. If you are concerned about memory loss and developing Alzheimer's disease, you need to make healthier choices about the quality and the quantity of the food you consume on a daily basis. Make blueberries, grapes and a piece of salmon part of your favorite food choices.

80

ACROSS
1 Pay
9 Poohs
15 Acquire
16 Slanted
17 Interest
18 First name in 60's pop
19 Letter series
20 Brewpub offering
22 Year in the reign of Ivan the Terrible
23 Like ___ on a string
25 Coin with the image of a springbok
26 "That's ___"
27 Damaging insects
30 Part of a capt.'s order
31 Has ___ (is connected)
32 Machine wedge
34 Wave, for one
36 Darned, in Dover
38 Schoolyard challenge
39 More husky
40 Foreign trio member?
41 Abbr. in many group names
42 Ready to go off-line?
44 Balance
48 What two dots may mean
49 Breakfast acronym
51 It has a code
52 Old Japanese coin
53 Mints, e.g.
56 Galoot
57 Want
59 One in training?

61 Cause to be absorbed
62 It's used to avoid listing
63 Pool parties
64 Something to shoot

DOWN
1 Ancient religious symbol
2 Begins quickly
3 Forum buyer?
4 "Malcolm X" director
5 One might be chronic
6 Kind of child
7 Sheer
8 "What a shame"
9 Unrealistic notions
10 Suffix with old
11 Skimmer, e.g.
12 Turquoise component
13 Symbol of success
14 Having no symmetry, in a way
21 Stumper
24 Ultimatum words
26 Infielder's failure
28 Fraternity letters
29 Beans and fries, e.g.
33 Aromatic resins
35 Game with trump cards
36 Most overbearing
37 Sorting criterion
39 Shags, say
43 "Sure"
45 Tailor, at times
46 Not going anywhere
47 Regarded to be
50 Murdoch University site
53 "Don't take ___ seriously"
54 Dash
55 Threw off
58 Actor Silver
60 W.W. II zone

by Rich Norris

ACROSS

1 Book of maps
6 Lounge
10 Lounge
14 Milk purchase
15 Actress Falco
16 Word before a verb, maybe
17 Pain inside
18 Taboo
19 Not timid
20 Cruising
21 1986 Detroit debut
23 Refuses
25 Tall tale
26 E.P.A. concern: Abbr.
29 Paint over
33 Government subsidy
38 This-and-that dish
39 21-Across, e.g.
40 Bruin Bobby
41 Singer __ James
42 Story line
43 1998 Peter Weir film, with "The"
46 Group of 100
48 "No sweat"
49 Six years, in the 46-Across
51 Period of greatest success
56 Amateurish
61 Prefix with -naut
62 Aware of
63 Without value
64 Express appreciation to
65 __ Clayton Powell Jr.
66 Help for a detective
67 "It's the truth!"
68 Region
69 Renaissance Italian family name
70 Carried with difficulty

DOWN

1 Shades of blue
2 Oklahoma city
3 Cagney's TV partner
4 Regions
5 Narrow waterway: Abbr.
6 Late-night name
7 Olfactory stimulus
8 Dance named after an aviator
9 Dance class wear
10 Grouped
11 It may get into a jamb
12 Humdinger
13 They may be split or tight
21 An ellipse has two of them
22 "__ you sure?"
24 Take-home
27 __ about (approximately)
28 Lash __, who played the Cheyenne Kid in old westerns
30 Pledge
31 Concerning
32 Unfreeze
33 Openings
34 It may begin "Do not . . ."
35 Lots
36 Out
37 "__ la Douce" (1963 film)
43 Actor Stamp
44 Tennis's Arthur
45 Bill __, TV's Science Guy
47 No. on a business card
50 Manhandles
52 "Hurray!"
53 Had control of the deck
54 Golfer Palmer, informally
55 Like farm oxen
56 Husband of Ruth, in the Bible
57 Take back
58 Funnyman Laurel
59 Oversupply
60 Peter Fonda title role
64 Explosion maker

by Alan Arbesfeld

82

ACROSS

1 Like a tack
6 Cape Cod town
11 Mercedes rival
14 Fencing sword
15 Tore down
16 Sculler's need
17 What to accentuate, to Bing Crosby . . .
19 Get mellower
20 Swift works
21 Gown material
23 Neat dresser's quality
27 Some radios
30 What to eliminate . . .
34 Terra ___
36 Málaga Mrs.
37 River to the Caspian
38 Home of the Jazz
39 Rocker John
41 Cost to cross
42 Abundant
43 Place to graze
44 Have a gut feeling
45 What to latch onto, with "the" . . .
49 Kobe currency
50 ___ ridgeback (hunting dog)
52 Unable to sit still
55 Pre-cable need
59 Halloween word
60 Whom not to mess with
64 Play for a sap
65 Really spooky
66 Lake ___, separating Switzerland and France
67 Mack who emceed TV's "The Original Amateur Hour"
68 Play for time
69 Bolt to unite

DOWN

1 Fliers from De Gaulle
2 "Good joke!"
3 Help in a heist
4 Adjust, as a brooch
5 Proportionately
6 See 32-Down
7 Squealer
8 Israeli weapon
9 Ministerial nickname
10 Ukrainian port
11 Ferry or wherry
12 Crèche trio
13 Small songbird
18 Genesis son
22 Shrewd
24 Administer the oath of office to
25 "I, Claudius" role
26 Alaska's first governor
27 Integra maker
28 Recurring theme
29 Shepherd's handful
31 O. Henry specialty
32 With 6-Down, Sibelius work
33 Popular 90's sitcom
35 Not ours
39 Patron saint of sailors
40 Heavy metal
44 Space Needle site
46 Rapper's improvisations
47 Sanford of "The Jeffersons"
48 Kudzu, for one
51 Staircase support
52 Border on
53 Cyrano's protrusion
54 Pigeon-___
56 Verre skipper
57 Kind of tide
58 ___ Boleyn, queen to Henry VIII
61 Emeritus: Abbr.
62 Nest egg letters
63 Nada

by Holden Baker

126

MEMOGUARD: AN IDEAL SUPPLEMENT FOR GUARDING MEMORY AND BRAIN HEALTH

In the crowded world of vitamin supplements, all promising to prevent something different from weight loss to age-related memory loss, a few are taking the lead. These candidates meet the necessary requirements of an ideal dietary supplement. They have been investigated in reputable epidemiological and basic research studies with convincing positive results, have minimal to no side effects at reasonable doses and are safe and cheap. The ultimate test, a randomized clinical trial, is now underway for many.

Having reviewed the literature in the field of supplements and brain health, and based on my own 20 years of research studies at Harvard and Johns Hopkins medical institutions, I vote for a cocktail that contains vitamin E, vitamin C, DHA and curcumin. I could not find such a supplement in the market and as such took steps to have it manufactured and distributed in North America. Called MemoGuard, it offers the best combination of natural nutrients to guard your brain health against the effects of aging.

I believe the clinical trials in several academic institutions around the country for either curcumin or DHA in combating early signs of Alzheimer's disease will soon prove successful. DHA, which is a fat-soluble compound, helps with the absorption of curcumin into the brain. In turn, vitamin E increases the viability and stability of DHA so that it remains active for a longer period of time. Vitamin E itself improves blood circulation in the brain. Vitamin C recycles the antioxidant properties of vitamin E and prolongs its effects.

As such, vitamin E, vitamin C, DHA and curcumin ingredients in MemoGuard are designed to provide a complementary and synergistic set of supplements for protecting your brain against inflammation, atherosclerosis and amyloid build-up. The dosage of each component is within the safe range and the combination does not have any significant side-effects. MemoGuard has the potential to help you keep your brain young without causing any harmful effects.

83

ACROSS
1 The Charleses' canine
5 Circus employee
10 Full of energy
14 Slick, in conversation
15 "I'd walk ___ for . . ."
16 Saharan
17 Doesn't keep
18 Hoarder's supply
19 Provide pro tem
20 Start of a quote by 53-Across, when asked to name his favorite song
23 Carbolic acid
24 Moving about
28 Quote, part 2
33 R.p.m. indicator
36 Lacks, in brief
37 Go for the gold?
38 Nickname of radio shock jock Greg Hughes
39 Monte ___
40 Chops, e.g.
41 Bobby on the ice
42 Slur over
43 Rainbows, e.g.
44 End of the quote
48 What "dis" is
49 Self-assured
53 Speaker of the quote
58 Chamber phenomenon
61 TV producer Spelling
62 Verve
63 Channel marker
64 Amount wagered

65 "Fashion Emergency" host
66 Buzzers
67 High bridge card
68 Talk back to

DOWN
1 "Get ___ on yourself!"
2 Sluggard's sin
3 Share with the church
4 Green liqueur
5 Angler's gear
6 Nanjing nanny
7 Flexible mineral
8 Like some textbook publishing
9 Item of 5-Down

10 Overshoe
11 Lode load
12 Card player's shout
13 Like all primes but one
21 Kabuki kin
22 1920's chief justice
25 Put darts into, as a garment
26 Singer Hayes
27 Carries on
29 The Andes, e.g.
30 Start to go?
31 Speck on a map
32 Rock's Brian
33 Characters in cels
34 Patriots' Day month
35 Approximately

39 Middle of the second century
40 Early shows
42 Hence
45 Relishes
46 Game one
47 H+, e.g.
50 1965 march city
51 Dutch treats?
52 Units of force
54 Talk (over)
55 Expanding grp.
56 Ollie's human friend
57 "The Mikado" character
58 Flow's partner
59 "The Hustler" prop
60 Ground breaker

by Sarah Keller

128

ACROSS

1 Pampering places
5 Pronunciation indicator
10 See 40-Across
14 Minor stroke
15 Loads of fun
16 Word with Bay or gray
17 Gray
18 Something not to talk about
19 Naval position: Abbr.
20 Leaves a center for cereal abuse?
23 Bard's nightfall
24 AWOL chasers
25 Go online
27 An hour of prime-time TV, often
29 Back muscles, for short
32 Grp. vigorously backing the Second Amendment
33 It's not the norm
36 @
37 Makes cereal more flavorful?
40 With 10-Across, place to get milk and bread
41 Divide, as Gaul
42 TV puppet voiced by Paul Fusco
43 Asian cookers
44 Kind of bulb
48 Mrs. Ceausescu of Romania
50 Galoot
52 Whole
53 Master cereal-maker's knowledge?
58 Spirit, in Islamic myth
59 42-Across, for one

60 Crowning
61 "I Want ___" (Rodgers and Hart song)
62 Kitschy film monster
63 Loafer, e.g.
64 Depend
65 Low-rent, maybe
66 Rancher's concern

DOWN

1 Went blank in the head
2 Narc's target
3 Armored Greek goddess
4 River to the underworld
5 Stayed awake
6 Heart-to-hearts

7 Wanderer
8 Rough bark
9 Ending with comment or liquid
10 Swaggering
11 French brandy
12 Good wood for cabinetry
13 Pit contents
21 Muscat dweller
22 Chicago transports
26 "Nope"
28 Skirt for the modest
29 Blue stone
30 Regrettably
31 Northumberland river
34 Palindromic guy's name
35 Gloom

36 Accusatory question
37 Play solitaire, perhaps
38 Hellish
39 Certain jazz combo
40 Al Capp's Daisy ___
43 Salon job
45 Abhor
46 Like some pools
47 Complained slightly
49 Fool
50 Having the most points
51 Copper
54 Galley workers
55 Arctic sight
56 Lunar effect
57 Unheedful
58 Food container

by Peter Sarrett

ACROSS

1 General assembly?
9 What leaky pens leave
14 Visited overnight
15 Predisposed
16 "Is that so?"
17 Shakespearean character in a "most extracting frenzy"
18 Monarch capturer
19 Hard rock band?
21 Very smooth
23 Cloth on certain tables
24 Opposite of peace
25 It might help you get up
27 Tom's cries
29 __ Hughes, former British poet laureate
30 Performed a cadenza, e.g.
32 Bamboozles
34 "Our Town" family name
36 Poet __ Wheeler Wilcox
37 Place for a brush
41 Some forensic evidence
45 Theory
46 Kind of collector
48 Stupid
49 Crankcase additive
50 "Stand and Deliver" star, 1987
52 Certain pens
53 Like an air-filled lifeboat
57 Mind the baby
58 Black-and-orange bird
59 Early motion picture projector
61 1980's South African president __ Botha
62 Working together
63 Brewers' kilns
64 Lack of color

DOWN

1 Also-ran for the 1992 Democratic presidential nomination
2 Play set mostly in Cyprus
3 Incomplete
4 Departure announcement
5 Interpret
6 Improvised
7 Low bow
8 Blocks
9 Put a coat on
10 Hideaway
11 Render unnecessary
12 Bridle attachment
13 Proteus and Nereus
15 Independent sort
20 Thunderstorm residue
22 Fry a bit
26 Comes together
28 Dependable
31 Legendary criminal played by Treat Williams in a 1981 movie
33 One stuck in the kitchen
35 Dances
37 Early 80's "S.N.L." comic
38 Resicential section of Queens
39 Suggests
40 Windhoek is its capital
42 Installment
43 File box contents, maybe
44 Some analysts' concerns
47 Spring signalers
51 Big-toed animal
54 Former Senate majority leader
55 Porters
56 Actor Morales
60 "This is __"

by Patrick Berry

BEST FOOD FOR A HEALTHIER BRAIN

Antioxidant Berries

black currants	cranberries	strawberries
blackberries	mulberries	
blueberries	raspberries	

Antioxidant Fruits

apples (red)	kiwifruit	papayas
avocados	kumquats	pineapples (fresh)
cherries	lemons	plums
grapes (red)	limes	pomegranates
guavas	oranges	

Antioxidant Vegetables

alfalfa sprouts	chard	olives
beets	collards	onions
bell peppers (red)	fennel bulb	spinach
bok choy	garlic	sweet potatoes
broccoli	green beans	tomatoes
brussels sprouts	green onions	turnip greens
cabbage	kale	
cauliflower	leeks	

Antioxidant Herbs and Spices

basil	licorice	rosemary
cinnamon	mint	thyme
chili peppers	oregano	turmeric
cloves	parsley	

Antioxidant Nuts

almond	hazelnuts	sunflower seeds
flaxseed	linseed	walnuts

Other Sources of Antioxidants

cocoa	green tea

Sources of DHA
algae   mackerel   tuna
blue fish   salmon
herring   sardines

For Reducing Amyloid Load in the Brain
curcumin
DHA sources (see above)
blueberries (to a lesser extent)

ACROSS
1 See 59-Across
6 Kachina performer
10 In very short order
14 Corday killed him
15 "___ in Berlin" (1960 jazz album)
16 Luncheon follower
17 Popular snack chip
18 Produce a faint image of
20 Stir up trouble
22 Picture with a posse, perhaps
23 Natural boundary
24 Holders of blessed bread
25 Scammed
28 Part of some Muslim households
29 Extensive variety
31 Asian waist product?
34 Old Testament book
35 They may leave a stain
36 Uintah and Ouray Reservation inhabitants
37 Early '50s soldier
38 American competitor
40 Set off
42 State follower, sometimes
43 Some steak preparers
45 "Fiddler on the Roof" star
46 Routine
47 They may be shifted in transit
51 Banks' go-between
53 Name on a compact
54 Roll and bind
55 ___ Dartle, woman in "David Copperfield"
56 One may be picky
57 Exercise options?
58 First-year Harvard law student
59 With 1-Across, pseudo-wits

DOWN
1 Like some tuners
2 Superman's mother
3 Nobelist poet ___ Axel Karlfeldt
4 Wedding expenses
5 Doing warehouse work
6 Providential
7 Like a big brother
8 Furthermore
9 Existential declaration
10 Make fizzy
11 "Eureka" or "Excelsior"
12 When some take a coffee break
13 Looks
19 Cooperative people?
21 Air-conditioned people?
24 Soup flavorers
25 Michael, for one
26 Contents of some barrels
27 Bird whose cry sounds like laughter
28 Flat
30 Swing
32 Primitive monetary unit
33 Cuba's ___ of Youth
36 July 4 parade figure
38 Simon of pop
39 Heroic poems
41 Some divers' booty
43 Shirt pair
44 Deplete
45 Make frizzy
47 Rocky or Bullwinkle
48 "___ Kett"
49 Buck, say
50 Rockefeller Center muralist
52 Dude

by Dana Motley

133

ACROSS

1 Office station
5 Arthur ___ Stadium
9 "Hurrah!," e.g.
14 School for princes William and Harry
15 Swing at a fly
16 Fool (around)
17 Bounce back
18 "Stop right there!"
19 Ringmaster
20 Judge's query
23 Foal's father
24 ___ League (56-Down's group)
25 Krazy ___
28 Bureaucratic stuff
31 "___, humbug!"
34 Cake topper
36 Little devil
37 Voice below soprano
38 Doctor's query
42 Sliver
43 18-wheeler
44 Desert spring
45 ___ Canals (Great Lakes connectors)
46 Light lager
49 Farm bale
50 Sidekick
51 See 40-Down
53 Bartender's query
59 See 8-Down
60 Beach composition
61 Shade of blue
63 Raise the curtain
64 Wings: Lat.
65 Deep ___ bend
66 Nose, slangily
67 Baby-sit
68 E-mailed

DOWN

1 Lousy grade
2 Carve in stone
3 Old warehouse district in New York
4 "Who ___ what evil . . ." (intro to "The Shadow")
5 On dry land
6 Moved to the music
7 Crown of light
8 With 59-Across, words before "Then fall, Caesar!"
9 Make ready for use, as library books
10 Warm and comfortable
11 SeaWorld whale
12 Not new
13 Titleist supporter
21 Sad song
22 Longstocking lass
25 Fuzzy fruits
26 Sneeze sound
27 Link with
29 Supermodel Cheryl
30 Morning hrs.
31 Turn red from embarrassment
32 Heart chambers
33 ___-totsy
35 Gun lobby, briefly
37 "Eureka!"
39 Dentist's tool
40 With "of" and 51-Across, a facial moisturizer
41 Religious scroll
46 ___ leather
47 Former White House speechwriter Peggy
48 Sidestepped
50 Outdoor party site
52 Foes of Rebs
53 Chirpy bird
54 Justice Black
55 Future atty.'s exam
56 New Haven institution
57 Barn topper
58 Neck and neck
59 Air rifle ammo
62 However

by Gregory E. Paul

ACROSS

1 Five Pillars of __
6 Tobacco wad
10 Prez's backup
14 Impact sounds
15 Heavenly circle
16 Not prerecorded
17 It may bring you back to reality
19 Warts and all
20 Pail problem
21 Queried
22 Splinter group
23 Cowgirl Evans
25 Enter
27 Exit
30 Not the main office
32 Opposite of spicy
33 Replay option
34 __-Locka, Fla.
37 Diamond __
38 Running things
40 Part of WWW
41 NBC weekend comedy, briefly
42 Thoroughly thumps
43 Nerd
45 Lifers, e.g.
47 Like heaven's gates
48 Bee's bundle
50 Say coquettishly
51 Sailor's hail
52 Warning wail
55 Nada
59 Fancy marbles
60 Academic enclave
62 Algonquian language
63 Understands
64 Laker star Shaquille
65 Aesop's also-ran
66 Big Board initials
67 Full of good cheer

DOWN

1 Result of a flea, maybe
2 "Get lost!"
3 Break in the action
4 Appended
5 Ed.'s pile
6 Picked out
7 Dove's opposite
8 Downwind, at sea
9 Scrabble or Boggle
10 Pickle brand
11 President whose grandson wed a president's daughter
12 Kick out
13 Trattoria topping
18 Sentry's command
24 Loud enough to hear
26 Coming
27 OPEC units: Abbr.
28 Lena of "Havana"
29 Nonmixer at a mixer
30 Ink stains
31 Column crossers
33 Go over
35 Part of a lemon
36 "Dear" advice-giver
39 Advertising lure
44 Combat area
46 Parisian palace
47 Undersized
48 Antismoking aid
49 Scarlett of Tara
50 Inherently
53 Actress Judith
54 Goes bad
56 Water pitcher
57 Spot for a spanking
58 Air France locale
61 Barnyard male

by Nancy Salomon

89

ACROSS

1 Composer whose music is often heard at graduations
6 Word on some diplomas
11 TV sked abbr.
14 Take for a while
15 When the Boston Marathon is held
16 It comes with a charge
17 Nondefensive military move
19 Shine, in product names
20 High dudgeon
21 Baby's ring
23 There are six of these in the middle of 17- and 56-Across and 11- and 25-Down
28 Razor brand
29 Hand or foot
30 "Well, well!"
31 Reassuring words
32 High muck-a-mucks
34 Of the flock
35 Ending of the Bible
36 Medium settings?
38 Punishment, metaphorically
41 Base tune
43 Garage figure
45 Old-hat
47 Santa ___ (hot winds)
48 "Paradise Lost," e.g.
49 Roguish
50 Jam producer
52 Scam artist
54 1995 court V.I.P.
55 Eastern way
56 "Just do it," e.g.
62 Lennon's lady
63 Sun Valley locale
64 Mirage sight
65 Theologian's subj.
66 Dot in the ocean
67 On the dot

DOWN

1 Tiny toymaker
2 Hula hoop?
3 Long-snouted fish
4 Basketball stat
5 Back in?
6 Place for a pin
7 Financing abbr.
8 Like sandpaper
9 "Just do it" shoes
10 Away from the wind
11 Fix
12 "10" music
13 Eskimo garb
18 Tour for Nicklaus
22 "Mon Oncle" star
23 1, 8 or 27
24 "Step ___!"
25 Some adult education
26 Dog star?
27 Emerging
31 Capital of old Moldavia
33 Crosby partner
34 Reveal accidentally
37 Future J.D.'s hurdle
39 Auricular
40 Knock flat
42 Connors contemporary
44 Hanukkah item
45 Flock leader
46 Like federal tax laws
47 From the heart?
50 Sweat units
51 Group values
53 Early 12th-century date
57 Leader in a beret
58 On a roll
59 ___ rule
60 Lady's man
61 Unproven ability

by Greg Staples

136

SIX

Exercise to Boost Your Brainpower

Exercise lowers your blood pressure, cuts your risk of diabetes, improves your metabolism, tones your muscles and minimizes your risk of heart attacks. But did you know that exercise also gives a boost to your brainpower?

The link between mind and body works in both directions. Just as your mind's choice of food and lifestyle decisions affect the shape of your body, the level of activity and the tone of your muscles impact the shape and ability of your brain. An active and a fit body fuels an active brain. Physical exercise sharpens your memories and can slow and reverse the toll of aging on your brain.

FIT BODY, FIT BRAIN

Dr. Kristine Yaffe from the University of California in San Francisco monitored the health and memory of 6,000 elderly women to determine if walking can slow the age-related mental decline. Some women walked only half a mile per week, while others walked as much as 17 miles per week. In the course of eight years, a linear association formed between more walking and enhanced memory. For every extra mile walked, there was a 13 percent chance of postponing cognitive dullness.

In a Laval University study in Canada, the elderly with couch-potato lifestyles were twice as likely to develop Alzheimer's disease as people with a mild level of physical activity per week. Among the 5,000 participants monitored for five years, those who had walked more were more successful in lowering their risk for dementia. In another Canadian study from the University of Halifax, scientists discovered that the earlier subjects started an exercise program the better the chances of their delaying Alzheimer's. At least a dozen other studies have provided strong evidence that exercise keeps the brain fit, but the most striking results came from a study of sedentary elderly after a six-month walking program.

Dr. Arthur Kramer and his team of colleagues at the University of Illinois monitored a group of volunteers in their 60's and 70's who had not exercised in more than ten years. They instructed the volunteers to begin a physical fitness program, starting with 15-minute sessions three times a week, then increasing to 45 minutes. They monitored another parallel group of elderly volunteers who remained sedentary and a third group who performed only simple stretching movements three times a week. For every 5 percent improvement in heart and lung health, there was a 15 percent improvement in their performances on memory and cognitive tests. A simple walking program, with no expensive gadgets or fancy equipments, resulted in larger brain capacity and sharper memories.

Improving fitness lifts your mood and helps to shake off your blues. Dr. James Blumenthal from Duke University divided 156 patients experiencing depression into three groups. One group received only medications, one received medication plus exercise, and the third group did not take any medications and simply exercised. He discovered that the exercise group gained the same degree of improvement as those on antidepressant drugs. Exercise seemed to have worked as well as medications, but without causing common associated side effects.

A PERSONAL STORY OF TRIUMPH OVER PRESUMED ALZHEIMER'S

Ms. Smith was a delightful 76-year-old retired schoolteacher with nicely combed thick white hair and a sad quiet smile. She and her husband came to my memory center wondering if she was developing Alzheimer's disease. Since the nine months after her sister died, she appeared less interested in participating in their social activities, did not talk much and refused to go out to restaurants as she had done in the past. She was otherwise in good health and took care of the day-to-day chores around the house.

During my evaluation, she answered questions slowly and paused often, as she did not appear enthusiastic to complete the tests. However, the parts she completed were mostly accurate and her blood tests and brain MRIs were normal. I realized that behind the sad face was a smart and capable brain. I spoke with her in detail about how mild depression in elderly patients is often mistaken as possible Alzheimer's disease. She refused to take medications for depression.

With help from the psychologist on our team, I convinced Ms. Smith to start a fitness program of walking 30 to 45 minutes a day four times a week. She reluctantly accepted when her husband promised to join her for every walk. When she returned three months later, her husband was smiling and said, "I have my wife back." A simple reassurance that she did not have Alzheimer's disease and that she simply needed stimulation to lift the fog in her mind was enough to help her rebound from mild depression.

I suggested they participate in a dance class. Three months later, they walked into my room holding hands and as they put it, were "on cloud nine." They even demonstrated some of the dance steps they had learned in my office!

While many neuroscientists focus on the benefits of exercise among the elderly, two recent studies demonstrate how exercise can boost brain health in younger adults and even children. Dr. Scott Small from Columbia University in New York obtained baseline scores on memory tests in 11 volunteers with an average age of 33. They were below average in terms of aerobic fitness at the beginning of the study, but after three months of exercising for one hour four times a week, they impressed the researchers by their much improved scores. In a small study of elementary school students, children participating in a regular exercise program performed better in their math, logic and reading tests.

No matter your age, a strong and active body is crucial for building a strong and active mind. Though hard to believe, some parts of your brain actually increase in size after several months of regular exercise.

EXERCISE STRETCHES YOUR BRAIN CAPACITY

Brain MRIs have for the first time captured biological evidence that people who exercise regularly cultivate more powerful brains. In the study of young volunteers at Columbia University who exercised for three months, Dr. Small detected a significant improvement in the size of the hippocampus, the part of the brain critical for your ability to memorize names, faces and directions.

Dr. Arthur Kramer also discovered an unexpected upgrade in brain volume among the elderly in the physical fitness program. The frontal and temporal lobes reaped the most benefits and grew larger. The larger size of frontal lobes, the part of the brain used for problem solving, planning, motivation and "executive functions," provides an explanation for faster and more accurate test scores among the members in the exercise group. After only three months, they had brain volumes equivalent to those three years younger than their actual age. The active group reversed the brain loss associated with a sedentary lifestyle and started a path toward a more powerful brain.

DIVING DEEP INTO THE BRAIN IN SEARCH OF ANSWERS

Scientists are attempting to look deeper into the brain to discover how toning up and expanding your muscles can have such a dramatic effect on your brain. Many scientists believe a neuroprotective chemical called "brain-derived neurotrophic factor" (BDNF) may be the key player. Physical exercise releases chemical signals from the muscles (the chemical is insulin-like growth factor, or IGF-1) that travel through the blood vessels to reach the brain. They then stimulate the secretion of BDNF, the healing protein serving the nervous system much like a fertilizer. When neuroscientists spray BDNF on neurons, they can see how these cells branch out their processes, make new connections and strengthen the old neurons.

EXERCISE TO FIGHT STROKE

Stroke is the third leading cause of death in the United States. Improving fitness is the best way to prevent the blockage of blood vessels, which cause stroke. Exercise enhances blood circulation to the brain cells so they can enjoy a rich source of nutrients and oxygen. Neurons thrive on a fresh blood supply that can come only from a steady flow through clean and open vessels. Your three-pound brain accounts for a small portion of your body size; however, it consumes more than 20 percent of the total oxygen and nutrients in your blood. The more than 100 billion cells each make connections with at least thousands of other neurons, accounting for the more than 100 trillion synapses acting in your brain. This complex network system cannot tolerate any limitation in the blood supply. It is your responsibility to keep the blood flow strong and steady by staying physically fit and healthy.

Exercise, even walking 30 to 45 minutes a day, three or four times a week, improves blood circulation to your brain by lowering atherosclerosis. It increases the levels of good HDL cholesterol, lowers levels of bad LDL cholesterol, improves blood pressure, and enhances metabolism in every organ in the body. People maintaining weekly and regular exercise habits are 57 percent less likely to have a stroke compared to their sedentary neighbors and coworkers. Stroke can be devastating and you need to do your best to prevent it. Exercise can be your main fight against this cruel disease.

STEP 6: *CHOOSE TO TAKE THE FIRST STEPS*

Your brain improves or decays based on your level of physical activity. Just as you boost your brainpower with mental exercises, you can expand your brain potential with an exercise program. Use the mind-body connection to foster positive choices to make your brain and body stronger simultaneously. Make getting off the couch and putting on your sneakers a routine part of life, and you will build a more powerful brain in as early as three months. Pumping oxygen and BDNF in your brain means a better brain reserve and a higher chance of top-notch brain function into your 70's and 80's. We now have solid data to prove an age-old expression that a sharper mind resides in a healthy body.

Once you appreciate the gigantic benefits of an exercise routine three to four times a week, for 30 to 45 minutes, it will be difficult to sink into your couch and fall asleep in front of the television. The hardest step is often the first, which is getting out of old routines to start a more active and dynamic life. You can begin gradually by parking your car farther away from your office or taking the stairs instead of the elevator. As you walk, realize new synapses are forming and that the blood circulation to your hippocampus is improving every mile you advance. Picture your brain cells thanking you for providing them with a better supply of oxygen and nutrients. As you continue regular exercise for three months, you will find that you walk with more confidence, stand taller, feel more energetic and think more clearly.

In all studies concerning the association between body fitness and brain function, the emphasis remains on continuity of exercise, not necessarily on the intensity and duration of any single session. A minimum of 20 minutes three times a week works much better than a completely sedentary life. Two hours of vigorous exercise seems to be only slightly better than one hour.

The predominance and abundance of computers, televisions, cell phones and pagers are turning our society toward an increasingly sedentary lifestyle. You must break away and make your brain health a priority. Nothing is as important as your ability to keep your brain in top shape. By converting the hour of passive TV watching into an active brain-nourishing hour, you turn your brain into a stronger working machine. You also ensure better mental agility into your 70's and 80's and reduce your chance of developing Alzheimer's disease.

TOP 10 REASONS WHY EXERCISE IS ESSENTIAL FOR YOUR NERVOUS SYSTEM

1. It increases the actual size of your brain volume and reverses the effects of aging.
2. It triggers the release of BDNF, nourishing and strengthening synapses between the hippocampus and the rest of the brain.
3. It lowers your risk of stroke by 57 percent.
4. It cuts your risk of Alzheimer's disease two- to threefold.
5. It enhances your balance and equilibrium.
6. It leads to the release of endorphins—the feel-good brain chemicals—bringing you a sense of euphoria.
7. It improves memory and decision making, and makes you smarter.
8. It reduces the risk of diabetes, hypertension and atherosclerosis (all of which harm the brain silently over decades).
9. It helps ward off stress.
10. It makes you look healthier, sexier, more confident and less depressed.

CROSSWORD CHALLENGE ■

You cannot buy BDNF in a drugstore. The only way you can sprinkle the cells in your brain with this natural growth stimulant is to get your body moving. Running on your treadmill can increase your chances of scoring higher on your next exam or completing your crossword puzzles faster. The following crosswords have a fill-in blank for you to record your solving time. Try timing yourself before and after you increase your exercise for three months, and watch as your time improves. ■

My Time: _____ min.

ACROSS

1 Miffed
5 Early in the morning
11 Bit of sugar, say: Abbr.
14 Historical chapters
15 Big ___ (German gun in W.W. I)
16 Olive ___
17 Slangy dissents
18 Vinegary
19 Baton Rouge campus
20 A driver may come to it
23 Pay back?
24 Number of weeks per annum
25 Brownish-orange
27 "28 Days" subject
29 Funny Philips
32 Great plays may be seen in it
33 TV dial: Abbr.
35 Sportscaster Cross
37 Far or down follower
38 Sound on a winter's night
41 Apple not for eating
43 Sawbones
44 Word repeated in the Beatles title "___ Said ___ Said"
45 Teasdale and others
47 Bridal-notice word
49 Robert Devereux's earldom
53 Stick one's nose (in)
55 Fed. construction overseer
57 Second person

58 Five-foot wading birds
62 Potpie morsel
63 Shell figure
64 "Look ___ hands!"
65 Superlative finish
66 "Newhart" actor Tom
67 Old accusation
68 Scores: Abbr.
69 Flunky
70 Catbird seat?

DOWN

1 Motion detector
2 One with a vision
3 Gung-ho
4 In ___ (actually)
5 Adders
6 Computer whiz
7 Afternoon hour in Bonn

8 Memo abbr.
9 Old bloc in Parliament
10 Cheesy snacks
11 It's not free of charge
12 A 6-Down may oversee them
13 Opposite of sing.
21 Piece of pipe
22 Francis and Dahl
26 Home land?
28 Shade of green
30 Not use plainly
31 Web address ending
34 Legal scholar's deg.
36 Bugs, briefly
38 Construction crew
39 It's not free of charge

40 "What's this ___ . . . ?"
41 Philosopher's study
42 "Myra Breckinridge" star
46 Single-masters
48 Yuletide offering
50 Nomination approver
51 Doings
52 Cancels
54 Center of Florida
56 At times it's stolen
59 "Wishing won't make ___"
60 Defense grp.
61 "You said it!"
62 Get-up-and-go

by Elizabeth C. Gorski

My Time: _____ min.

ACROSS

1 Drifter?
5 Answering device?
15 ___ winds (herald of warm and muggy weather)
16 Love poem of 1849
17 Start of something small?
18 Guns N' Roses music
19 "No ___!"
20 Foolish
21 Motor add-on
22 Relative of the custard apple
24 Place-to-sign indicators
25 French president before De Gaulle
26 "All My Children" vixen
27 Controversial agcy. since 1862
28 It may be seen by a bank
29 Swab
31 Don't believe it
32 Anna May of "Shanghai Express"
33 Pigeonhole
34 Outcome
37 Do a charade
41 They're just below heads
42 War stat.
43 Transported
44 Be metrical
45 Whoop
46 Grudge
47 Walt Frazier, for the Knicks
48 Prime-time time
50 Threaded fastener
51 Where Merlin is imprisoned in "Idylls of the King"

53 Give an edge
54 Phone line
55 Hot server
56 Extraordinary perception
57 Stone's throw

DOWN

1 Vamoosed
2 Medium, maybe
3 Germane
4 In the past
5 Island known as "The Gathering Place"
6 Ceaseless
7 Briefly
8 New York's ___ Center
9 Tartarus, in Greek myth
10 "Let It ___" (Everly Brothers hit)
11 Encouraging word
12 Penn State campus site
13 One with lots to sell
14 Flight board message
23 Cries at a Wild West show
25 "Got me beat"
28 38-Down area natives
30 Social worker
31 Bunk
33 Surgical tray array
34 Opens, as a bottle
35 Eugenio ___ (Pope Pius XII)
36 Gym wear
37 Banking aid?
38 River to the Atlantic
39 Makes a string flat, maybe
40 Wobbles
42 Crème flavorer
45 "Holy cow!"
48 "The Bronx? No thonx" writer
49 Ancient dweller in modern Azerbaijan
52 Kind of bran

by Manny Nosowsky

ACROSS

1 Verboten: Var.
5 Boats' backbones
10 "The Nazarene" writer Sholem
14 Park and Lexington, e.g., in N.Y.C.
15 Decorated Murphy
16 Starlet's goal
17 Ceremony for inventors
19 In alignment
20 Off the track
21 Rankled
23 Lager holder
24 Burlesque star Lili St. ___
25 One of Alcott's "Little Women"
26 Jean Arp's art
28 Stair part
31 Greeting for a villain
34 Holy Iraqi
37 In reserve
38 Bat material
39 Is headed for a fall
41 Baseball rarity
42 Ill will
44 Lantern-jawed celeb
45 Hide's partner
46 High-strung
47 Shiites or Amish
49 Easy card game
50 Place to relax
52 Sophisticates they're not
56 Soak through
59 Coin flipper's phrase
60 "How sweet ___!"
61 Low-cal beer in reserve?
63 Ides of March rebuke
64 Actor Delon
65 In perpetuity

66 Leak slowly
67 Jack who was famously frugal
68 Laura of "I Am Sam"

DOWN

1 Spanish appetizers
2 Sailor's "Stop!"
3 Midler of stage and screen
4 Cyber-handles
5 Name in a stuttered 1918 song title
6 Where Lux. is
7 Uplift spiritually
8 Pepsi bottle amount
9 Meets, as a bet
10 Sister of Apollo
11 Bad place to build?
12 Whodunit board game
13 Pay mind to
18 "Peter Pan" dog
22 Gogol's "___ Bulba"
24 Caravan beast
27 Conk out
29 Falco of "The Sopranos"
30 Need a bath badly
31 Dish that's "slung"
32 Culp/Cosby TV series
33 Word processor for sailors?
35 Munched on
36 Brainy group
39 ___ Haute, Ind.

40 Sturgeon delicacy
43 Joins forces (with)
45 Silenced
48 Crack from the cold
50 Played out
51 Praline nut
53 Critic Barnes
54 Check falsifier
55 Howard of morning radio
56 They're cut into wedges
57 Sermon ending?
58 Simple rhyme scheme
59 Big Apple college inits.
62 They're related

by Fred Piscop

My Time: _____ min.

ACROSS

1 "Star Wars" gangster ___ the Hutt
6 Basilica center
10 Police dept. alerts
14 Bubbling on the burner
15 Part of 5-Down: Abbr.
16 "Star Trek" speed
17 Belt tightenings
19 Director Kazan
20 Hearty hello
21 Draft dispenser
23 Play one's part
24 Directed skyward
27 Silly 70's fad
29 Pitcher's tour de force
31 Factor in shipping costs
32 Sling mud at, say
33 Composer Satie
35 Bother persistently
38 Nightmarish street
39 Trite truth
41 Tony-winning Hagen
42 Big name in polls
44 Fill till full
45 Nest builder in the eaves
46 Thunderous sound
48 Motorist's stop
50 Reddish-brown
53 Endangered bamboo eaters
54 Nabokov title heroine
55 Sign of a full house
56 Dessert wine
57 Course listing
59 Title of this puzzle, in reference to 17- and 39-Across and 11- and 26-Down

64 Program problems
65 Finishes (up)
66 Love a lot
67 X and Y, on a graph
68 Cold cuts, e.g.
69 Hill broadcaster

DOWN

1 Pugilist's poke
2 ___ Dhabi
3 Physique, so to speak
4 Result of teasing?
5 Yankees' div.
6 Table salt, to a chemist
7 ___ Darya (Asian river)
8 Sporty Chevy, briefly
9 Fake
10 Leave dumbstruck
11 Protection for the royal family
12 Building block
13 Small rows
18 Nervous laugh
22 Facedown
24 Family name at Indy
25 Chihuahua chicken
26 Not much moolah
27 Early political race
28 "Not ___ bet!"
30 Love personified
34 Flying toy
36 Clueless
37 Spanish snacks
39 Toots one's own horn
40 Tyrant

43 "Telephone Line" grp.
45 Job-seekers' reading
47 French fragrance
49 Runway surface
50 Deadly snake
51 For two, in music
52 Hubbub
56 "Hey, over here!"
58 Naval inits.
60 Stephen of "Still Crazy"
61 Go one better than
62 All competitor
63 One with a six-yr. term

by Nancy Salomon

My Time: _____ min.

ACROSS

1 Result of a handshake, maybe
5 Athlete's foot symptom
9 Musical ability, slangily
14 Yours, in Tours
15 It borders Mayfair
16 Behavior pattern
17 Start of a quote by 9-Down
20 Oz visitor
21 For each
22 Natl. Humor Month
24 Norms: Abbr.
27 Some wool
32 Argentine aunt
33 Guest welcomers
35 Hodgepodges
36 Glossary part
38 Western tribe
39 Skater Lipinski and others
40 Eastern tribe
41 "___ as a winter swallow": Balzac
42 Connect with
43 Read
44 Like this puzzle's grid
46 Not bad, as an argument
48 One of the family
49 Overused
51 Teamster
56 Dummy
59 Mailing to a record exec
61 Like a bialy
62 Like a decal
63 One of four in 80
64 Bicycle buyer's request
65 "The Ladykillers" star, 2004
66 Construction ___
67 Finish (up)

DOWN

1 Fed. Election Commission registrant
2 ___ Z
3 One who doesn't do what's expected
4 Popular video recorder
5 Second half of the quote
6 Little one
7 A.L. and N.L. city
8 Bucket
9 See 17-Across
10 Shakespearean prince
11 Middle piece of Tokyo?
12 Locale in a Poe story
13 Pork place?
18 S.A.T. administrators
19 Cultural org.
22 Swear
23 Puncture
25 Computer program input
26 News feature
28 Part of R.S.V.P.
29 Broadcaster
30 Cousin of a raccoon
31 Like some profs.
34 "It ___ to me . . ."
37 Highway sign
45 Nearest the center
47 Pickling solutions
50 Emends
52 Roman road
53 Quo ___?
54 Lyric poem
55 Take up again
56 Snack
57 ___ Trail in the Andes
58 Noun suffix
60 ". . . ___ saw Elba"

by Mike Torch

My Time: _____ min.

ACROSS

1 "Blitzkrieg Bop" group, with "the"
8 Carrier's carrier
15 Chapter
16 Old-time actress Taylor
17 Be docile
19 Hit too high, say, with "out"
20 Diamond status
21 Logos and such: Abbr.
22 Bats
23 Hägar the Horrible's dog
24 Wool gatherer?
25 Mehmet __, builder of Istanbul's Blue Mosque
26 Tests the waters, in a way
27 Dutch treat
28 They've been known to cause a stink
30 Praised loudly
31 Super bosses?
33 Drink since 1961
36 Wall Street workers
40 Rodgers and Hart's "__ Love"
41 How golf's Gary Player was named?
42 Make tracks
43 Knock-down-drag-outs
44 Letter opener?
45 Northumberland river
46 N.Y.C. subway
47 German boulevard
48 It's rolled in a bar
49 "Calm down!"
52 Sent with a click
53 St. Louis's __ Airport
54 Legal paper
55 Definitive answer

DOWN

1 Danger sign
2 Quarrel stopper, maybe
3 TV news tool
4 Prefix with plastic
5 L'Étoile du __, Minnesota's motto
6 __ Period, depicted in "The Last Samurai"
7 Like some motions
8 They may be running along a street
9 Comparatively warm
10 L.A.-to-Jacksonville route
11 Syr. neighbor
12 Obscure
13 See 50-Down
14 Blows one's stack
18 Good one
23 Lyon's river
24 Punk
26 Lynyrd Skynyrd's "__ Your Name"
27 Pietistic
29 Snakes' eyes
30 Skipping notes
32 Behind one's back
33 This won't work
34 "Call!"
35 Instance of unfairness
37 Pettifogger
38 Small potatoes player
39 X-ray, for example
41 Refer
44 Fugard's "A Lesson From __"
45 Supercharger
47 "The Shelters of Stone" heroine
48 Saxophonist Zoot
50 With 13-Down, a diner order
51 "O Tibbie, I __ seen the day": Burns

by Sherry O. Blackard

96

My Time: _____ min.

ACROSS

1 Allures
8 Little angels
15 Exercises
16 Handout for tourists
17 Whitney Houston song used by NBC for the 1988 Summer Olympics
19 Nickname on the range
20 Wearing a small crown
21 Opening words of "Travelin' Man"
22 Schmaltz
24 Piano composer ___ Nancarrow
26 Contrary to the spirit of 37-Across
36 It separates Sicily from the rest of Italy
37 Football coach's admonishment
38 Start of some games
39 "Doughnut," in baseball lingo
46 Stink
47 Access the contents of
49 Popular apéritif
50 Dumber than dirt
54 Said one's piece
55 Mouth, slangily
56 Some poker players
57 They get left behind

DOWN

1 Anaïs Nin, for one
2 Like a pregnancy
3 French Beaux-Arts painter Cabanel
4 Common calculator button
5 Spanish bear
6 Tom and Jerry ingredient
7 Concrete proposals?
8 Prefix with linear
9 Lover of Eos
10 Alternative to bowties
11 Spreads
12 Puts out
13 Not electric
14 Cannonballed
18 Drama with lots of fans
22 Dinner companion?
23 Seconds, e.g.
25 Iago, notably
27 "The Sopranos" figure
28 Martian rover?
29 Confrère
30 Scottish seaport
31 "This ___ a drill!"
32 Onetime Aerospatiale products
33 Links strings
34 Not picked up
35 Scouting outings
39 So-called "royal herb"
40 Got off the dime
41 U.S. air base site in Greenland
42 Kind of fluid
43 English children's author Blyton and others
44 "___ help a lot!"
45 Lose it
47 Daredevil
48 Classic Bruin nickname
51 One at the kids' table, perhaps
52 This, in Thiers
53 Response when something hits you

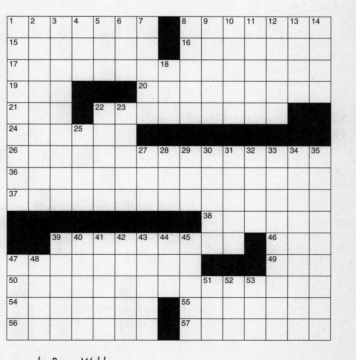

by Byron Walden

My Time: _____ min.

ACROSS
1 True-blue
6 Toy gun poppers
10 Smooch
14 "Good Night" girl of song
15 Arthur ___ Stadium in Queens
16 Peak
17 River triangle
18 Signify
19 Horn's sound
20 Logic
23 ___ capita
24 Buffalo's lake
25 Money in the bank, e.g.
30 Declare
33 Seizes without authority
34 Old what's-___-name
35 George W. Bush's alma mater
36 Michael who starred in "Dirty Rotten Scoundrels"
37 Snorkeling accessory
38 Wolf calls
39 Broadway hit with 7,000+ performances
40 With it
41 Immobilize
42 Swelling reducer
43 Highway stops
45 Ritzy
46 Little rascal
47 Question of concern, with a hint to 20-, 25- and 43-Across
54 Corner square in Monopoly
55 Den
56 Unsophisticated
57 Loafing
58 Dublin's home

59 Lyrics accompany them
60 2000 "subway series" losers
61 Toy used on hills
62 Commence

DOWN
1 Eyeball covers
2 Nabisco cookie
3 Shout
4 Against
5 Weapon in the game of Clue
6 Tripod topper
7 On the open water
8 Adds gradually
9 Mexican misters
10 Couric of "Today"
11 Computer symbol

12 Haze
13 Movie backdrop
21 Commies
22 Tiny criticism
25 Emmy-winner (finally!) Susan
26 Author ___ Bashevis Singer
27 Truly
28 Vases
29 Harbor sights
30 Took care of
31 Totally tired
32 Sí and oui
35 Quotable Yank
37 Swerve back and forth, as a car's rear end
38 Very short shorts
40 Big bothers
41 Soccer star Mia
43 Caught
44 In layers

45 Sees a ghost, maybe
47 Walk through water
48 Sword handle
49 Put on the payroll
50 Tightly stretched
51 Turner who sang "I Don't Wanna Fight"
52 At any time
53 Sabbath activity
54 ___-dandy

by Lynn Lempel

My Time: _____ min.

ACROSS
1 10K, e.g.
5 Wheedler's tactic
10 Jungle crushers
14 ___ Bator
15 Land of a billion
16 Basilica area
17 Start of an Oscar Wilde quote
20 Revolutionary Allen
21 Comic shriek
22 Out of bed
23 Bakers' wares
25 Strange sightings
27 Quote, part 2
31 Cost-controlling W.W. II agcy.
34 Jacob's twin
35 Et ___ (and the following)
36 Cozy spots
38 "I cannot ___ lie"
40 Make a knight, e.g.
42 Utter disorder
43 See 61-Down
45 Dr. Seuss's Sam ___
47 "Rule Britannia" composer
48 Spain's Juan Carlos, for one
49 Quote, part 3
52 ___ En-lai
53 Slinky's shape
54 Bawdyhouse manager
57 Bleachers cry
59 ___ Jean Baker (Marilyn Monroe)
63 End of the quote
66 Excursion
67 Met offering
68 Civil wrong
69 Coin flip
70 Theroux's "endless night"
71 Summers in Québec

DOWN
1 Deserving a slap, maybe
2 Touched down
3 Country singer Johnny
4 Summarize
5 Tonic's partner
6 Brand-new
7 ___ fixe (obsession)
8 Meeting of spacecraft
9 "Mangia!"
10 Groundwork
11 Chooses, with "for"
12 1975 Wimbledon winner
13 Perceived
18 "Sleep ___"
19 Like many an O. Henry story
24 Pothook shape
26 Half a sawbuck
27 Awful smell
28 Grenoble's river
29 Come from behind
30 Furnish with gear
31 Midwest air hub
32 Hacienda drudges
33 Pack animals
37 A Brontë sister
39 Cause of wheezing
41 Graph with rectangular areas
44 "___ 'nuff!"
46 Meadow call
50 The Continent
51 Actress Lollobrigida
52 Roughs it
54 Feminist Lucretia
55 Michael Jackson's old do
56 Honored guest's spot
58 Neighborhood
60 Knee-slapper
61 With 43-Across, approximately
62 Little scurriers
64 Auction assent
65 "Uh-uh!"

by Ed Early

151

My Time: _____ min.

ACROSS
1 Nonplussed
6 Winter hookup
10 Nudges
14 15-Across's instrument
15 ___ Shankar
16 View from Toledo
17 Show of smugness
18 Thunderclouds, perhaps
19 Put away
20 Astounded by how much weight you've gained?
23 Beach lotion letters
25 Born in France
26 Dirty looks
27 "Really!"
29 Little swabs
32 Actress Verdugo
33 "___ giorno!"
34 From ___ Z
37 Deprived of fast food chains?
41 "Help!"
42 Just-for-fun activity
43 Even if, briefly
44 Source
46 One offering securities
47 Pageant wear
50 Geologist's time
51 ___ Plaines, Ill.
52 Tireless in pursuit of weight control?
57 Hardly chivalrous
58 Pedestrian sign
59 Em and Polly
62 Son of Aphrodite
63 Lui's opposite
64 "Ciao!"
65 Bad impression?
66 Practically devoid of customers
67 Cravings of a sort

DOWN
1 Nincompoop
2 Tiny ___
3 Stretching may relieve it
4 Sandwich man?
5 Bill Clinton, e.g.
6 Exploratory spacecraft
7 Poor, as excuses go
8 Kaput
9 Birds take this
10 James and Jackson
11 Use a soapbox
12 Unselfish sort
13 Garden bagful
21 Get into a pool
22 High peak
23 Peels off
24 Salk's conquest
28 Compass heading
29 Berries buy, at a supermarket
30 Honky-___
31 Ltd., in the U.S.
33 Food for regular folks?
34 4.0 earners
35 [titter]
36 Signs of spoilage
38 Kind of shot
39 Lives it up
40 They, in Marseille
44 Most liberal
45 Loutish sort
46 Roth ___
47 Wiped out
48 Accustom
49 Building wing
50 Urged, with "on"
53 Sent packing
54 Mosaic piece
55 "To Live and Die ___"
56 Island feast
60 ___ Offensive
61 Sophs. in two years

by Seth A. Abel

My Time: _____ min.

ACROSS

1 Jest
5 Chekhov's "Uncle ___"
10 "Ape"
14 Actor McGregor
15 Acid/alcohol compound
16 Long ago
17 "Use brighter colors!"?
20 Cape Sable locale: Abbr.
21 Classic 1950 film noir
22 "Mack the Knife" composer
23 Like "Water Music"?
28 Leachman who won an Oscar for "The Last Picture Show"
30 Seep
31 High, in couture
32 Feeling of elation
37 Puts on . . . or things that are put on
38 Person who kneads
39 What a 38-Across needs
40 Teeny
42 What "yo mama" is
43 Bluesy James
44 "The Princess Bride" director, 1987
45 Multicolored yarn?
49 Georges who wrote "Life: A User's Manual"
50 Net alternative
51 Reliever's stat
54 What an old sci-fi comics fan might see?
59 Wept (for)
60 Spritz
61 Inspiration
62 ___ Trueheart of "Dick Tracy"
63 Cleveland nine, with "the"
64 Attorneys' degrees: Abbr.

DOWN

1 Bridges in Hollywood
2 Illegal way to go
3 Trysters, perhaps
4 Basic school subj.
5 Nixes
6 Take ___ at
7 Utmost
8 "___ haw!" (cry of delight)
9 Dada "daddy"
10 Snooped
11 Free
12 Immune system agent
13 Cut one's losses, maybe
18 Haskell of "Leave It to Beaver"
19 Bearded, as grain
24 Pretentious
25 Embryonic attachment
26 Poppycock
27 Côte d'___
28 Spiced milk tea
29 Milk, abroad
32 Subtly mean
33 "Truth!"
34 Three-time U.S. Open winner
35 Hawaiian goose
36 M.I.T. grad: Abbr.
38 Nosh
41 Sir Toby of "Twelfth Night"
42 Clinch
44 LAX to J.F.K. choice
45 Rumble
46 Some 47-Down
47 Exams
48 People kick things here
49 Go ___ (fizzle)
52 Cattail, e.g.
53 "___, how love can trifle with itself!": Shak.
55 Suffix with Mao or Tao
56 "Car Talk" carrier
57 Part of TNT
58 Be indisposed

by Paula Gamache

153

101

My Time: _____ min.

ACROSS

1 Gets ready to play
8 All done, as a movie
15 Last stops
16 Billboard listing
17 Adriatic port
18 Close enough
19 Claim
20 Having one's nose to the grindstone
22 Org. that publishes Playback magazine
23 El ___
24 Reserve
26 Time abbr.
27 With 44-Across, part of a children's song refrain
29 "___ Dinah" (1958 Frankie Avalon song)
30 Determinedly following
31 Gist
33 Was a bad influence on
36 Cause of delirium in farm animals
39 TV station inventory
43 "___ Cinders" of old funnies
44 See 27-Across
47 Fruity drink
48 Debut
49 Shrink
50 La ___, port near Buenos Aires
52 College Park player, informally
53 Arise (from)
54 Dovetail (with)
56 Flipper
58 It might accompany a pan

59 Unconventional delivery of supplies
60 Candy counter selection
61 Ebbs

DOWN

1 Staple of campaign oratory
2 Soothing medicine
3 Emulated Mikey in the cereal ads
4 Kind of room at a hosp.
5 Family nickname
6 Remove, as a notice
7 Oven container
8 Big wave
9 Thousandth of a yen
10 Popular razors
11 Mom-and-pop grps.
12 Like tickets and some stomachs
13 "Get ready!"
14 Really far-out?
21 Confused
24 "Yeah, you're right"
25 Funny business
28 Medium brown
29 "Well, lah-___!"
32 Cereal box stat.
34 Certain preowned vehicle
35 Ones making house calls
36 Go after, as a rebound
37 Reactionary
38 Suitable for gripping
40 It's uncultivated
41 Level
42 Sheets with stars
45 On the back
46 Up-and-coming type
48 Totcled
51 Cookbook author ___ Boyle
53 Benchmarks: Abbr.
55 Make a doily
57 They're rolled in Mexico

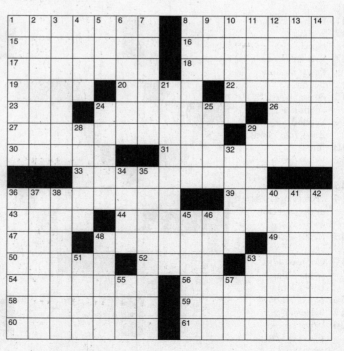

by Sherry O. Blackard

154

My Time: _____ min.

ACROSS
1 Makeup artist?
5 Paired: Prefix
10 "Woe ___ . . ."
14 Archipelago component
15 One of the Saarinens
16 "D"
17 Country legend dropping in?
19 Track
20 Rollerjam participant
21 Pincered insects
23 "Topaz" author
25 Prepares to propose
26 Onomatopoeically named legume
30 Break
31 Claiborne of fashion
32 Polar explorer dropping by?
37 Hip to
39 It may need stroking
40 Small combo
41 Supreme Court justice dropping out?
46 See 62-Down
47 "Ladders to Fire" writer
48 Gabby was his sidekick
50 Gregg experts
53 W.W. II villain
54 Western burg, unflatteringly
55 Smell in "Apocalypse Now"
59 Jon Arbuckle's dog
60 Labor leader dropping off?
63 Tops
64 Religion, to Karl Marx
65 Physical

66 Comic book supergroup
67 Droplets
68 Sixth-brightest star in a constellation

DOWN
1 They may be locked or sealed
2 "Out of Africa" name
3 Neighbor of Mont.
4 Get some sleep
5 Disparaged publicly
6 "___ be!"
7 It's just past three
8 Vichyssoise ingredient
9 David Mamet play
10 Not resting on the shoulders, say
11 Salad orderer's request
12 Salad maker's need
13 N.A.A.C.P. and others
18 ___ Buena (island in San Francisco Bay)
22 Unaltered
24 Unaltered
26 Dove home
27 Historical ship
28 Russia's Sea of ___
29 Almost
33 Origin
34 Sweater letter
35 Nada, across the Pyrenees
36 Steeple sound
38 It barely misses a score
42 Rat Pack nickname
43 Con
44 Those who lend their names
45 Oriental royal
49 Singer with the 1999 #1 hit "If You Had My Love"
50 Vice venue
51 Cord
52 Take potshots
54 Wheedle
56 Fire
57 Map figure: Abbr.
58 Baby's word
61 One of Frank's exes
62 With 46-Across, marsh-dwelling bird

by Henry Hook

155

103

My Time: _____ min.

ACROSS

1 Literature Nobelist Bellow
5 Slender
9 Gregorian music style
14 Port or claret
15 Left a chair
16 Edmonton hockey player
17 Vicinity
18 Out of the wind
19 Handsome wood design
20 Place to pull in for a meal
23 Seafood in shells
24 Site of one-armed bandits
27 Place for a pig
28 New York ballplayer
29 Ryan of "When Harry Met Sally"
30 Four-star officer: Abbr.
31 F.D.R. radio broadcast
34 As well
37 Responses to a masseur
38 German chancellor ___ von Bismarck
39 Highest-priced boxing ticket
44 It may be served with crumpets
45 Snoop around
46 Old cable inits.
47 "Sesame Street" broadcaster
50 Modern affluent type
52 Teen meeting place
54 Kindly doctor's asset
57 Setting for Theseus and the Minotaur
59 Plumb crazy
60 Skin outbreak
61 Broadcasting
62 Whiskey drink
63 Display
64 Desires
65 Statement figures: Abbr.
66 "Bonanza" brother

DOWN

1 Groups of bees
2 Clear of stale smells
3 Apprehensive
4 Clues, to detective
5 Movie preview
6 Not change course
7 "Gotcha"
8 Must-have item
9 Just-made-up word
10 Actor/dancer Gregory
11 O.K.
12 Org. that funds exhibits
13 Have a go at
21 Big rig
22 Decorated, as a cake
25 Well-groomed
26 Not fooled by
29 Fail to qualify, as for a team
31 London weather, often
32 That girl
33 Barracks bunk
34 Bohemian
35 In ___ of (replacing)
36 Vegetable in a crisp pod
40 Tarantulas, e.g.
41 Angers
42 Captivates
43 Tennis star Kournikova
47 Pullover raincoat
48 ___ Aires
49 Scatters, as petals
51 Mini, in Marseille
53 Grind, as teeth
55 Rick's love in "Casablanca"
56 Fate
57 It may be put out to pasture
58 Genetic stuff

by Craig Kasper

My Time: _____ min.

ACROSS

1 Rugged rock
5 Incite
9 Unlike a dirt road
14 Whopper
15 White-tailed eagle
16 Spry
17 Fusses
18 Makes lace
19 Like maples but not firs
20 Area between two scrimmage lines
23 Jul. follower
24 Largest of the British Virgin Islands
29 Chemical process also called hyperfiltration
33 Attention-getter
34 Radio feature
35 Successful
36 Flared-spout pitcher
38 Military newbie
41 Heredity unit
42 Grief
44 Rotators under the hood
46 ___ Lingus
47 Make crazy
51 Increased
52 Took off
53 Yellowstone employees
59 Video game pioneer
63 Bluish green
64 "The Grapes of Wrath" figure
65 Get ready for Web-surfing
66 Northern Oklahoma city
67 Take a break
68 Hard stuff
69 Lightning catchers
70 Inquires

DOWN

1 Family group
2 Obnoxious
3 Baseball brothers' name
4 Holst who composed "The Planets"
5 "Stop living in your fantasy world!"
6 Kind of hygiene
7 1998 animated film with the voice of Woody Allen
8 Spanish explorer who discovered the Mississippi
9 Capital of Sicily
10 Get on in years
11 By way of
12 Keebler worker?
13 Susan of "L.A. Law"
21 Regretted
22 Rejections
25 Chinese mafia
26 Bony
27 Toy train maker
28 "___ your instructions . . ."
29 Express differently
30 Lash site
31 Mineo of "Exodus"
32 Vote in
33 Gossipy Hopper
37 Gad about
39 Relative of "Phooey!"
40 Green gems
43 Timber from Maine
45 Long-necked bird
48 Hagen of Broadway
49 Luggage carrier
50 Some wool
54 Gambler's game
55 Policy cry
56 Stretches (out)
57 Hazard
58 Nears the western horizon
59 Vestment for a priest
60 As well
61 Back then
62 Role on "Frasier"

by Nancy Kavanaugh

105

My Time: _____ min.

ACROSS

1 Lowlife snitch
4 Woman of distinction
8 With 67-Across, author of "Ulysses"
13 Catherine who was the last wife of Henry VIII
14 Sacked out
15 The chosen, socially
16 Tinted windows locale
17 Tax-exempt bond, briefly
18 Wife of 56-Across who said 69-Across
19 Setting for "Ulysses"
22 Aussie outlaw Kelly
23 Industrial pollutant
24 Ancestry
28 Journalist/author Rick
30 Egyptian sun god
32 Roman sun god
33 Resort island near Venezuela
35 Nice, as clothes
38 1904 date in "Ulysses"
41 Cord that you hope doesn't break
42 Bert who hosted "Tattletales"
43 "___ Over but the Shoutin'" (book by 28-Across)
44 Go south, as a market
46 Stand for a portrait
50 Not stick to the path
53 Part of r.p.m.
55 Some germ cells
56 Hero in "Ulysses"
59 Three-toed animal
62 Others, to Cicero

63 Aleutian island
64 Dwight's two-time challenger
65 In the mail
66 Dear, in a billet-doux
67 See 8-Across
68 Outfits
69 Last word of "Ulysses"

DOWN

1 Oakland athlete
2 Force mounted by Philip II
3 Setting for a Homeric epic
4 Curses
5 Gulf emirate
6 Carte du jour
7 Fit for the dinner table

8 Pack tightly
9 Single-handedly
10 Measure of thickness
11 Night school course: Abbr.
12 Oink pad?
13 Secondary strategy
20 "Same here"
21 Flowering shade tree
25 Kind of prof.
26 "Oh my ___!"
27 English cathedral city
29 Tattoo identification, maybe
31 Mexican silver mining center
34 Comfortable with

36 Reflected sound effect
37 "Orinoco Flow" singer
38 Composer Styne
39 The Runnin' Rebels of coll. sports
40 Overthrowing
41 Lousy
45 What's for dinner
47 Alleviate
48 Brings to mind
49 Politico Alexander from Tennessee
51 ___ artery
52 Hawk's home
54 Prunes, say
57 Food item sold in bars
58 Like some lingerie
59 ___ Mahal
60 Furor
61 Thickness

by Paula Gamache

158

My Time: _____ min.

ACROSS

1 Cry from the block
5 Welcoming
9 Dust bits
14 "If I ___ . . ."
15 Et ___
16 See 29-Down
17 Pay back
19 Main male
20 Provoke
22 Biblical shepherd
23 Already off
24 Be indisposed
26 Blocks
29 Of an atrioventricular valve
30 Phil who sang "I Ain't Marching Anymore"
31 Sensitive things
32 Court call
35 Noted guerrilla
36 Scram . . . or a hint to solving 17-, 20-, 50- and 57-Across and 11- and 28-Down
38 Words of promise
39 Light source
40 ". . . ___ and hungry look": Shak.
41 Nabokov novel
42 Comparatively compliant
44 Composer Prokofiev
46 Spot to order a spot
48 Farm unit
49 Goals
50 "Understand?"
55 Go around
57 Be a hindrance
58 Pointer mover
59 Symbol of Apollo
60 Percolate slowly
61 Substitute (for)
62 Rowers' muscles, for short
63 Cub or Red, briefly

DOWN

1 Clinic fluids
2 In charge of
3 Forebear of one of Israel's 12 Tribes
4 Shifts
5 46-Across vehicles
6 Unalaska inhabitant
7 Run amok
8 1980 Andrzej Wajda film in which Lech Walesa appears
9 Inits. on N.Y.C. buses
10 "Verrry sexy!"
11 Star
12 Waters of jazz
13 Are going to
18 Not e'en once
21 Dos
25 Originally, once
26 Shot orderers
27 Parrot
28 Move it
29 Large 16-Across
31 Marathoner's challenge
33 Actress McClurg
34 Novelist Morrison
36 Bad cut
37 "Middlemarch" author
41 Not call it quits
43 Umbrian town
44 Things between cuts
45 European tongue
46 Heat and Lightning
47 Short concluding stanza
48 Lifeless, old-style
51 "The Memory of Trees" Grammy winner
52 Truant, in a way
53 It may be steely
54 Viewer
56 Habitable hole

by Robert H. Wolfe

SEVEN

Brain Health Quiz

HOW WELL ARE YOU TAKING CARE OF YOUR BRAIN?

You can determine how well you attend to and pamper your brain by answering a few simple questions. Each person is unique and requires individual assessment for a brain health check-up. However, the following 10 questions do provide a general picture of your level now. After you've finished the quiz, add up the numbers preceding each answer to get your score.

If you discover you have multiple risk factors, you will have a higher incentive to adopt the necessary lifestyle modifications. You also have more to gain from every minor improvement. Discuss the results with your doctor. On the other hand, if you have been in perfect health all your life, have no medical conditions, do not take medications and already feel very sharp, you may not need to make changes in your lifestyle. Just give yourself a pat on the back and enjoy the crossword puzzles.

BRAIN HEALTH QUIZ

Average Daily Blood Pressure
(1) Normal or low blood pressure (below or around 120/80)
(2) Mildly elevated high blood pressure (around 130/85)
(3) High blood pressure (around 140/90)
(4) Very high blood pressure (above 160/100)

Diabetes
(1) No diabetes
(2) Diet-controlled diabetes
(3) Mild-to-moderate diabetes, on medications
(4) Severe diabetes for more than 10 years, poorly controlled

Diet
(1) Eat fruits and vegetables five times a day, with a smart, balanced diet of meats, carbohydrates, bread and fish (2–3 servings a week)
(2) Eat fruits and vegetables once or twice a day, with a fairly good, balanced diet
(3) Occasional fruits and vegetables, no particular attention to diet
(4) No fruits and vegetables, fast-food hamburgers more than 2–3 times a week

Brain Stimulation
(1) Interested in solving problems, crossword puzzles and sudoku puzzles, playing card games, fixing things around the house, other brain-teasing activities
(2) Occasional brain-stimulating activities
(3) Do not enjoy solving problems or puzzles of any kind
(4) Avoid active thinking as much as possible, let other people figure things out

Stress and Anxiety
(1) No stress, feeling happy and in control of life, have a positive attitude
(2) Occasional stressful situations, such as dealing with deadlines weekly
(3) Frequent stress and anxiety most days of the week, rarely relax
(4) Running around all the time, always feeling behind, constantly feel worried, stressed and anxious

Cholesterol
(1) Normal cholesterol profile (LDL <100, HDL >40), controlled with diet and exercise
(2) Mildly elevated cholesterol, on medications
(3) High cholesterol (total cholesterol >200), on medications, but not under good control yet
(4) High cholesterol, not on medications

Weight
(1) Thin to normal
(2) Mildly overweight
(3) Overweight (with abdominal size of >40 inches for men, and >35 for women)
(4) Obese

Smoking
(1) Never smoked, or quit more than 10 years ago
(2) Quit, with occasional smoking in bars or restaurants
(3) Smoke up to one pack per week
(4) Smoke one pack per day or more

Leisure Activities
(1) Enjoy hobbies (gardening, dancing, movies, day trips, fishing, crochet, etc.), keep busy with them once a week
(2) Occasional hobbies, about once or twice per month
(3) No regular leisure activities, may travel once or twice a year
(4) No hobbies, no leisure activities, watch noneducational programs on TV more than 3–4 hours a day

Exercise
(1) Walk or engage in some form of exercise for more than 30–45 minutes, at least four days a week
(2) Walk or engage in some forms of exercise once or twice a week, for at least 30 minutes each time
(3) Do not participate in any regular exercise program, may take a long walk occasionally
(4) No exercise ever, sedentary (coach-potato) lifestyle

YOUR SCORE

Less than 15: Green zone, keep up the good work.
Between 16 and 30: Yellow zone, need improvement.
Between 31 and 40: Red zone, need major improvements, see your doctor soon.

CHANGING HABITS FOR A HEALTHIER BRAIN

The Brain Health Quiz is intended to show you that you can achieve a healthier and sharper brain through simple modifications in your lifestyle. Now that you have learned about the impact of your blood pressure, weight, stress level and choices of food on the brain, you should find it easier to optimize your brain fitness. Your risk of developing Alzheimer's in your 70's and 80's rests on your general health throughout your midlife and the actions you take today to maximize your brain and body fitness.

A simple modification, such as saying no to second servings of meals or too many sweet desserts and snacks, adds up to the preservation of millions of synapses. Much like saving 20 dollars a day translates into millions of dollars in your retirement years, walking 30 minutes a day translates into larger frontal lobes and a much lower risk of developing Alzheimer's. Fortunately, most of the factors responsible for rapid decay in brain function are the same issues causing heart disease. You can combat them simultaneously by making smart choices regarding your health habits; in the process you will buy yourself a longer life with a sharper brain.

LATEST DISCOVERIES IN THE FIELD OF MEMORY AND ALZHEIMER'S

Metabolic Syndrome Harms the Brain Too

Patients suffering from diabetes often have multiple medical problems. They readily develop nerve damage in their toes, cataracts, skin infections, pneumonia, strokes and heart attacks. Scientists have now unveiled a connection between diabetes and loss of mental capacity. In a study of 8,056 nurses monitored for up to 18 years, those with diabetes were 50 percent more likely to lose their mental ability and become demented. The longer they had diabetes, the worse their memory problems got. Metabolic syndrome, a prediabetes condition, also increases risks of cognitive impairment. The central feature of metabolic syndrome consists of mildly elevated high blood pressure, lower levels of good HDL cholesterol and abdominal obesity, defined as a waistline of 40 inches or wider for men and 35 inches or wider for women.

Sleep Apnea, Diabetes and Smaller Brain

Overweight people who snore during the night may have "obstructive sleep apnea." Sometimes their snoring is punctuated by brief episodes of silence during which they actually stop breathing. Their brains suffer from low oxygen during sleep and, as expected, they awake feeling tired, drowsy and groggy. They may doze off at a drop of a hat, at meetings, movie theaters or even when stopped at a traffic light.

Sleep specialists have recently made two major discoveries. Aside from increasing risk of hypertension, stroke and heart attacks, sleep apnea over decades leads to 18 percent shrinkage in an array of brain areas including the frontal lobes. According to a study by Dr. Nader Botros at Yale University School of Medicine, sleep apnea also elevates the risk of developing diabetes by 2.7 fold.

These discoveries demonstrate how vascular risks often go hand-in-hand to decrease mental agility; a large percentage of patients with obesity have a combination of sleep apnea, diabetes, high blood pressure, poor cholesterol profile, atherosclerosis, heart disease, ministrokes and sedentary lifestyle. Each of these conditions can eat away at synapses and harm the brain.

YOUR TEETH, YOUR BRAIN

You brush your teeth twice a day. You floss them regularly and see your dentist for a cleaning about once a year. You realize how important dental hygiene is to maintaining a beautiful, healthy set of teeth. Shouldn't you do the same for your brain? You need to realize that your brain—just like your teeth, skin and heart—needs care and attention. It takes simple steps to keep your brain in top condition. Make it a priority to laugh more often, enjoy fruits and vegetables every day, go for a walk (or hit the gym) after work or before you start your day, and keep your brain engaged with brain-teasing crosswords.

ACROSS

1 Stay positive and show a lot of 37-Across (2 wds.)
5 Endorphin, released during exercise, can be classified as this type of compound
9 Leptin will not be able do its job if this link stops working (2 wds.)
10 Entered (2 wds.)
12 Prefix after milli-, nano- and pica-
13 Live and breathe
14 One reason for the buildup of amyloid plaques in the brain
16 Teachers' org.
17 Opposite of "relaxed"
20 Affected by unhappiness, as a person with depression
22 Chocolate, ice __ and candy (foods you shouldn't eat every day)
24 Rub out, as text
26 Physicians' degs.
28 Beginning
31 Yang's counterpart
32 Chemical formula for water, spelled out letter by letter
34 Vegetable with antioxidant and anti-inflammatory properties
35 Sleep disorder that deprives the brain of oxygen
36 Hemoglobin deficiency that can contribute to memory problems
37 Positive outlook on life that can help prolong the health of your hippocampus
38 Finis (2 wds.)
39 __ leg syndrome (disorder that can interfere with your ability to sleep well)

DOWN

1 Kind of diet that can raise your risk of a heart attack (2 wds.)
2 __ E, antioxidant compound implicated in better brain function in the elderly
3 Cortisol, adrenaline or leptin
4 Railroad worker Gage with frontal lobe damage
6 "Old dogs" can learn new tricks because the brain is flexible and __
7 DHA is an example of __-3 fatty acid, the best food for the brain
8 What you should do to improve your hand, eye and foot coordination
11 Meditation is one way to distract it from your daily thoughts
15 Purple fruit rich in antioxidants that help fight inflammation
18 Planet between Venus and Mars
19 Captain's cry for help
21 Assistance
23 What you can do to increase the levels of BDNF in your brain
25 Limbic lobe is responsible for its production
26 Certain brain scans, for short
27 Contact point between brain cells
28 Trying to lose weight (3 wds.)
29 Early morning phenomenon
30 Emotional or physical injuries that can play a role in memory problems
32 Anxiety and stress can affect this organ in your body
33 Overweight, as people with a higher risk of hypertension and Alzheimer's disease

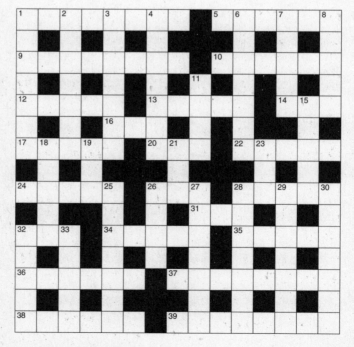

by Michael Shteyman

ACROSS

1 1995 Robin
Williams film
8 Exalt
15 That's what
you think
16 NASA, e.g.
17 Kind of table
18 It has its outlet
in the East
China Sea
19 Onetime Camaro
alternative
20 Dump
22 Book before Neh.
23 Language from
which "galore"
comes
25 Rash decision?
26 Starr and
Thompson
27 Control,
symbolically
29 Bar stock
30 Electronic control
system, for short
31 ___ chicken
33 Clinton, e.g.
35 Need to make
a difference
37 Noted Carmelite
mystic
40 Having
more bass
44 Pool accessory
45 Football
playoff grp.
47 Pit
48 Brief bylaws
49 Palm tree locale
51 Opposite
of adios
52 Schubert's
"The ___-King"
53 Some resins
55 Unit of 100
ergs per gram
56 Mutinied ship
of 1839
58 Leaders in pits
60 Detail
61 Less than stellar

62 View
63 Reproduces,
in a way

DOWN

1 Band on the run?
2 Stuck
3 Basic cell division
4 Chemical suffix
5 Sight in Memphis
6 Down Under
youngsters
7 Ready to roll
8 Terminal
headaches?
9 "See if ___"
10 Neighbor of
Eure-et-Loir
11 Beaten punch
12 Completely
overjoyed,
perhaps

13 Tropical insect
whose name
is the last word
in the Official
Scrabble Players
Dictionary
14 "Nature" essayist
21 Wily
24 Gives a
protective cover
26 Poet Rexroth
28 Smug expression
30 White-haired
types
32 Course setting:
Abbr.
34 Yeaned youngster
36 Debut of
9/15/1982
37 Riots
38 Due to heat
39 Identifying
phrase

41 Some Monopoly
players pay it
42 Swell
43 Primes
46 High
49 "___ of Blue Eyes"
(Thomas
Hardy novel)
50 Split
53 Woman's
name suffix
54 One with future
prospects?
57 Juliet, to Romeo
59 Breaking
capacity, briefly

by David Quarfoot

ACROSS

1 Dainty piece of delicate workmanship
6 "A truer measure of man's ability" sloganeer, once
11 It has a variety of schedules: Abbr.
14 Nursery supplies
15 Nut source
16 Struggle
17 Dispirit
18 Not currently
20 Occupational ending
21 Site of some famous hangings
22 Consideration
23 Humanities degs.
24 Canadian capital?
25 "Angie Baby" singer, 1974
26 "The point being . . . ?"
27 Biker's bike, colloquially
29 Suffix with two
30 Line from a classic tongue twister
36 Lenape orator who inspired Pontiac
37 Anticipates an imminent disaster, maybe
38 Ten follower
39 Long haul
40 "___ Time transfigured me": Yeats
41 Owner of a famous thumb
44 Ricky Nelson's "___ Late"
45 Solution, on an Rx
46 Big benefit, say
47 They're impulsive
50 "Friends" actress, familiarly

51 Vaunt
53 Spent
55 Richard Gere title role of 2000
56 North Sea tributary
57 Dispatch boat
58 Emolument
59 Composer Warlock
60 Stately home

DOWN

1 Italian color
2 View from Calabria
3 "Medical Center" star
4 Taliban mullah
5 Salts are in it: Abbr.
6 It's free for a limited time
7 David George Gordon's "The ___-Bug Cookbook"
8 Polo competitor
9 Match game?
10 Paul Bunyan's blacksmith
11 Like some walls
12 Put a winter coat on?
13 Poorly kept
19 Doctor's order
21 Field worker
23 Yum-Yum, Peep-Bo and Pitti-Sing in "The Mikado"
24 Excoriate
25 Marinates more
28 Hospitality target

29 Hare hunters
31 Sink item
32 LaserJet 2100, e.g.
33 Brought by dolly
34 Jocosity
35 Court citation abbr.
41 Staff lines?
42 Dance studio feature
43 Really turn on
47 Answer to the folk riddle "Worker in yellow clothes"
48 Strike
49 English river to the Wash
50 Mud
52 Increase, with "up"
53 Fix
54 Unknown name

by Brendan Emmett Quigley

ACROSS

1 End-of-week cry
5 Makes, as tea
10 Wise __ owl
14 Folk singer Guthrie
15 Soprano Callas
16 Popular building block
17 1959 Doris Day/Rock Hudson comedy
19 Actress Singer of "Footloose"
20 Victor's entitlement
21 Errors
23 See 24-Across
24 With 23-Across, Neptune, e.g.
26 Back street
27 Clearance item's caveat
29 Wrestler's win
30 Had a bite
31 Disposable pen maker
32 Davenport
33 Church official
37 What a full insurance policy offers
40 Bronze and stainless steel
41 Bed size smaller than full
42 __ Paul's seafood
43 Spider's prey
44 Conger or moray
45 Mosquito repellent ingredient
46 First lady after Hillary
49 Put two and two together?
50 California's Big __
51 Evidence in court
53 Tetley competitor
56 Radio tuner
57 Piano player's aid

60 France, under Caesar
61 "__ Doone" (1869 novel)
62 Not us
63 Building additions
64 Vote into office
65 Jekyll's alter ego

DOWN

1 Bugler's evening call
2 Hang on tight?
3 Not according to Mr. Spock
4 Shakespearean volumes
5 Some luxury cars
6 Squealer
7 Time in history
8 "The Flintstones" mother
9 Pseudonym of H. H. Munro
10 Post-danger signal
11 1988 Olympics host
12 Be of one mind
13 Clamorous
18 Outdated
22 Lustrous fabric
24 Go (through), as evidence
25 Made into law
27 "Mamma Mia" pop group
28 Window box location
29 Verse-writing
30 Tablet with ibuprofen
32 Bygone space station
34 Averse to picture-taking

35 Meanie
36 Home in a tree
38 Without any extras
39 Was beholden to
45 University of Minnesota campus site
46 Overhang
47 Like some symmetry
48 Mover's rental
49 Playwright __ Fugard
50 Uncle __
52 Ireland, the Emerald __
53 Ballpark figure?
54 Went out, as a fire
55 Pinnacle
58 Before, in 29-Down
59 Business letter abbr.

by Craig Kasper

ACROSS

1 Luau instruments, for short
5 Noted plus-size model
9 Nice to wear
14 Like Playboy models
15 "Hud" Oscar winner Patricia
16 Be nuts about
17 Qatari V.I.P.
18 Turns abruptly
19 Novelist Ephron
20 Old telephone feature
23 Proofreader's mark
24 G.P.A., slangily
25 Put a value on
27 When summer starts
30 Cry over
32 Geographical septet
33 Kabob holder
35 Pitcher part
38 See 41-Across
40 Historic time
41 With 38-Across, what the four key parts of this puzzle are
43 Uno + due
44 Conductor Toscanini
47 State openly
48 Brawl site in a western
50 Horrifies
52 Yalta's peninsula
54 Stowe equipment
55 Hearty party
56 Gymgoer's goal
62 Earth's __ layer
64 19-Across's sister
65 Medieval chest
66 Wades across, say
67 "The heat __!"
68 Bring up
69 Rendezvous
70 Rock's Rundgren
71 The end of each of 20- and 56-Across and 11- and 29-Down is a popular one

DOWN

1 Addict
2 __ sabe
3 Turnpike toll-paying locale
4 Big Orange of college sports
5 Pepsin and rennin, for two
6 Gettysburg victor
7 Yule trio
8 Adamson's lioness
9 Crude dude
10 Ukrainian port
11 Fuji flow
12 Part of a Happy Meal
13 "The Second Coming" poet
21 Seek a seat
22 Poor, as excuses go
26 Put into slots
27 "__ that special?!"
28 Within earshot
29 "Howards End" director
30 Kicked off
31 Fancy pitcher
34 Green Hornet's sidekick
36 Hit Fox show, in headlines
37 Mass seating
39 Mall attraction
42 Eminem and Dr. Dre, for two
45 Gad about
46 Bay Area city
49 Makes right
51 Pizza order
52 Video game heroine Lara __
53 Stubble remover
54 New England catch
57 Complex dwelling
58 "Eh"
59 Black-and-white treat
60 Final Four org.
61 Tombstone lawman
63 Ballpark fig.

by Allan E. Parrish

PERSONAL TRIUMPH TO FINALLY LOSE FIVE POUNDS

Ms. Brown was a 52-year-old secretary in a busy law office in New York. She and her husband were paying the college fees for their two daughters and she worked a second job to stay on top of the bills. She weighed 185 pounds and felt frustrated that after 10 years of trying to lose weight, she actually gained 20 pounds. She had limited time to exercise or pay attention to her diet. When she arrived at home, she was too exhausted to do anything other than eat dinner and watch television.

Lately, she noticed increasing memory lapses and began wondering if these were early signs of Alzheimer's. She had watched her mother suffer from Alzheimer's disease and dreaded the idea that she too would one day lose her independence and mental abilities. She came to my memory clinic anxious about what diagnosis she would receive.

I talked with her, obtained blood tests and gave her paper and pencil and a set of questions, including the Brain Health Quiz. I soon discovered her memory and cognitive functions were normal for her age and educational background. I invited her to come for a follow-up visit and spent 40 minutes reviewing her test results and encouraging her to take steps toward better brain health. Her score on the Brain Health Quiz was 28. I assured her she was not showing the first glimpses of Alzheimer's and encouraged her to improve her brain fitness. She decided to actively change her lifestyle and turn her life around 180 degrees.

She bought a blood pressure cuff from Walmart for 25 dollars and measured her pressure daily while at work. She noticed that the stress from work caused her blood pressure to spike as high as 160/95. She decided to become more organized and asked her manager to reduce her workload. She took 20-minute meditation breaks during her lunch hour, followed a heart-healthy diet and forced her husband to join her for walks after dinner instead of watching television. They not only exercised and improved their fitness, but also talked and relaxed with one another, too.

Over six months, she felt her self-esteem had escalated; she was less stressed, more in control and generally happier. She walked with stronger and more confident strides. She lost only five pounds but was determined to maintain a healthy lifestyle and lose two pounds a month. She knew with her new approach in her daily routine she was starting a path to a stronger heart and a more powerful brain.

ACROSS
1 Lobbying grps.
5 Bigot's comment
9 Skim, as soup
14 "___ Rhythm"
15 The Old Sod
16 Fred's dancing partner
17 Bass brass
18 It lacks roots
19 Baseball squads
20 Karl's confused query in Córdoba?
23 Masseur's target
24 "Washboard" body parts
25 Etna spew
28 Without proper planning
31 Jurist Fortas
34 Treat unfairly, slangily
36 Wish undone
37 Q.E.D. part
38 Colin's confused query in Como?
42 May event, for short
43 Now published
44 Actor Davis
45 Low isle
46 Pedal-to-the-metal sort
49 Suffix with racket
50 Place to sweat
51 Laudatory lyrics
53 Knut's confused query in Cannes?
61 Roswell crash victim, supposedly
62 Highlands tongue
63 Dizzy of the Gas House Gang
64 Bounded along
65 Walk like a sot
66 Hostile one
67 Chances upon
68 Order (around)
69 Marginal mark

DOWN
1 Nitty-gritty
2 Lago filler
3 Baseball's Georgia Peach
4 Bean's support
5 Add zing to
6 Demon of Semitic lore
7 Push
8 Scan
9 Waltzer's river
10 Touches up
11 Boggy places
12 Smart ___
13 Radio host John
21 Writer Loos
22 Packed away
25 Tasty jelly
26 Journalist Alexander
27 One in "another fine mess"
29 Sharp ridge
30 Boy in a Johnny Cash song
31 Pop up
32 Count in music
33 It'll knock you out
35 Succeed, as a proposal
37 Some rails
39 November stone
40 Cry's partner
41 Bridge authority
46 Shells out
47 Puts out
48 Rangers and Corsairs
50 Unwelcome forecast
52 They're jerked
53 Conceal, in a way
54 Relative of the yucca
55 Ready
56 Hop, skip or jump
57 Food item whose name appears on its side
58 Not own
59 Fill to surfeit
60 Contract into folds

by Jim Goodsell

ACROSS

1 Doubled, a Polynesian capital
5 Animals of the species Pan troglodyte
9 Doubled, a 1969 #1 hit song
14 The Phantom of the Opera
15 Make way?
16 "Century"
17 Figure in a math function
19 Replies to a host
20 Partly doubled, a call in a game
22 Explorer ___ Anders Hedin
23 Working in a galley
27 Doubled, a Hollywood star
30 Guess: Abbr.
31 "Well, let me think . . ."
32 Part of a roller coaster
33 Center of Florida?
35 Pro shop item
36 ___ Ridge (1972 Derby winner)
37 Partly tripled, a lyric from a 1964 #1 pop song
41 Head of Haiti
42 Resident's suffix
43 Ottoman Empire title
44 Sooner than
45 ___ Ten
46 TV component: Abbr.
48 Doubled, a drumbeat
49 Kind of bridge
51 Boxer Spinks
53 Partly quadrupled, a 1963 comedy
59 Orphan of old comics
62 Yarn spinner
63 Peckish?
64 "My Way" lyricist
65 Mystery author Buchanan
66 Doubled, home of Whitman College
67 Revel, in a way
68 Doubled, a pen

DOWN

1 Gourd fruit
2 Asia's ___ Sea
3 Miss
4 Approves
5 Mountaintops
6 Brainchild protector
7 Unexcitable
8 Feudal drudge
9 Laugh riot
10 Four-time Indy winner
11 Geo. Bush, once
12 Chem. neurotransmitter
13 ___ judicata
18 Relocate in
21 Beau
24 Most reserved
25 Kind of blanket
26 Coarse flour
27 Added spice to
28 Realm
29 Winning card combo
31 Tripled, Yogi Bear's catchphrase
34 Vaudevillian Olsen
35 Doubled, a tropical menace
36 Scandinavian rug
38 Perfume bottles
39 Tripled, a line from "The King and I"
40 Stylish and expensive
45 Old film
46 Knocking sounds
47 Some hardwood
50 Formed by inflow and outflow
52 Scribblings
54 Show horse
55 "Give that ___ cigar!"
56 Quick, in trade names
57 Sally ___ (teacake)
58 Zip strip?
59 Cousin of a crow
60 Oocytes, eventually
61 Nothing

by Patrick Merrell

114

ACROSS
1 Barefaced
8 Some air lines
15 Greasy kid stuff
16 Boutros Boutros-Ghali, by birth
17 Where to get in on the ground floor
19 Equate, in a way
20 Staff notes?
21 Tidy sum
22 Mother of Horus
23 Some hats
24 Innocent
25 Affirmative action?
26 Fields
27 Swiss canton or its capital, old-style
28 Stick out
30 Goes back over
32 Now unemployed
34 ___ hole in (corrodes)
35 Got off topic
38 Great desire
41 Late actress Uta
42 Twists in a bar
44 "___ favor, amigo"
45 Mullah Muhammad ___
46 Four Holy Roman emperors
47 He loved Lucy
48 "___ for Innocent" (Grafton novel)
49 Bang up
50 Monopolize
51 Hard to grasp
54 The Crossroads of America
55 Hug, maybe
56 Itty-bitty
57 Soft tissue

DOWN
1 Knot that won't slip
2 Link
3 "Seriously . . ."
4 Small fry
5 Not accepting nohow
6 Security Council vote
7 Just so
8 Short parade-goer's complaint
9 Nostrils
10 Little birds
11 Ready for combat
12 Watch closely
13 Dignify
14 Living room furniture
18 Like the end of the world
23 Liberator
24 Boito's Mefistofele and others
26 "I Love a Parade" composer
27 They may be drawn
29 Dairy outlet?
31 Not just aversions
33 Alpha particle's emission
35 Reply to a knock
36 He wrote "You and I have brains. The others have fluff"
37 Lightheaded
39 "Big deal . . . I was wrong"
40 Multiscreen cinema
43 De Niro's do in "Taxi Driver"
46 Warning signals
47 Class underachiever
49 Cross words
50 Make a bundle
52 Sticker
53 Sclt, in Sauternes

by Manny Nosowsky

115

ACROSS
1 Gets out of the way
11 Bass output
15 They don't react well
16 N.F.L. Hall-of-Famer Ronnie
17 Perilous thing to cross over
18 Prune
19 Tend to brood?
20 Mathematical extreme
21 Incurred
22 Grooming gizmo
24 Three-time 55-Down champs
25 What an optimist envisions
28 Quoits pegs
31 It can't be played on a trumpet, e.g.
32 Fire
33 Revelation response
34 18th-century French inventor of a temperature scale
36 Boric acid target
37 Common rugby score
38 Baseball, slangily
39 Estimate follower
40 Take a city bus, perhaps
44 Podiatric concern
45 Enthusiastic show of approval
49 Worked (up)
50 Persona non grata
52 Cry of horror, in poetry
53 Director Reitman
54 Statistical calculation
56 Campbell of "Wild Things"
57 Movie mini-marathon
58 Looking like rain
59 Passing events

DOWN
1 Thick
2 Pleasant way to walk
3 Twenty, in Trieste
4 Bit of work
5 One associated with fire
6 Goes along
7 Figures in major-league baseball
8 Protector of the dead, in myth
9 Something hammered out
10 Liverpool-to-Nottingham dir.
11 Some wool
12 Auto garage courtesy
13 Tuscan ancients
14 Boards
21 Weary worker's wish
23 "___ Brown" (Judi Dench film)
24 Its highest point is Huascarán
26 Holy Arks' homes
27 "Get your pretty self over here!"
28 Cooling one's jets?
29 Belle of Louisville's beat
30 Mountain-climber's hood
34 Rose on the hind legs, with "up"
35 "Odyssey," e.g.
39 Home to Queens U.
41 President Ford's chief of staff
42 Too
43 Less trusting
46 Column choice
47 Frère de la mère
48 Present times
50 It may be tribal
51 Set, Egyptian god of ___
54 Hdqrs.
55 See 24-Across

by Byron Walden

175

ACROSS

1 Crossword pattern
5 Dinner and a movie, perhaps
9 No longer fresh
14 Prefix with space
15 Sharif of "Funny Girl"
16 Swatch competitor
17 Convention group
18 Sitarist Shankar
19 Christopher of "Superman"
20 Polyester, e.g.
23 Battering device
24 Words before tear or roll
25 Astroturf, e.g.
34 Everest or Ararat
35 Comic strip orphan
36 Country singer Brenda
37 Johnson of "Laugh-In"
38 Vision-related
39 Darn, as socks
40 Lunar New Year
41 Grand Canyon transport
42 Contemptible person
43 Oleomargarine, e.g.
46 Airport monitor abbr.
47 Blonde shade
48 Fake 50, e.g.
57 Throng
58 Banjo-plucking Scruggs
59 Hand lotion ingredient
60 Indy-winning Al, Jr. or Sr.
61 Canal of song
62 It's trapped on laundry day
63 Sirs' counterparts
64 Give temporarily
65 Falls behind

DOWN

1 Chews the fat
2 Depend (on)
3 "Pumping ___"
4 Marxism, for one
5 Starting notes in music
6 Amo, amas, ___ . . .
7 Rikki-Tikki-___
8 Guitarist Clapton
9 Eerie
10 Item of men's jewelry
11 From the United States: Abbr.
12 Jeans purveyor Strauss
13 Business V.I.P.
21 Sword handle
22 ___ acid (B vitamin)
25 Maker of precious violins
26 Composer/author Ned
27 ___-frutti
28 Isle in the Bay of Naples
29 Emcee's spiel
30 Negatively charged particle
31 Alaskan native
32 "Common" thing that's not always common
33 Passover feast
38 Bizarre
39 Closet larvae repellent
41 Does deals without money
42 Earthy desire
44 Bicycle for two
45 Tried to save a sinking boat
48 Buddy
49 Ore of the O'Neills
50 ___ Major
51 Rod's partner
52 Price of a ride
53 "___ go bragh"
54 Pelvic bones
55 Beyond the end line
56 Answer to "Shall we?"

by Sarah Keller

ACROSS

1 Opportunity to hit
6 Shoots 18, say
11 Rocks in a bar
14 Long green
15 The Beatles' "Eight Days ___"
16 Turf
17 Result of eating ice cream too fast, possibly
19 Moth-eaten
20 Best guess: Abbr.
21 Fastens with a band
22 "That is ___ . . ." (in other words)
24 Town next to Elizabeth, N.J.
26 Flexible, electrically
27 Fondue dip
32 Bops hard
35 Light as a feather
36 Pot's top
37 Spa wear
38 En ___ (all together)
40 Place for a ham
41 Where Schwarzenegger was born: Abbr.
42 "Lost our lease" event
43 Airplane seating option
44 Entreater's words
48 Asta's mistress
49 The whole ___ (everything)
53 Must, slangily
55 Debaters debate it
57 Shaq's alma mater: Abbr.
58 Copy
59 Sunshine State vacation area
62 Snore letter
63 3 on a par-5 hole, e.g.
64 Largish combo
65 Golfer Ernie
66 Collar inserts
67 Quaint footwear

DOWN

1 Color of waves of grain, in song
2 Sculpted figure
3 Bath toys
4 2001 role for Will Smith
5 Comb stoppers
6 Attic
7 Was in the red
8 Dregs
9 Shriner's topper
10 Missing many details
11 Kind of triangle
12 RC, for one
13 Whirling water
18 "___ 'er up!"
23 Pindar work
25 One-named supermodel
26 Plot unit
28 Studio prop
29 Insult, slangily
30 Spot for a warm pie
31 Falco of "The Sopranos"
32 Shawl or stole
33 Billing unit
34 Some voters
38 Yucatán native
39 Grand Paradiso, for one
40 Per ___
42 Attacks from the air
43 Sub sinkers, in slang
45 Young 'un
46 Catches sight of
47 Like gastric juice
50 Dementieva of tennis
51 So far
52 Corrodes
53 Stare intently
54 Kadett automaker
55 Fraternity party attire
56 Paris airport
60 Long. crosser
61 Keystone lawman

by Jim Hyres

118

ACROSS

1 "Hardball" channel
6 Tim of "WKRP"
10 Actor McGregor
14 Car hitch-up
15 Best of theater
16 Put on a scale
17 Mic check #1
20 Coverage co.
21 Gets across?
22 Like a sad sack
23 Long, long time
24 Within: Prefix
26 Mic check #2
31 Like hawks and auks
32 Words to an "old chap"
33 Genetic letters
36 Fix up
37 One of the Jacksons
39 Utah national park
40 A no. that's good when under 3.00
41 Laundromat loss, maybe
42 A beatnik may beat it
43 Mic check #3
47 Minister to
48 Carry on
49 Burger King or The Gap
52 Call after a toss
54 Toward the rear
57 Mic check #4
60 ___ Sea, east of the Ustyurt Plateau
61 Italian wine town
62 Latish bedtime
63 Puts on
64 40-Across, e.g.
65 Campus buys

DOWN

1 "How ___?"
2 Impostor
3 Prefix with second
4 Bull's urging
5 Draw near
6 Move, as a picture
7 Shangri-la
8 Sort of
9 Patriotic org.
10 Heretofore
11 Diminish
12 Straddling
13 Eye of ___ (witches' brew need)
18 Straddling
19 Thurber's fantasizer
23 Slightly
25 Straight, at the bar
26 Broken, in a way
27 Constantly
28 1967 war locale
29 Sounds from pens
30 Certain gasket
34 Scrapped, at NASA
35 Before long
37 Sportscaster Madden
38 Conclusive trial
39 Type of court defense
41 Court reporter
42 One in charge
44 Photos
45 Like dusk
46 Something seen with the Virgin Mary
49 Election hanger-on?
50 Sub
51 Actor Rickman
53 Prov. bordering Mont.
54 Michael J. Fox's role on "Family Ties"
55 Cyclist's problem
56 Some gobblers
58 Suffers from
59 Vane dir.

by Brendan Emmett Quigley

ACROSS
1 Gobbled
6 "__ Lisa"
10 Press down
14 Deep performer
15 Parts of Japanese bridal costumes
16 S-shaped curve
17 Reunion group
18 It comes out of a trunk
19 Monthly expense
20 Was evasive
23 Spleen
24 Good news for an angel
25 Emulated Ethel Merman
33 Old Chevys
34 "Time's a-wastin'!"
35 Salon application
36 Outstanding
37 Oozes
39 Robin Cook thriller
40 Material for a whitesmith
41 Arizona river
42 Having more karats
43 Stake
47 Wedded
48 Colorado native
49 Worse than slapped
58 Toll unit, sometimes
59 "Got it"
60 Wedge drivers
61 Sinn __
62 Plumlike fruit
63 Plumbing fitting
64 Grandson of Adam
65 Setters
66 Snappish

DOWN
1 Primer material
2 Make a deal with the feds, say
3 Actor Morales
4 "Back in the __"
5 Document attachments
6 Worked by hand
7 Final notice
8 "The Secret of __" (1982 animated film)
9 Danger in old homes
10 Some sculptures
11 Seemingly forever
12 Remote control button
13 Fountain of music
21 "A little __ the mightiest Julius fell": Shak.
22 Bit of Kurdistan
25 __ State (Arkansas nickname)
26 Roulette bets
27 Shaver
28 Main
29 Person in a mask
30 They're released
31 Shea player, for short
32 A mask, for a 29-Down
33 Punishment for some kids
37 Beans or rice
38 "Bingo, __ Yale" (fight song)
39 Nod, maybe
41 Characteristic carrier
42 Bump
44 Some coins
45 Pupils
46 Biblical verb ending
49 Dependable
50 Alternatives to mules
51 Advertiser's award
52 Beach site
53 Gaudy sign
54 "Six Feet Under" son
55 "This Love of __" (1945 film)
56 Thin strip
57 Glimpse

by Nancy Kavanaugh

ACROSS

1 Many a Standardbred
8 Aid in raising cane?
15 San Remo setting
16 One who's trying
17 Member of NATO
18 Hard at it
19 Like some checks: Abbr.
20 Rodgers and Hammerstein musical setting
22 Inner: Prefix
23 __-El (Superman's birth name)
24 It may interfere with delivery
27 10 marks, once
29 Tank top
30 "Just because"
32 City where Mark Twain is buried
36 Foundation, often
37 People known to have germs?
38 Noted Hollywood exec
39 Refuse to change
40 Imposts
42 In headlinese, say
43 Minor expenses
47 Spanish pronoun
48 Baseball's Drabek
49 Man who's taken vows
50 Cottontail's tail
51 RCA rival
54 Catch
56 Target of a flick
57 Moped
58 They send up jets
59 Things fault-finders study

DOWN

1 It may require joint checking
2 Popular side
3 Rulers' rulers
4 The earth is on one
5 Kind of service
6 Novelist Jünger
7 Fireplace alternative
8 Austrian physician whose work laid the foundation for hypnosis
9 Digital communication?: Abbr.
10 11-member grp.
11 Be on easy street
12 Checking out
13 Kappa's position
14 Cereal killer
21 Pull __ on
24 Jelly plant
25 "Band of Gold" singer Payne
26 Lets up
28 Broadway sights
31 Assist
33 Curse
34 No longer worried
35 Hill predators
37 Statement made with a tsk, tsk
39 __ record
41 Cloisonné clusters
43 Label
44 Wild West justice
45 Hardly hard
46 Cavalry soldier
50 Judgment passer, perhaps
52 Boiling blood
53 Tender place?
55 "__ wise guy, eh?"

by Sherry O. Blackard

Conclusion

Healthy lifestyle choices can delay the effects of aging and allow your brain to stay young. Living to your 90's and remaining sharp is now a reasonable goal. During the past five years, neuroscientists have discovered that you can indeed tone up your brain and make it larger, just as you can strengthen and expand your muscles. It is amazing to believe that your daily choices of food, exercise and stress can literally change the shape of the brain. But now for the first time there is convincing and powerful research that supports this new concept.

BRAIN RESERVE, RETIREMENT PLAN

Throughout life you have many opportunities to create new synapses in your brain and expand your mental agility. In contrast to the old dogma, brain plasticity and potential for growth are possible at any age and are not limited to children. Increased mental and physical activity over decades, combined with a diet rich in antioxidant vitamins, will translate into a larger pool of synapses and new neurons. This larger capacity, called the brain reserve, is similar to creating a larger retirement fund after many years of saving money and investing for your senior years. The more synapses generated throughout your life, the better your chances of resisting the loss of those synapses with the wear-and-tear of aging or Alzheimer's disease.

THE SEESAW PHENOMENON FOR MEMORY LOSS

The chance of developing memory loss and slowing mental agility depends on the balance of positive and negative factors affecting the number of synapses in your brain, especially in your hippocampus.

During your senior years, you remain sharp as long as your brain reserve outweighs the negative influences damaging your synapses. You may experience only occasional memory lapses. If at some point the effects of aging, atherosclerosis and varying degrees of Alzheimer's outweigh your brain reserve, you begin to show signs of cognitive decline; you may start forgetting what a key is used for or get lost while driving in your own neighborhood. Needless to say, to ward off memory loss and Alzheimer's, you must start today to expand your brain reserve.

THE HEALTHY BRAIN INITIATIVE

Thanks to advances in medical care, as well as public education about reducing risks for heart attacks and early screening for cancer, more people are living into their 80's. By 2030, the number of senior Americans will double to 70 million; one out of every five will be older than 65, and nine million citizens will be older than 85. Sixty-two percent of the elderly citizens worry about their mental capacity. There is also worry from the Medicare system and the government concerning the need for more funding to care for those with impending dementia and mental loss. Congress has recognized the gravity of this health care tsunami and in 2005 appropriated funds to the Centers for Disease Control and Prevention (CDC) to launch "The Healthy Brain Initiative."

The CDC, in collaboration with the Alzheimer's Association, invited 60 of the top research scientists to a meeting in May 2006. They hoped to develop recommendations for a national initiative focused on promoting brain health, to map a course of action to ward off Alzheimer's. After much discussion, the scientists determined that identifying and treating vascular risk factors as well as improving physical activity offer the best chances for achieving optimal brain fitness. The vascular risk factors include high blood pressure, diabetes, smoking, high cholesterol and obesity.

OBSTACLES TO CHANGING YOUR LIFESTYLE

Hopefully this book has helped you appreciate the day-to-day impact of diet and activity choices on your mental agility, sharpness and overall brain health. Now you can take the first steps to improve your lifestyle. Like most, you have probably tried to lose a few pounds, exercise or join a gym but have not been quite successful. Luckily, now you have an added incentive to improve your fitness, as most lifestyle choices needed for a stronger heart are also essential to build a more powerful brain.

Denial is one of the common obstacles preventing people from changing their health habits. Smokers often feel they will not develop lung cancer or heart attacks because they believe such major problems will likely happen to their neighbors or friends but not to them. When trying to quit, they often fall back into old smoking habits as the craving for nicotine proves unbearable. However, most quit instantly and permanently as soon as they develop cancer or heart attacks; unfortunately it is often too late. Take your first step to lower your chance of developing strokes, large or small, today before anyone has the chance to say, "I told you so."

A hectic lifestyle is another factor commonly preventing people from achieving their goals for diet and exercise. When challenged with deadlines and neverending loads of work, there is limited time to tone muscles or make an effort to eat fish two or three times a week. People would love to have a few extra minutes to take care of their bodies but feel too stressed and overwhelmed with their job and home responsibilities. You need to act smart by finding intelligent ways to lower your workload in order to maintain a healthy balance between taking care of your health and attending to your career goals and family joys.

STRATEGIES FOR OVERCOMING THESE OBSTACLES

I have found that focusing on priorities is a simple way to get around these obstacles. I ask my patients if they would make changes to their lifestyle habits if I paid them (hypothetically) $100,000 in cash every week. When confronted with such a simple choice, they appreciate the ease of making changes in their lives whether it is quitting smoking, managing their blood pressure, or walking 45 minutes three to five times a week. They see positive results within weeks and subsequently incorporate diet and exercise into their daily routine. If your brain health and cognitive sharpness is worth millions to you, then start taking steps and making changes in your daily habits, starting today—not tomorrow.

I invite you to review your Brain Health Quiz (page 161) to discover which areas need improvement. If you choose to make three changes in your lifestyle, you'll increase your chance of success by starting one change at a time. For example, focus on managing and treating your hypertension for three months. After you notice improvement in your blood pressure, add brain stimulation as the next component to tackle. After another three months, focus on reducing stress or losing weight, as needed. You can chart a one-year plan for achieving perfect brain health, with setting reasonable goals at three-month intervals.

You will be confronted with making choices about what you eat and how you handle stressful situations every day, and almost every hour. Stay strong and make the right choices. If you want to shed a few pounds, don't be tempted to eat chocolate, take second servings or accept snacks. Just firmly say no. These small victories over simple daily temptations will soon fill you with confidence and help you make better decisions to enhance your brain reserve.

Remember, should you be given the choice between $100,000 and eating a piece of chocolate cake, you would not think twice. Your brain's lasting health is worth millions. Use this approach and compliment yourself every time you make intelligent choices toward achieving your health goals. The most important step is the first: getting out of old routines and making new changes. Once you overcome the initial inertia, you will be on your way to better physical fitness and better memory, and you will feel happier about yourself overall.

CONGRATULATIONS: YOU NOW HAVE A BIGGER AND MORE POWERFUL BRAIN

Since you started reading this book, you have learned a dozen new concepts. You now can talk about the hippocampus, brain plasticity, BDNF and cortisol. You also have completed dozens of crossword puzzles. You may have even started walking more or joined a dance class. Just like the research volunteer subjects who learned how to juggle three balls in the air for three months and later found out their brains had grown, you too have created thousands of new synapses with learning new concepts and challenging your brain with crossword puzzles. Your brain is now actually slightly bigger.

As you realize how simple it is to upgrade your brain, I hope you continue to take advantage of every opportunity in your daily routines to work on creating new synapses and expanding your hippocampus as well as the frontal, parietal and temporal lobes of your cortex. You can indeed achieve lobes of steel if you continue to eat right, avoid stress, increase your physical activity and tease your brain. Building a more powerful brain is easier than sculpting strong abs.

TOP 10 STRATEGIES TOWARD BOOSTING YOUR BRAINPOWER

1. Start with passion. You won't succeed unless you honestly believe you need to make changes in your lifestyle habits to improve your brain fitness.

2. Get organized. Look at your results from the Brain Health Quiz on page 161 and decide on the top four areas that require the most help. Write them down in your date book. Start with the first area, work on it for three months, and then add the second and third areas at three-month intervals. Every Sunday, set up reasonable and succinct goals for the coming week. Every morning, set up priorities toward reaching your goals. Maintain a balance of work, family, pleasure and personal needs.

3. Delay gratification. Give up on daily temptations that prevent you from reaching your weekly goal. If you decide to walk 30–45 minutes a day, then you may have to forgo watching your favorite television show. If you have decided to shed a few pounds, then do not even consider touching cookies or brownies. Visualize

---

how wonderful you will feel once you reach your goals at the end of the week. Stay determined, persistent and strong. Soon these choices become routine habits and you will no longer even consider the unhealthy alternative.

4. Meditate. Once a day, find a quiet place to relax for 15 minutes. Let go and release tension in your body. Turn off your phone, pager, Blackberry and everything else that beeps. Remember that stress kills brain cells in your hippocampus. Enjoy the tranquility of your mind as you get ready for the rest of your day.

5. Pamper yourself with microadventures. Once or twice a week, do something you really enjoy. As a means of confirming you are in control as well as getting positive feedback for yourself, indulge in something fun and exciting. Reward yourself with massages, shopping, a getaway or flowers for keeping up with your goals and fighting distractions and temptations.

6. Tease your brain. When stuck in traffic or waiting in line at the post office, take advantage of the time and think about math questions (subtract 13 from 100, and then keep counting down by 13), spell long words backward, or recall phone numbers of old friends. While on trains, planes or buses, try crossword puzzles, sudoku puzzles or other mind teasers. This is similar to improving your fitness by taking the stairs any time you get a chance.

7. Get quality sleep. If you have trouble falling sleep or staying asleep or if you wake up too early in the morning, see your doctor. Most sleep problems affect quality of life but are readily treatable. Routine use of sleeping medications should be the last choice.

8. Eat well. Make sure to include fruits and vegetables in your meals, starting with 1–2 servings per day. Over the months increase it to 4–5 servings per day. Eat fish, especially salmon, 2–3 times a week. If possible, drink 1–2 glasses of wine with your dinner.

9. Walk, jog, swim or do any other activity you prefer; refuse to be a couch potato. Walking has at least a dozen health benefits, ranging from improving your sexual function and extending your life to creating new neurons and expanding the size of your brain.

10. Have a positive and respectful attitude toward others. If you see the world through other people's eyes, you will understand them on a different level. Respect their choices and preferences, and you will find yourself among people who enjoy working with you. The more love in the air, the less stress you will feel, and the more you will enjoy your home and your work environment. Your hippocampus will thank you for it.

The New York Times

CROSSWORDS

SMART PUZZLES PRESENTED WITH STYLE

Available at your local bookstore or online at nytimes.com/nytstore.

St. Martin's Griffin

Answers

Crossword Puzzles

1

A	D	A	G	E	■	■	■	B	R	O	O	M	S	■
R	E	P	L	A	N	■	F	A	U	X	P	A	S	■
R	E	P	O	S	E	■	S	I	D	E	L	I	N	E
■	P	O	W	E	R	S	T	E	E	R	I	N	G	■
I	F	I	■	D	U	O	■	S	P	I	E	L	■	■
S	A	N	D	L	■	E	R	S	E	■	O	R	E	■
O	T	T	O	I	V	■	M	A	X	E	R	N	S	T
■	W	A	S	H	C	Y	C	L	E	■	■	■	■	■
A	I	R	D	R	O	M	E	■	H	U	M	E	R	I
S	H	E	■	P	O	N	Y	■	L	O	C	O	S	■
H	A	D	J	I	■	T	A	O	■	H	S	T	■	■
■	T	R	U	S	T	M	E	O	N	T	H	I	S	■
M	E	E	I	T	H	E	R	■	C	R	E	D	I	T
D	I	S	C	O	R	D	■	D	I	A	N	N	E	■
I	T	S	Y	O	U	■	■	B	R	A	I	N	■	■

2

A	D	A	M	■	T	H	E	R	E	■	S	U	N	G
G	E	N	E	■	R	E	L	A	Y	■	K	N	E	E
H	E	A	R	T	I	N	T	H	E	■	I	V	A	N
A	R	T	■	A	E	R	O	■	B	R	E	T	T	■
■	H	A	N	D	I	N	T	H	E	T	I	L	L	■
A	V	E	R	S	■	O	U	R	■	L	Y	E	■	■
S	E	M	I	■	A	S	S	A	Y	■	■	■	■	■
H	E	A	D	I	N	T	H	E	C	L	O	U	D	S
■	■	■	N	O	I	S	E	■	L	S	A	T	■	■
A	P	T	■	D	O	L	■	R	E	E	D	Y	■	■
F	O	O	T	I	N	T	H	E	D	O	O	R	■	■
F	L	O	R	A	■	A	T	O	M	■	B	E	D	■
E	L	L	A	■	R	I	G	H	T	P	L	A	C	E
C	O	E	D	■	A	T	E	A	T	■	A	S	O	F
T	I	D	E	■	P	E	N	N	Y	■	B	E	N	T

3

C	B	S	■	R	E	V	I	L	E	■	S	H	O	P
A	N	A	■	O	L	I	V	E	R	■	P	U	Z	O
P	A	N	A	M	A	C	A	N	A	L	A	R	A	B
P	I	G	L	A	T	I	N	■	A	S	T	R	O	■
■	■	I	N	E	■	T	O	Y	■	S	K	Y	■	■
G	L	O	B	■	S	L	A	M	■	■	■	■	■	■
R	A	M	A	D	A	C	A	T	A	M	A	R	A	N
A	L	A	B	A	M	A	M	A	H	A	R	A	J	A
B	A	N	A	N	A	R	A	M	A	S	A	G	A	S
■	■	■	T	E	R	I	■	L	A	R	A	■	■	■
R	P	M	■	D	I	D	■	A	D	S	■	■	■	■
E	L	O	P	E	■	C	U	T	I	E	P	I	E	■
B	A	B	A	W	A	W	A	S	A	V	A	T	A	R
U	Z	I	S	■	C	A	M	E	R	A	■	A	G	O
S	A	L	T	■	T	H	E	S	I	S	■	S	O	S

4

B	E	S	I	E	G	E	R	■	E	M	M	E	T	T
O	V	E	R	R	A	T	E	■	T	O	O	T	H	Y
W	E	W	O	N	D	E	R	■	O	U	C	H	E	S
I	R	E	N	E	■	O	B	I	S	■	I	T	O	■
E	T	R	E	■	H	O	W	E	L	S	E	C	A	N
■	,	■	D	E	A	L	■	D	E	E	R	■	■	■
A	L	A	■	S	L	A	P	■	■	A	S	T	A	■
B	I	R	D	S	O	F	A	F	E	A	T	H	E	R
S	E	M	I	■	■	L	I	M	P	■	Y	E	T	■
■	■	■	S	U	R	E	■	D	I	E	M	■	■	■
F	L	O	C	K	I	F	N	O	T	■	O	N	E	S
A	O	K	■	A	S	T	O	■	S	T	O	V	E	■
U	P	R	O	S	E	■	T	O	G	E	T	H	E	R
N	E	A	R	E	R	■	S	H	E	L	L	I	N	G
A	S	S	E	S	S	■	O	M	E	L	E	T	T	E

5

L	A	B	S	■	D	A	H	L	■	M	E	M	O	S
E	L	E	C	■	A	G	E	E	■	A	L	A	N	A
T	A	R	O	■	R	U	I	N	■	R	E	C	A	P
S	M	A	R	T	C	A	R	D	■	I	M	A	N	■
G	O	T	N	O	■	■	L	E	N	■	R	D	S	■
O	S	E	■	W	H	O	S	■	R	E	T	O	O	L
■	■	L	E	A	K	A	G	E	■	I	N	F	O	■
I	N	T	E	L	L	I	G	E	N	T	L	I	F	E
N	O	U	N	■	T	E	A	R	O	U	T	■	■	■
S	T	R	O	V	E	■	S	E	W	N	■	S	R	A
T	A	N	■	E	R	S	■	■	I	M	P	E	L	■
■	R	I	T	E	■	W	I	S	E	C	R	A	C	K
M	I	T	E	R	■	I	D	E	S	■	B	R	A	Y
A	Z	U	R	E	■	S	E	A	S	■	I	T	L	L
T	E	P	I	D	■	H	A	L	E	■	G	A	L	S

6

S	A	I	L	■	P	S	H	A	W	■	C	H	A	R
K	I	T	E	■	R	A	I	S	E	■	H	I	R	E
I	R	O	N	O	U	T	T	H	E	K	I	N	K	S
■	■	■	S	A	N	I	T	Y	■	O	L	D	I	E
R	I	M	■	T	E	R	I	■	C	L	I	N	T	■
U	S	A	G	E	■	E	N	O	C	H	■	■	■	■
M	A	Y	O	R	S	■	G	O	O	■	T	H	A	I
B	A	B	E	S	I	N	T	H	E	W	O	O	D	S
A	C	E	S	■	R	A	H	■	D	I	S	M	A	L
■	■	■	■	J	E	T	E	R	■	T	H	E	M	E
A	T	S	E	A	■	L	E	C	H	■	S	S	T	■
P	R	A	N	K	■	P	I	G	L	E	T	■	■	■
P	U	T	T	E	R	I	N	G	A	R	O	U	N	D
L	E	E	R	■	M	C	K	A	Y	■	A	V	O	N
E	D	D	Y	■	N	O	S	E	S	■	D	A	D	A

7

```
S P A R S   L A M B   G O B S
W O M A N   U S E R   R A R E
A T O N E   C I T I   I K E A
T H R E E Y E A R S   D R A G
H E T E R O     I T S   I D A
E R S   A G O I C O U L D N T
    S T A I D   L E A G U E
C A S E   L I D   S E T S
A L T A I R   O O M P H
S P E L L A U T H O R   C A P
T A N   L I T   N O M O R E
I C O N   N O W I A R E O N E
R I P E   S P I N   A L L O W
O N A N   O I N K   T O I L E
N O D E   N A G Y   A N O D E
```

8

```
P A D S   C A L M   I C K E S
E L E E   A M A S   C L I P S
A S S T   R I N G L E A D E R
L O P S I D E D   A B I D E S
S P E A R S   S O B E R
    R I S E   A N E R O I D S
A R A L   L A T E X G L O V E
S A D   W E S   I P S   N I A
A T O M I C P I L E   L O I N
P A S Y S T E M   R U E S
    C H I N A   I N A P E T
T U P E L O   G A M E S H O W
W H E N I N R O M E   H E S A
A U R A S   P E E N   E R I N
S H E E T   I S N T   D E N G
```

9

```
S T A G E R S   D A W N S O N
W I S H Y O U W E R E H E R E
I N S E C T R E P E L L A N T
S W A N K   T A U N T   B I G
H A U T   W I T T S   D A T A
E R L   K A T H Y   S U S H I
S E T S M I L E   T H E S O N
    W A T E R B O A T
I N T E R S   B O O K S H O P
N E W A T   L E Y T E   A F L
L O O T   T E A C H   R I F E
A G S   N O D T O   C I T E D
B E T T E R G E T M O V I N G
O N E M O M E N T P L E A S E
R E P I N E R   S H A T N E R
```

10

```
S A S Q U A T C H   S N O R T
N E T A N Y A H U   H A U E R
O R A N G E R E D   A P T L Y
C O N T E S T E D   W A L E S
O S C A R   A P L U S   O A T
N O E S   G R E E N H O U S E
E L S   C R U D   P A D D E D
    W O E S   C A N E
O N S A L E   L I C K   H I P
F O U R O C L O C K   M A M A
F R A   R E A C H   L O V I N
C E S T A   C A L C U L A T E
A L I E N   E R I E C A N A L
S C O T T   U N D E R R A T E
T O N E S   P O S S E S S E D
```

11

```
W H A T S N E W   C R O W D S
H U S H H U S H   R E S H O E
I S S U A N C E   I N T E N T
S T A G   N O N E E D   R T S
K L U     R I P S   S E A T
S E L L   A T M O   A C T S O
  S T U R M   S C H N O O K
    M I A M I H E A T
  S A M E S E X   S T I F F
S O L O N   A T E S   A L E R
I M A X   I D Y L   O D E
F E M   S T E F A N   A R O D
T O O T O O   O P E N F I R E
E N D A L L   U S A T O D A Y
D E E M E D   R E P H R A S E
```

12

```
S P A S   M A S H   B A Y E R
C O R P   O R E O   E L I Z A
A S I A   D R A W I N G P I N
M I S C U E   M E M O   S O T
S T E E P L E   S P I T
    N O S I R   A T H O M E
L I N E N   D E L I   I H O P
O N C E   S E W E R   M I R E
M E A D   T R E E   T B O N E
A Z A L E A   D R O O L
    E N Y A   S T R E E T S
U S E   D E M S   H O W L I N
T H R E A D B A R E   E I N E
E A S E L   L I A R   E T T A
S H E L L   E L M S   D E S K
```

13

```
E R A T . B E L I E . A M E N
L A S H . A R E N T . N O N E
B I T E . T I N K E R T O Y S
A N I M A T E D . . D E T A T
. . A R E . . H A N . . . .
T A I L O R M A D E . N A S A
A T O L L . A F A R . A C T I
S A T . L E C A R R E . E E L
S L A M . S A L E . L O R N E
E L S A . S O L D I E R B O Y
. . L A O . . R C A . . . .
A U D I T . . E M I T T I N G
S P Y G L A S S E S . O V A L
S T E N . P A S T E . R A T E
N O D S . B L E S S . S N E E
```

14

```
M U M . D E C A F . P A G E R
O L E . E R A T O . A C O R N
U N A . C E L T I C C R O S S
R A N D R . . S A T E D . .
N E T R E S U L T S . . T A P
. . J E U N E . T A H I T I
P E A . R I G S . D E M O N
S P U R O F T H E M O M E N T
A C T O R . S O L D . S E A
T O O T O O . R I C C I . .
S T P . K I N G C O T T O N
. I C E I N . . I S E R E
B U L L S E S S I O N . N B A
A L O E S . E L I D E . S I T
M E T O O . T O N E D . E T O
```

15

```
N I N E . S P A C E . G R I D
O N O R . H U M A N . A U N T
O L D E . A N I L S . M T N S
S A D I S M . E L I J A H .
E W E . A P B . G U L L E D
S S R . T O U C A N S . E X O
. . B I O T I C . T V S E T
A F T E R . T A C . S I S S Y
B A H A I . T O E C A P . .
E L I . C R O S S L Y . I S A
L A R V A E . S O N . T L C
. S E L D O M . S O W H A T
T O T E . S T A G E . H A L O
S U E R . O R N O T . I C O N
K I D S . X A N D O . G A M E
```

16

```
E L I S A . P R A M S . S O S
T U N E D . L E T A T . L U C
O N C E A . A T O N E W I T H
. C R A G . C A M B R I D G E
T H E F I X E R . I O N I U M
A B A T O R . E T I E N N E
R O S E S A R E R E D . .
A X E R . T A C O S . A S S T
. . M E T H O D A C T O R
U S E R I D S . O P T I M A
P U R I S M . B A G P I P E S
K N O T H O L E S . O V E R .
E N D E A V O R S . S E N S E
E E E . P I N E Y . E L D E R
P D S . S E G A R . S Y S T S
```

17

```
A R E A O F E X P E R T I S E
S I G O U R N E Y W E A V E R
I T A L I A N D R E S S I N G
F E N . D I E . A R T . E D O
. . S A L A A M . . P S S T
A N N A . . D R I V E R . .
C O U N T S . I D A R E Y O U
C A D D I E S . S I T C O M S
T H E B L A H S . L E E R E D
. . A T L A S T . . P E N A
S P A R . . M A I N S T . .
H I D . G Y P . S E P . A R K
E V E R Y M O T H E R S S O N
P O L A R C O O R D I N A T E
S T A T E A S S I S T A N C E
```

18

```
T A B L E . B I O S . R A S H
I L I A D . A D U E . A N T E
M A R T I N R I T T . L O O S
S I D E B E T . S A M P R A S
. . L E A S T . I H A T E
L U T H E R B U R B A N K
B L E U . . F I R M A . .
J E A N A R P . P A I D O F F
. . T I A R A . . E R L E
. K I N G O F T H E R O A D
A M O N G . T R I A D . .
L O W G E A R . E L E C T O R
L O T T . J U N I O R H I G H
A R O O . A D I N . L I L L E
H E W N . R E P S . E S T E E
```

19

```
E L A L   S P A S   A D O B E
M A M E   P R I M   L A N E D
T W O F O R O N E O F F E R S
  C U T T Y   T A P   T I N E
H O N   T E N   R E C   L I L
M U T T   R E P   N O B L E S
O R T H O   H E A T E R
  T O O F O R E B O D I N G
    S U B U R B   S N E R D
T A L E S E   S O C   E X I T
A L E   E Y E   T A B   T D S
S C A T   E L M   M E R C I
T O F O U R M O R E Y E A R S
E V E N T   E V I L   A S O F
R E D Y E   R E D S   L E N O
```

20

```
W H I G S   N U B   A L S O
R E T R O   C A S A   L I E U
A R E A S   Z I N G   A S P S
P E R S O N A L A D Z   Z I T
    S O A R S   A O R T A S
D E C   N O S E   D R O P
E R O S   M E T Z   B A R G E
S O M A L I A   O N A D I E T
C O M B O   T O N E   S C A N
  O R G S   R E S T   E R A
D O N E I N   A S T R A
O N E   C A T C H S O M E Z S
S I Z E   P O L O   J I V E S
E C R U   A B E T   A N E N T
D E A R   T E S   N O N O S
```

21

```
N O C A T C H   W H A T S U P
I N A P I L E   H O V L A N E
C A R E F O R   E P I C U R E
E D A   F U E L R O D   S A W
J A M A   T W E E N   S A V E
O R B I T   E T S   A W G E E
B E A R H U G S   S T E E L S
    H O R O S C O P E
C A V E R N   L A Y A N E G G
O C E A N   C I N   R E T R Y
L A N D   M A D A S   Y E A R
D D E   L A T E R O N   R N A
D E E P E N D   I M E A N I T
A M R A D I O   E M A N A T E
Y E S M A A M   S E T T L E D
```

22

```
T E A M E D U P   G R A M P S
O N P A R O L E   L A H O R E
P R E C I N C T   E V A D E S
H O R S E H E A D N E B U L A
O B I   O R L O N   L A M
L E E R S   S E W   C R A T E
E D S E L S   D E C L A R E S
    G A I N   L O A M
A L C A T R A Z   T R E P I D
T E A L S   M O M   A N I T A
T A R   M E D I C   L A Y
A S F A R A S I C A N T E L L
C H A R O N   A R P E G G I O
H E R M O N   C O R R I G A N
E D E S S A   S N I F F I N G
```

23

```
D E L E   U S M C   J U M B O
A P E X   P H I L   A C U R A
S E N T   T I L E   C O L O R
H E A R T O F D A R K N E S S
  A B I T   R A I N
B A R D O T   F I R E   O P T
A G A I N   T I N E   O P E R
C E N T E R O F G R A V I T Y
O N C E   E Y E S   G E N E S
N T H   C U S S   A R R E S T
  C E S T   A G E D
M I D D L E O F T H E R O A D
A M O R E   R I T A   A S T O
R A Z O R   E L I S   F L O P
E N E M Y   S E C T   T O M E
```

24

```
A D L I B   H O U S E   G S A
L E O N A   E P S O M   A W L
L E G A L B R I E F S   Z A P
O R I   B E R E F T   D E M O
R E C O O L   U T N E
  L A T E B L O O M E R S
B R A E   S R A   P H O B I A
A U R A S   A N T   O L O G Y
S T I N T S   J A W   I N A S
S H A D O W B O X E R S
  E P E E   B E H A V E
B A R R   E T U D E S   V I A
O V A   O P E N D R A W E R S
Z I T   C E L I A   L A R G E
O D E   T A S T Y   E X T O L
```

25

```
S T A T S █ C O A T █ A B E L
M U R A L █ H I L O █ P E T E
A D E N I N A D E N █ I N T O
R O N █ T O W █ R E B A T E S
T R A I T S █ M O U E S █ █ █
█ █ R E E V E █ P L A T T E █
S T R A D █ E E R █ A W A R D
A M E N █ T R A █ A R I E █ █
B E E F S █ S K I █ S P O O N
U N D O E R █ A D L A I █ █ █
█ █ R E A C T █ E N A B L E █
C O R I N T H █ O F F █ O A R
O V E R █ T O G O T O T O G O
S E L A █ A S A P █ R A Z E D
A N O N █ N E T S █ D E E R E
```

26

```
T A R P █ T A W S █ C S P A N
I D O L █ A L O T █ O H A R A
T E L E █ F I R E █ L O R E N
A L F A L F A S P R O U T S █
N E E D I E S T █ I N T █ █ █
█ █ █ E M T █ S T E A M U P █
█ B A R B A R A W A L T E R S
F A N █ █ I D A █ █ █ L I I █
C I N C I N N A T I R E D S █
C L E A N E D █ N I A █ █ █ █
█ █ █ L A T █ O B S E R V E S
█ S H O S H O N E I N D I A N
S H A R P █ G L A D █ R O T O
R A T I O █ R O M E █ O L I O
S H E E T █ E W E R █ P A N T
```

27

```
J A N E W A Y █ H E A D S U P
A M I L A T E █ A X L R O S E
B R E A K I N █ V O L U M E S
B A L L E T █ █ E T A G E R E
E D S █ █ B U N I N █ W I T █
D I E M █ D U R O C █ N A D A
█ O N C R E D I T █ B O Y S █
█ █ █ J U G █ █ S O N █ █ █ █
█ I G O R █ G A Z P A C H O █
S N O B █ D E W E Y █ E A C H
N C O █ R A T E D █ █ M A E █
O L D D A Y S █ █ L A T I N A
C O M I N G S █ R A R I T A N
A S A R U L E █ I N T R U D E
T E N S P O T █ B A S E P A Y
```

28

```
E L S E █ N E T S █ P R O W L
L E O N █ O L I O █ R E M I T
E A S T █ V A N S █ E L A N D
C H A R I O T S O F F I R E █
█ █ █ A N T E █ █ █ R E V █ █
A V E N G E █ L O R E L E I █
C I R C E █ S H O W █ █ O R R
T O W E R I N G I N F E R N O
E L I █ █ N U T S █ O N E I N
D A N C I N G █ S Y D N E Y █
█ █ █ A N E █ █ I K E A █ █ █
█ I S P A R I S B U R N I N G
A L L O W █ S O O N █ G L E N
D I A N A █ A M O K █ E S A U
D E W E Y █ Y A K S █ R A T S
```

29

```
N O T V █ S W A G █ D W A R F
I D E A █ T I T O █ I O N I A
N I T S █ I N T O █ A R D O R
O N E S E C O N D P L E A S E
█ █ █ A S K S █ G E M █ █ █ █
P H E L P S █ A R T █ A V I D
A O L █ R O S S I █ P R I D E
T W O M I N U T E D R I L L S
C S P O T █ N O F E E █ L E K
H O E D █ S S R █ S M E A R S
█ █ █ D O H █ A C I D █ █ █ █
T H R E E D A Y W E E K E N D
B E I N G █ D E A N █ O D A Y
A M A N A █ E N I D █ C I N E
R I L E S █ S S T S █ H E A D
```

30

```
□ K I T E █ A P U █ S H O E □
C O C O A █ P E P █ A M P L E
A L E U T █ E A R E D S E A L
R A S P █ □ S C O R E █ R I D
█ █ █ E E L █ O A R █ W A N E
I R R E G U L A R █ H A T E R
N E E █ O N I T █ M A L I █ █
□ O F F I C E █ B A L L O T □
█ █ █ L U S H █ B I T S █ N A E
□ R E S T █ P R O C E S S O R
R A C E █ B O O █ H Y P █ █ █
E M T █ M U S I C □ █ A L O T
A S I R E C A L L █ P R I M O
D E V I L █ D E E █ E S S A Y
□ S E A T █ A R F █ G E A R □
```

31

```
W A N N A   B A E Z   I C E S
A S I A N   L I N A   D A M P
R I G H T H A N D P R O P E R
N T H   S E N T   S A T I R E
  W T S   A C H E   N O T I E
S E C O N D H A N D G O A L
A R A B Y   E Y E D
P E P S U P     S C A M P I
      B R A C   O N E O N
  O F F H A N D R U N N I N G
S N A R E   A D O S   A N Y
O L D I E S   O W E S   H T S
F I E L D H A N D S T R E A M
A N I L   A N T E   A E R I E
S E N S   M O O D   B E R L E
```

32

```
E G A D   A D D A   P E A B O
S I L E N C E I S G O L D E N
T R I N I T R O T O L U E N E
A L E U T I A N I S L A N D S
      D E N T     F U N
E D B E R G   B L O T T E R S
T I E R S   Z A I R E   C U T
H A G S   R U L E D   J O N I
O N A   B I L L S   T A L O N
S E N S U O U S   F A Z I N G
      E Z R     F O N Z
M A G A Z I N E A R T I C L E
A N I M A T E D C A R T O O N
G E N E R A L D E G A U L L E
S T A N D   L Y T E   P A L S
```

33

```
A R T I S A N S   O A T E S
B E A R U P O N   U N R E S T
B A N K R A T E   N E A R T O
E R A S E R H E A D   B R I M
Y U K   T O R R E S   A M A
S P A S   M A C R O   P A C
    T O G E T H E R W I T H
R E S I N Y   A T O N E S
E X T R A M A R I T A L
A P U   I N L A W   F I S T
R I D   R A T I O S   N A H
M A I D   S O N J A H E N I E
O B O I S T   G I L E V A N S
S L U R P S   O M E L E T T E
T E S T Y   D A M P N E S S
```

34

```
G O T M I L K   E N G L I S H
O N A N D O N   T A R A N T O
C A B O O S E   A M A T O R Y
A D A   S E W S   E N T R E
R I S K   I S A K   D E B T S
T E C H   T O T A L P R I C E
S T O A T   M O T O R   T H E
    N O S E   I B I D
S S S   W H O L E   X A C T O
P U T O N A N A C T   R O R Y
A G I N G   E L O I   T W A S
  A N E R A   A U R A   P I T
A R T D E C O   R A T H O L E
B E E G E E S   I N V O K E R
A D D E N D A   C A S T E R S
```

35

```
A T L A S   S I S I   A N T E
C H A L K   E D E N   T A R A
R A B B I T E A R S   I S I S
E T S   I O N   G Y M S H O E
    E N D   H I N E S
  K A N G A R O O C O U R T
I N N S   T A P   W E A R Y
T O V   K E E P E R S   Z E D
S P I R O   E E E   J O Y S
  F L E A M A R K E T E R S
    S L A T S   S U B
W A R P A T H   E E R   T A I
A L O E   T O A D S T O O L S
D I S C   E M M A   L E G A L
S T E T   R E A M   E R A S E
```

36

```
T O M E   O R E M   S P A D E
O N E S   N A D A   A L I E N
A R E S   E Y E D   M A D T V
M A K E I T S N A P P Y
A M E N D E     M I A S A R A
N P R   I N I S   A N K L E T
    S O T T E D     O O N A
  G E T T H E L E A D O U T
F E A R   M E S C A L
C A V I E S   S I C K   A B A
C R E P T U P   R A N G E R
  M O V E Y O U R T A I L
K A U A I   R U D I   E T R E
O N A L L   I M I N   S H U N
P E R L E   L A N G   T A T E
```

37

```
T A B O O . G A M E . . B A I T
A L L A H . I B A R . . O N C E
O P A H S . J E S T . . S T I R
. C U T T O T H E Q U I C K . .
E L K . O D E . . . U N C L E .
S I T U P S . G A L A . S E L .
P A I R . P R O O F S . . . . .
. R E L I G I O U S F A S T . .
. S N A P A T . . . L I O N . .
I M P . E D E N . T I E D O N .
N A A C P . . P O D . E N E . .
J O N A T H A N S W I F T . . .
O R E S . A R I A . D A R T S .
K I L T . W E N T . I R I S H .
E S S E . N A E S . T E P E E .
```

38

```
W A S H . W O R E . . . P I T Y
E T T E . A S E A . C A C A O .
T H E M I S S U S . U P E N N .
N O W I N P A P E R B A C K . .
A M E N D . S U E . . L A N . .
P E D . I D A . P O P C O R N .
. . S A U N A . C L A U D E . .
. N O T I N T H E C A R D S . .
B O N I N G . S A U C E . . . .
C L E R K E D . T R E . U B I .
D O T . O R A . . B I S O N . .
N O D I N A G R E E M E N T . .
A G O R A . P O I N T E D T O .
L E N I N . E G G Y . A T O N .
P R E P . S O S A . N O N E . .
```

39

```
I L E . . T H E O . O P I E .
C E L L O . H A L L . F I L M .
A M A I N . A B I D . A C L U .
M O N K E Y D W I T H . S T A S
E N D E A R . B E A R O U T . .
. . L R O N . T O R R E S . .
W A V Y . M E T . S T E A L .
A B A . N O W ♡ H I S . I S A .
R O L L O . S U N . I T E M .
P L E A S E . D A M N . . . .
. I N T E N S E . L A C A S A .
A S T I . M I D D L W E I G H T
C H I N . E D G E . S T O A T .
R E N O . S L A V . T E R R A .
O D E S . H E R O . . A I R .
```

40

```
H E I S T . G L A D E . A F T .
A L L A H . L A T E R . L A O .
L I L L E H A M M E R . B U T .
. . . R U S E . . A R E N A .
F A S T E N S . N A T U R A L .
A C Q U I T . S O V I E T . .
C H U R N . R E L I C . V A L .
T E A K . S A L A D . V I S E .
S S W . C O V E N . P O L K A .
. V E R S E S . C A L L E R .
P L A T O O N . E A S T E R N .
H O L E S . A L L S . . . .
A W L . S A I N T M O R I T Z .
S E E . L L A N O . U N T I E .
E R Y . Y E M E N . T A S T E .
```

41

```
A L P H A . T A L L . A J A R .
B E A U T . O R E O . M U L E .
U N I T E D K I N G D O M O F .
T O N . . C Y D . . D U P E S .
. T A B O O . A T A R I . . .
U P T U R N . Q U A Y . N B A .
N E H R U . P U N T . J A N .
G R E A T B R I T A I N A N D .
E S T . A I L S . V I C A R .
R E O . F A C T . H E C K L E .
. W H I S K . J O S E F . .
U L N A S . E A U . L A O .
N O R T H E R N I R E L A N D .
T R E E . W A I L . Y E S N O .
O D D S . E N D S . E T H E R .
```

42

```
O S C A R . S T A G . . B E T .
K I O W A . P A D R E . E V E .
S T O O L P I G E O N . N I L .
. . . L E A K S . O R A C L E .
B B C . I T E . A M I S H . .
L E H I G H . S Z E C H W A N .
A W A S H . R E T R O . A D O .
M A I M . D I M E S . G R A D .
E R R . M E D I C . D U M P S .
D E P R A V E S . P E S E T A .
. E A G E R . R E V . R S T .
V I R G I L . E E R I E . . .
E D S . C O U C H P O T A T O .
E L O . S P A R E . U N I O N .
P E N . S W U M . S A R G E .
```

43

```
M A C K   W E A K   A K R O N
I C O N   A M M O   D I A N E
T H R E E G U Y S W A L K E D
T A K E R S     H I P N E S S
S T Y L I   S C E N T
      C O L O R   T R E N D
I N T O A B A R   T O O T O O
M O O G   E M O T E   O U R S
P A R L A Y   N E X T T I M E
S H E E R   N E A T O
      C L E R K   T E R R A
H O T S H O T   S A L O O N
I H O P E T H E Y L L D U C K
S I T A R   E R I E   E T C H
S O O T Y   R E N D   R E O S
```

44

```
A V I V   B E G A T   Z A P S
M I D I   A R O L E   E R A T
I V E S   S I T O N   R A G A
D O A H A T C H E T J O B O N
      N S A       H A H
B I D U P   A T M   N O C A L
E D U   C A L A I S   U R G E
H A V E A N A X T O G R I N D
A R E A   G R E E D Y   M E G
R E T R O   M R S   R E E S E
      M O P       V O N
T O M A H A W K M I S S I L E
O M A R   P A N I C   I N O N
R A N K   A R O M A   G R A D
I N X S   S E W E R   N E D S
```

45

```
S N O B   P O P P A   B U S S
H I K E   A U R A L   E P E E
O N I T   S T O R K   E T N A
W E N E V E R S A Y I T I S
E V A   I O U   D O L L A R
R E W A X   N O R   S E T T O
S H A D E S   S A C   S E E
      O N L Y A G A M E
H U G   Y A K   B A R E S T
I N U R E   P A D   Y E N T A
C A N O N S   A R A   T E N
  I F W E A R E W I N N I N G
A R I A   Y A R D S   O T T O
B E R N   S T I L E   A L O E
O D E S   O A K E N   H E R D
```

46

```
T O M B S   O P E D   M A R S
O B E A H   P O R E   A L O U
D O W J O N E S A V E R A G E
D E L A W A R E   E N V I E D
      M I A   A L D E N T E
N O R M A L S C H O O L
A T H E N S   E S P N   B O K
P I E T   F L O   M O N A
A S A   T E A L   S M O O T H
      B O S T O N C O M M O N
A C C E P T S   E A R
C L A M O R   S P L O S H E D
R E G U L A R P A Y C H E C K
E R E S   D E A L   C A R O N
S K Y E   A N T I   O D D L Y
```

47

```
E A S T   S W A M P   S T A B
R U L E   L A K E R   T A X I
E G A N   A R I S E   A C I D
C U T D O W N T O S I G H S
T R Y O N   A N S A
      N E V E   M A N N A
L E T   B A T T H E B R I E S
A Q U A   S C R O D   K N O T
P U R P L E H A Y E S   E N O
P I N T O   A N E W
      E D A M   G A S P E
  T H E W I Z A R D O F A H S
J A I L   T U N E R   E D I T
U C L A   C R O N E   R I L E
G O O N   H E R O D   S E E R
```

48

```
P A U L   A L A W   P L E B E
A N N E   L A L A   R I V A L
S O C I A L D A R W I N I S M
T I L   S E I S M I C   L S T
E N O   E N D   U N E   D I R
L T G O V   A M P S   H O S E
      R E O   O T T   B E T E
    P A R T Y P O O P E R
S I L L   H E E   N R A
O P U S   E S S A   E M B E D
F A N   D L I   G A S   R I M
A N G   E L K H A R T   A L I
B E E I N O N E S B O N N E T
E M I R S   O R S O   O D E R
D A N S E   W E I R   T O N I
```

49

F	E	A	R		M	A	S	H		M	A	N	S	E
A	L	P	O		A	G	U	E		I	D	E	A	L
R	I	O	T		R	E	B	A		M	A	U	N	A
	A	P	O	L	L	O		P	R	O	G	R	A	M
		O	O	F	S		O	S	E					
	U	P	B	O	W		I	S	A		R	C	A	
	S	H	I	P	E	A	R	T	H		B	A	R	I
M	A	Y	A	S		D	E	I		S	O	B	E	R
A	G	T	S		W	A	T	C	H	T	H	I	S	
N	E	E		E	A	R			E	A	R	N	S	
		A	V	A		C	A	L	I					
	T	I	M	E	C	O	N	T	I	N	U	U	M	
O	I	L	E	R		P	O	O	P		K	N	I	T
U	P	S	E	T		E	T	N	A		E	I	R	E
T	S	A	R	S		D	E	E	D		S	T	Y	X

50

R	O	W	E	D		R	A	S	P		Q	U	I	T
I	M	A	G	E		E	M	I	R		U	N	D	O
B	O	X	O	F	C	H	O	C	O	L	A	T	E	S
S	O	Y		E	R	A	S		C	A	R	O	M	S
			T	A	O	S		S	E	N	T			
H	E	A	R	T	S	H	A	P	E	D		N	A	B
A	R	G	U	E	S		M	A	D		H	O	M	E
Z	O	N	E	D		C	A	R		T	E	P	I	D
E	D	E	R		N	O	T		A	R	I	A	N	E
L	E	W		C	U	P	I	D	S	A	R	R	O	W
			J	U	R	Y		R	I	P	S			
O	S	I	E	R	S		S	O	A	P		E	B	B
S	T	V	A	L	E	N	T	I	N	E	S	D	A	Y
L	O	A	N		R	E	A	D		R	H	E	T	T
O	W	N	S		Y	E	N	S		S	E	N	S	E

51

J	U	L		M	P	S			R	A	N	A	T	
O	N	O		O	A	H	U		S	O	N	O	M	A
B	E	W	A	R	Y	O	F		C	U	T	U	P	S
	A	N	Y	O	N	E	W	H	O	G	I	V	E	S
S	T	E	R	N	E			A	L	E		E	R	E
R	E	C			P	I	N	A		G	A	E	L	
A	N	K	L	E		E	N	O	R	M	O	U	S	
			Y	O	U	A	D	V	I	C	E			
	C	R	O	S	S	T	I	E		D	R	I	E	D
R	O	A	N		U	B	E	R			N	Y	U	
O	C	T		O	R	O		A	B	A	S	E	D	
T	H	A	T	B	E	G	I	N	S	W	I	T	H	
A	L	T	A	I	R		B	E	W	A	R	Y	O	F
R	E	A	L	E	S		M	E	A	N		L	O	O
Y	A	T	E	S			D	N	A		E	K	E	

52

B	L	A	R	E		O	R	B	S		D	A	M	P
B	A	Y	E	D		R	E	E	K		E	S	A	U
C	I	N	C	I	N	N	A	T	I		S	T	I	R
			T	E	A	L		T	B	I	R	D	S	
A	L	S	O		A	T	I	T		A	R	O	S	E
P	E	E	R	P	R	E	S	S	U	R	E			
H	O	R	S	E		M	A	N	N		R	C	A	
I	N	F	O	R	C	E		R	O	O	T	O	U	T
D	E	S		S	Y	N	C		N	E	W	T	S	
			F	I	D	D	L	E	D	E	E	D	E	E
F	A	I	R	S		O	O	N	A		M	Y	R	A
I	N	N	A	T	E		S	T	U	N				
E	D	A	M		B	E	E	R	B	A	R	R	E	L
L	I	N	E		B	R	I	E		P	A	U	L	A
D	E	E	D		S	A	N	E		A	N	T	I	C

53

L	I	L	A	C		T	O	M	B		O	M	E	N
I	R	A	B	U		O	M	A	R		N	O	V	O
B	E	R	E	T		W	I	S	E	A	C	R	E	S
E	N	G	L	I	S	H	T	E	A	L	E	O	N	I
L	E	E		E	T	E		R	D	A		S	T	E
S	S	S		P	I	E	T	A		R	E	E	F	S
			B	I	N		A	T	T		G	L	U	T
	G	R	E	E	K	O	L	I	V	E	O	Y	L	
P	L	E	D		O	U	I		S	T	S			
A	I	D	E	S		T	A	T	E	R		J	L	O
I	M	F		H	A	S		B	T	U		O	A	T
S	P	A	N	I	S	H	M	O	S	S	H	A	R	T
A	S	C	E	N	S	I	O	N		C	O	N	D	E
N	E	E	D		A	N	N	E		A	S	N	E	R
O	D	D	S		Y	E	A	S		N	E	A	R	S

54

C	A	N	S		S	W	A	P		S	C	A	L	E
I	D	O	L		E	R	A	S		O	R	L	O	N
N	E	M	O		A	E	R	I	A	L	I	S	T	S
C	L	A	P	T	R	A	P		C	A	P	O	S	
H	E	N	P	E	C	K		C	C	C	P			
		S	E	T	H		S	H	I	E	L	D	E	R
M	O	L	D		P	I	P	E	D	R	E	A	M	S
U	V	A		A	D	O	R	E			T	U	V	
T	E	N	D	E	R	L	O	I	N		W	I	S	P
I	N	D	E	N	T	E	R		T	W	I	N		
			I	R	I	S		S	P	A	N	G	L	Y
	A	L	G	A	E		C	A	R	N	E	G	I	E
T	H	I	N	G	S	T	O	D	O		S	A	R	A
E	M	C	E	E		O	R	A	N		A	M	A	S
N	E	E	D	S		P	E	T	E		P	E	S	T

55

T	I	R	A	M	I	S	U	■	■	F	E	D	U	P
I	N	E	L	E	G	A	N	T	■	O	V	I	N	E
S	C	A	L	L	O	P	E	R	■	R	E	C	U	T
■	■	R	O	O	T	■	■	E	X	T	R	E	M	E
D	E	W	Y	■	■	S	H	E	E	D	Y	■	■	■
E	L	I	■	L	A	T	E	■	D	E	T	A	C	H
B	A	N	D	O	L	E	R	O	■	V	I	L	L	A
R	I	D	I	N	G	A	C	A	D	E	M	I	E	S
I	N	O	N	E	■	M	U	T	I	N	E	E	R	S
S	E	W	E	R	S	■	L	E	N	S	■	N	I	L
■	■	E	A	S	T	E	R	■	■	R	A	C	E	■
A	S	S	A	N	T	E	■	■	P	S	A	T	■	■
B	O	U	R	G	■	S	C	A	R	E	D	O	F	F
A	D	E	L	E	■	H	O	N	O	R	A	R	I	A
S	A	T	Y	R	■	■	S	O	M	E	R	S	E	T

56

A	T	O	■	A	S	K	E	D	A	L	O	T	O	F
L	O	P	■	T	H	E	R	E	Y	O	U	A	R	E
P	O	T	■	M	A	N	I	F	E	S	T	O	E	S
A	K	I	M	■	■	C	O	S	■	M	I	L	T	■
C	A	M	E	R	A	B	A	G	■	M	A	S	S	E
I	N	U	T	E	R	O	■	C	A	N	T	E	R	■
N	A	M	E	D	R	O	P	P	E	R	S	■	■	■
O	P	S	■	C	O	N	G	A	M	E	■	D	R	U
■	■	■	N	E	W	S	A	G	E	N	C	I	E	S
T	R	A	I	L	S	■	■	E	N	G	A	G	E	S
H	O	V	E	L	■	P	A	S	T	O	R	A	L	E
E	C	O	L	■	T	E	C	■	■	T	H	E	N	■
H	O	U	S	E	B	R	E	A	K	S	■	O	D	A
A	C	C	E	S	S	O	R	I	A	L	■	L	I	T
J	O	H	N	Q	P	U	B	L	I	C	■	E	N	E

57

H	A	S	L	E	A	D	S	■	A	N	T	I	C	S
O	N	T	A	R	G	E	T	■	C	L	O	T	H	E
R	O	O	M	R	A	T	E	■	T	E	N	S	E	R
D	I	K	E	■	P	A	R	L	O	R	G	A	M	E
E	N	E	■	R	E	I	N	A	■	■	F	I	N	■
S	T	R	A	Y	■	L	U	L	U	■	P	A	C	A
■	■	N	N	E	■	M	A	G	■	A	C	A	D	■
F	O	N	D	E	S	T	■	W	H	I	S	T	L	E
I	N	O	R	■	T	E	T	■	S	S	T	■	■	■
E	T	T	E	■	A	R	I	A	■	P	A	S	H	A
F	H	A	■	■	S	P	R	A	Y	■	P	U	B	■
D	E	R	E	K	J	E	T	E	R	■	C	A	D	S
O	L	I	V	I	A	■	O	N	E	H	O	R	S	E
M	A	Z	I	E	R	■	E	D	N	O	R	T	O	N
S	M	E	L	L	S	■	S	T	A	G	N	A	N	T

58

W	E	B	B	S	■	O	H	M	E	■	W	O	W	S
A	T	O	U	T	■	J	U	A	N	■	H	A	R	T
S	T	A	G	E	C	O	A	C	H	■	A	S	I	A
H	U	R	L	E	R	■	C	H	A	S	T	I	T	Y
■	■	D	E	L	I	A	■	I	N	C	I	S	E	S
B	M	W	■	E	M	B	R	A	C	E	S	■	■	■
L	E	A	K	■	P	R	O	V	E	N	A	N	C	E
O	G	L	E	D	■	A	Y	E	■	T	R	E	E	S
W	A	K	E	U	P	C	A	L	L	■	T	W	I	T
■	■	■	P	A	R	A	L	L	E	L	■	S	L	O
S	C	O	R	N	E	D	■	I	D	O	L	S	■	■
M	E	D	I	E	V	A	L	■	G	L	U	T	E	S
O	L	E	G	■	A	B	O	V	E	I	T	A	L	L
K	I	T	H	■	I	R	A	E	■	T	E	N	S	E
E	A	S	T	■	L	A	D	Y	■	A	D	D	E	D

59

B	A	S	■	F	R	A	U	D	S	■	P	E	T	S
I	D	O	■	L	A	B	R	E	A	■	O	L	E	O
C	O	R	N	E	D	B	E	E	F	■	T	A	R	A
■	■	R	O	S	I	E	■	M	E	A	T	I	E	R
I	R	I	S	H	I	S	M	■	T	E	N	S	E	■
S	T	E	T	■	■	S	O	D	A	B	R	E	A	D
R	E	S	E	W	S	■	B	O	R	E	■	■	■	■
■	S	T	P	A	T	R	I	C	K	S	D	A	Y	■
■	■	■	G	A	U	L	■	S	T	A	L	A	G	■
G	R	E	E	N	B	E	E	R	■	■	B	A	D	E
H	E	N	C	E	■	S	E	A	S	O	N	A	L	■
E	S	C	O	R	T	S	■	S	W	A	M	P	■	■
T	O	O	L	■	A	N	D	C	A	B	B	A	G	E
T	I	R	E	■	P	I	C	A	R	O	■	G	I	N
O	L	E	S	■	S	P	I	N	E	T	■	E	G	G

60

S	P	A	S	■	S	M	A	S	H	■	A	D	A	M
H	A	L	L	■	T	A	M	P	A	■	L	E	N	A
A	R	L	O	■	A	L	P	E	S	■	S	M	O	G
S	T	O	P	O	R	I	L	L	S	H	O	O	T	■
T	O	T	E	M	■	■	E	L	L	E	■	C	H	E
A	N	S	■	A	S	A	■	E	N	T	R	E	E	■
■	■	■	A	N	I	M	A	L	■	■	E	A	R	L
■	T	H	I	S	I	S	A	B	U	S	T	■	■	■
O	G	R	E	■	S	P	O	O	R	S	■	■	■	■
P	R	I	M	A	L	■	■	S	O	B	■	A	A	R
T	A	B	■	R	O	S	A	■	■	A	I	S	L	E
■	P	U	T	Y	O	U	R	H	A	N	D	S	U	P
A	N	N	A	■	M	A	G	I	C	■	L	A	M	A
P	E	A	R	■	E	V	O	K	E	■	E	I	N	S
E	L	L	A	■	D	E	T	E	R	■	S	L	I	T

61

```
F A T S . C H A D . S I G M A
U L E E . H A T E . A F T E R
D I E T S A R E F O R F O L K
G O P H E R . M E R C Y . . .
E T E . Z I P . R C A . F L A
D O E R . S I S . A S H L E Y
. . E M M E T S . T E A S E .
. W H O A R E T H I C K . . .
A H E A D . S M O O C H . . .
B E R B E R . S O U . E D O M
C H E . R E F . P S I . E M O
. . S N A R E . E I S N E R .
A N D T I R E D O F I T A L L
C A D I Z . S I L L . E L E E
T H E R E . H E D Y . P I T Y
```

62

```
F A S T . S A U C E . J O C K
I M N O . U P P E D . A I R Y
E Y E P O P P I N G . B L U R
S T E A M E R . S E T . S E A
T A Z Z A . A G O . R I P . .
A N Y . H A I R R A I S I N G
. . B A L S A . D O L L O P .
A L L Y . T E N A M . A L D A
D E A R T H . D R E A M . . .
J A W D R O P P I N G . M A D
. M S U . O A S . I N U S E .
C H A . E S C . T O N I G H T
H I K E . L O S I N G F A C E
E V E N . A N O D E . T B A R
Z E R O . B O X E R . Y E N S
```

63

```
D E A T H . J A W S . B O O K
A R T O O . A L A N . L O D E
M A T Z O M I A T A . I Z O D
P T A . P A L . E P O N Y M S
S O R E L Y . G R U N T . . .
. . T A T A R . P U Z Z L E .
T A C O . A S I P . S K O A L
A R O N . G O D O T . R O M E
R E A C H . F L O E . I T E M
P A T H O S . O H A R E . . .
. . A N N E X . P E G L E G .
N E W L E A F . O O P . O S U
O P E L . T R E N T L A T K E
R E B A . C E D E . A P S E S
M E S H . H M O S . Y E A R S
```

64

```
A D D . O S M A N . S P R I T
L E A . R H O D E . A R E N A
I V Y . L O V E O F L A B O R
B O O . E R I N . A L T A R S
I N F L A T E . B R I E . . .
. . B O N Y . T A M E . F E D
C O R P S . N E C E S S A R Y
O D E A . S E N O R . T R O N
B O A T L O A D S . R E E S E
O R K . A R T S . P A L O . .
. . A C T H . B R I E F L Y .
G L A D T O . A R I D . B E E
L I F E O F S P I C E . I M A
E A R P S . A S N E R . L A T
E M O T E . D E E D S . L Y S
```

65

```
O T I S . D F L A T . G A S P
D E N T . I R A Q I . I T T O
E L S A . P I N U P . Z E A L
. L O R D P L E A S E M A K E
H A L . O Y L . . L O S E R
A L E U T . P H I L . E D S
R I N G . S T O O G E S . .
M E T H E P E R S O N T H A T
. S W E L T E R . Y O U R
S E M . I D E S . B E T T E
Y E A R N . E A U . W O E
M Y D O G T H I N K S I A M
B O M B . H I N D I . S T A T
O R E O . I N F U N . N E T S
L E N T . S T O P S . T R E K
```

66

```
A P H I D . C O R K . H A S H
C R O C E . R E I N . O H I O
H E W A N T E D T O . R E N O
E V E N O U T . E X T R A C T
. . T R E S . H I D E S
S H R I E K . A I R E D . .
A E O N . M I N O R . I D S
T R A N S C E N D D E N T A L
S O N . T A S T Y . A C L U
. N O R S E . Z E P H Y R
S P E A K . D I O N . .
C O N T E S T . D I L E M M A
R I O T . M E D I C A T I O N
I S L E . O L E O . C A N T O
P E A R . G L O M . E L T O N
```

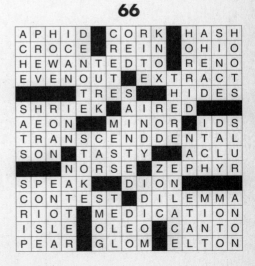

67

I	T	S	█	C	L	A	P	█	A	S	I	A	N	S
T	I	E	█	H	I	V	E	█	T	U	C	K	E	D
E	V	E	█	O	M	E	N	█	O	R	E	A	D	S
M	O	S	T	M	O	R	N	I	N	G	S	█	█	█
S	L	A	V	S	█	█	N	E	E	█	A	S	P	█
█	I	W	A	K	E	U	P	G	R	O	U	C	H	Y
█	█	Y	E	T	I	█	█	N	A	T	A	L	█	█
A	C	R	E	█	L	E	N	T	O	█	W	I	D	E
B	R	I	N	E	█	O	R	E	O	█	█	█	█	█
B	U	T	O	N	S	A	T	U	R	D	A	Y	S	█
A	X	E	█	S	I	R	█	█	D	I	V	E	S	█
█	█	I	L	E	T	H	I	M	S	L	E	E	P	█
S	T	A	L	A	G	█	I	D	E	A	█	T	O	A
A	R	R	I	V	E	█	D	E	A	R	█	T	U	T
T	E	P	E	E	S	█	E	S	T	E	█	E	T	E

68

B	A	D	E	█	W	A	D	I	█	D	A	M	E	█
E	A	R	L	█	V	A	S	E	S	█	A	G	O	G
T	H	E	S	M	I	T	H	Y	M	A	K	I	N	G
A	S	I	█	E	S	T	E	S	█	L	O	O	K	S
█	█	█	D	O	T	█	█	█	L	E	T	█	█	█
H	A	R	D	W	A	R	E	F	O	R	A	N	E	W
B	O	A	T	S	█	U	N	A	P	T	█	A	D	A
O	R	B	S	█	K	N	O	B	S	█	A	D	I	N
M	T	A	█	E	N	T	R	E	█	O	N	I	C	E
B	A	T	H	R	O	O	M	R	E	P	O	R	T	S
█	█	O	A	T	█	█	█	L	E	N	█	█	█	█
S	C	O	T	T	█	A	L	G	E	R	█	T	O	O
H	E	S	F	O	R	G	I	N	G	A	H	E	A	D
A	R	L	O	█	A	R	R	A	Y	█	E	L	S	E
D	O	O	R	█	G	O	A	T	█	P	E	T	S	█

69

A	S	H	E	█	I	P	A	N	A	█	I	S	L	E
S	E	E	K	█	R	O	T	O	R	█	T	O	A	D
A	G	R	E	E	K	S	T	O	I	C	S	A	I	D
P	O	B	O	X	█	T	Y	R	O	L	█	P	R	Y
█	█	█	U	A	R	█	█	S	A	M	█	█	█	█
T	H	A	T	M	E	N	S	H	O	U	L	D	B	E
H	A	D	█	█	B	A	T	E	█	S	K	E	I	N
I	G	O	█	G	A	R	O	T	T	E	█	L	L	D
E	A	R	T	O	█	C	R	U	E	█	H	B	O	█
F	R	E	E	F	R	O	M	P	A	S	S	I	O	N
█	█	D	I	E	█	█	█	R	A	N	█	█	█	█
C	P	L	█	S	N	E	A	D	█	G	A	L	A	S
H	E	Y	W	H	A	T	D	O	E	S	Z	E	N	O
A	N	N	A	█	T	E	E	M	S	█	Z	I	O	N
W	A	X	Y	█	A	S	N	O	T	█	Y	A	N	G

70

L	I	N	U	S	█	S	H	A	H	█	W	A	G	E
A	D	O	P	T	█	A	M	M	O	█	A	V	E	R
F	E	E	L	I	N	G	S	U	P	E	R	I	O	R
F	E	L	O	N	Y	█	█	L	I	L	█	A	D	E
█	█	█	A	T	E	A	S	E	█	P	I	N	E	D
G	I	L	D	S	█	K	I	T	B	A	G	█	█	█
A	D	O	█	P	I	N	█	I	S	O	L	D	E	█
T	O	U	C	H	I	N	G	S	T	O	R	I	E	S
O	L	D	H	A	T	█	L	O	S	█	S	A	S	█
█	█	█	A	N	S	W	E	R	█	C	H	A	R	O
C	E	L	T	S	█	A	T	T	I	R	E	█	█	█
O	L	E	█	E	A	R	█	S	E	N	O	R	A	█
H	A	N	D	L	I	N	G	C	H	A	R	G	E	S
A	T	T	U	█	N	E	E	R	█	K	I	L	N	S
N	E	O	N	█	T	R	O	Y	█	S	K	E	E	T

71

M	O	N	S	█	G	A	O	L	█	S	Y	N	E	█
A	M	A	H	█	L	E	N	T	O	█	H	O	O	D
L	E	G	O	M	U	T	T	O	N	█	A	G	E	D
A	G	A	W	A	M	█	S	E	G	O	L	I	L	Y
R	A	T	E	D	P	G	█	█	O	R	O	█	█	█
█	█	█	D	A	Y	O	J	U	D	G	M	E	N	T
A	L	B	U	M	█	T	A	N	D	Y	█	D	E	Y
P	E	R	P	█	W	H	I	P	S	█	Y	E	A	R
E	V	A	█	C	H	I	M	E	█	R	A	N	T	O
R	I	G	H	T	O	C	E	N	T	E	R	█	█	█
█	█	█	I	N	C	█	S	O	L	D	I	E	R	█
F	A	I	L	S	A	F	E	█	D	I	A	N	N	E
E	L	A	L	█	R	I	N	G	O	T	R	U	T	H
E	D	G	E	█	E	L	V	E	S	█	M	I	R	E
T	O	O	L	█	S	L	Y	E	█	S	T	E	M	█

72

S	H	A	M	A	N	█	█	C	H	A	P	E	L	█
H	O	S	A	N	N	A	█	C	H	A	L	I	C	E
I	W	O	N	D	E	R	W	H	E	R	E	T	H	E
P	E	K	E	S	█	T	A	O	█	E	T	H	O	S
█	█	█	D	O	C	U	D	R	A	M	A	█	█	█
A	M	F	█	A	R	I	E	L	█	█	T	A	E	█
M	A	E	S	T	R	O	█	S	I	M	M	O	N	S
M	O	T	H	E	R	█	█	█	B	E	A	R	I	S
A	R	C	A	D	E	S	█	G	A	G	R	U	L	E
N	I	H	█	R	E	H	A	B	█	█	S	S	S	█
█	█	█	I	C	E	P	A	L	A	C	E	█	█	█
A	V	I	L	A	█	A	N	O	█	O	N	E	I	S
F	A	M	O	U	S	L	A	S	T	W	O	R	D	S
O	N	A	S	S	I	S	█	H	E	L	L	I	O	N
R	E	N	T	E	R	█	█	A	S	S	E	S	S	█

73

```
C A T S   M I L N E   B A S K
A L I T   I D E A L   R I C E
P E E R   A L A R M   U R A L
  C R E A M E D C O R N E L L
    A S I S     T E D D Y
S C A M P     C A D E T
I O U   C R E A S E   T A C O
P O R T A U P R I N C E T O N
S P A R   S E D A T E   O R E
    A S H E S   L U M P S
S I E V E     S I L T
O B J E T D A R T M O U T H
U S E R   O P E R A   R A I D
S E C S   D E B U G   N U K E
A N T E   O R A T E   S T E W
```

74

```
L A R D   P R O M O   A M M O
E T U I   O A T E R   R A I D
G O N G   E D A M S A P P L E
O P T I C   R B I S   L E T
    T H E M U E N S T E R S
P E P S I C O   R O T H
I C E   C R O W   U F O S
T H E G O U D A B Y E G I R L
Y O K E   N E O N   S E A
    E W E N   E Y E S H O T
J I M R O Q U E F O R T
A N E   O U T S   O R L O P
C H E D D A R B O X   O A H U
K I T E   L I A N E   B R O Z
O S S A   S A T E D   E S S O
```

75

```
C R E W   I N S E T   B E C K
H E R O   T O R R E   E L I E
E N G R   S T A R T E V E R Y
Z O O M L E N S   F E N C E
    H I L O   S A L L I E S
D A Y O F F W I T H A
E X I L E   M O O T   B O A
L O P E   R E P A Y   R O B B
E N S   A O N E   A E R I E
    S M I L E A N D G E T
W E A R I E D   D R N O
R A P I D   N I C O L A U S
I T O V E R W I T H   E T N A
T I R E   H A N O I   N E I L
E N T R   O H A R E   T E S T
```

76

```
C L O G S   O L E S   J I F F
H O V E L   D E B T   E D I E
A G A N A   O V E R   D O N E
D E L I V E R Y R E V I L E D
    E E L     T A I
C B S   S E M I   M O S T E L
H O P I   N O D E   L O R R E
E R O S S A W I W A S S O R E
S N O O P   N O E L   A T O Z
T E N N I S   T R I G   S R A
    R I A     E O S
P A R T O N D I D N O T R A P
O M A R   K O B E   G R A V E
P A C E   E R I N   O A T E S
S T Y X   R E S T   O P A R T
```

77

```
S I L A S   A L F A   R I L E
K N E L T   R I A L   E D E N
I F Y O U W A N T L I F E T O
R U D E   A C E   C R A S S
T S E   G R A M E R C Y
S E N O R   R A R E   A S A
  B E G I N A T F O R T Y
A W E I G H   C A N C A N
D O N T G O E I G H T Y
D O E   S A G A   E X A M S
  P E T U N I A S   T A P
E T H E L   O T T   D O R A
W H E N Y O U R E T W E N T Y
E R I C   U S E R   H E C H E
S U R E   R O D S   O R E A D
```

78

```
R O M P   T U B A S   C H I C
U N T O   I N E R T   O A T H
N E W S   N O L T E   U R S A
I N T E N D   F R O G M A N
N O F R E E L A U N C H
    T R O L L   A E T N A
E M M A   B O O   O L D I E S
B E A T T O T H E P A U N C H
B O L L I X   A C E   P O K E
S W E E T   S O U N D
    I H A V E A H A U N C H
C A T S E Y E   O N S A L E
A L O U   E L I H U   A V I D
S T I R   A T L A S   G A N G
H O L E   R E E S E   E L K E
```

79

```
S U M A C ▪ J E T S ▪ ▪ P O E T
I T A L O ▪ O B I T ▪ ▪ O S L O
P E R T H ▪ N A N A ▪ ▪ W R E N
▪ T H E R I Y A L T H I N G ▪ ▪
▪ E I E I O ▪ ▪ ▪ A C A C I A
D I N A R A T E I G H T ▪ ▪ ▪
O L E ▪ S N E A D ▪ R A P I D
H A T H ▪ S A R I S ▪ N O D E
A T S E A ▪ S L O O P ▪ N E W
▪ R U P E E T U E S D A Y ▪ ▪
A L K A L I ▪ ▪ N O T E S ▪ ▪
G U I L D E R R A D N E R ▪ ▪
L E N D ▪ R O A R ▪ I R O N Y
O G E E ▪ C A N T ▪ E N S U E
W O R D ▪ E D D Y ▪ S A A B S
```

80

```
S H E L L O U T ▪ P S H A W S
C O M E I N T O ▪ I T A L I C
A P P E A L T O ▪ P E T U L A
R S T ▪ R Y E B E E R ▪ M D L
A T O Y ▪ R A N D ▪ L I F E
B O R E R S ▪ D I R ▪ A N I N
▪ ▪ S H I M ▪ G E S T U R E
▪ B L O O D Y ▪ M A K E M E
H O A R S E R ▪ A M A T ▪ ▪
A S S N ▪ D R Y ▪ S T A S I S
I S T O ▪ I H O P ▪ G E N E
R I N ▪ I S S U E R S ▪ A P E
D E A R T H ▪ B R A K E M A N
O S M O S E ▪ E T C E T E R A
S T E N O S ▪ T H E W O R K S
```

81

```
A T L A S ▪ L O L L ▪ I D L E
Q U A R T ▪ E D I E ▪ N O U N
U L C E R ▪ N O N O ▪ B O L D
A S E A ▪ F O R D T A U R U S
S A Y S N O ▪ Y A R N ▪ ▪ ▪
▪ ▪ E C O L ▪ R E C O A T
G R A N T I N A I D ▪ H A S H
A U T O ▪ O R R ▪ E T T A
P L O T ▪ T R U M A N S H O W
S E N A T E ▪ E A S Y ▪ ▪ ▪
▪ ▪ T E R M ▪ H E Y D A Y
B U S H L E A G U E ▪ A E R O
O N T O ▪ N U L L ▪ T H A N K
A D A M ▪ C L U E ▪ N O L I E
Z O N E ▪ E S T E ▪ T O T E D
```

82

```
S H A R P ▪ T R U R O ▪ B M W
S A B E R ▪ R A Z E D ▪ O A R
T H E P O S I T I V E ▪ A G E
S A T I R E S ▪ ▪ S A T I N
▪ ▪ N A T T I N E S S ▪ ▪
A M S ▪ T H E N E G A T I V E
C O T T A ▪ S R A ▪ U R A L
U T A H ▪ E L T O N ▪ T O L L
R I F E ▪ L E A ▪ S E N S E
A F F I R M A T I V E ▪ Y E N
▪ ▪ R H O D E S I A N ▪ ▪
A N T S Y ▪ ▪ A N T E N N A
B O O ▪ M R I N B E T W E E N
U S E ▪ E E R I E ▪ L E M A N
T E D ▪ S T A L L ▪ E L O P E
```

83

```
A S T A ▪ T A M E R ▪ G O G O
G L I B ▪ A M I L E ▪ A R I D
R O T S ▪ C A C H E ▪ L E N D
I T H I N K H A I L T O ▪ ▪
P H E N O L ▪ ▪ A S T I R
▪ ▪ T H E C H I E F H A S A
T A C H ▪ H A S N T ▪ P A N
O P I E ▪ C A R L O ▪ M E A T
O R R ▪ E L I D E ▪ A R C S
N I C E R I N G T O I T ▪ ▪
S L A N G ▪ ▪ P O I S E D
▪ J O H N F K E N N E D Y
E C H O ▪ A A R O N ▪ E L A N
B U O Y ▪ S T A K E ▪ E M M E
B E E S ▪ H O N O R ▪ S A S S
```

84

```
S P A S ▪ S C H W A ▪ M A R T
P U T T ▪ A H O O T ▪ A R E A
A S H Y ▪ T A B O O ▪ C M D R
C H E X O U T O F R E H A B ▪
E E N ▪ M P S ▪ ▪ L O G I N
D R A M A ▪ L A T S ▪ N R A
▪ ▪ A N O M A L Y ▪ E A C H
▪ K I X I T U P A N O T C H
M I N I ▪ T R I S E C T ▪ ▪
A L F ▪ W O K S ▪ ▪ T U L I P
E L E N A ▪ ▪ A P E ▪ O N E
▪ T R I X O F T H E T R A D E
J I N N ▪ A L I E N ▪ A T O P
A M A N ▪ R O D A N ▪ S H O E
R E L Y ▪ S E E D Y ▪ H E R D
```

85

```
T O P B R A S S ■ ■ G L O B S
S T A Y E D A T ■ L I A B L E
O H R E A L L Y ■ O L I V I A
N E T ■ D I A M O N D R I N G
G L I B ■ B A I Z E ■ ■ A D O
A L A R M ■ M E O W S ■ T E D
S O L O E D ■ S N O O K E R S
■ ■ W E B B ■ E L L A ■ ■ ■
P A I N T C A N ■ F I B E R S
I S M ■ S O L A R ■ D O P E Y
S T P ■ O L M O S ■ B I C S
C O L L A P S I B L E ■ S I T
O R I O L E ■ B I O S C O P E
P I E T E R ■ I N T A N D E M
O A S T S ■ ■ A S H I N E S S
```

86

```
A L E C S ■ H O P I ■ A S A P
M A R A T ■ E L L A ■ E T T E
F R I T O ■ A D U M B R A T E
M A K E W A V E S ■ O A T E R
■ ■ R I V E R ■ P A T E N S
T A K E N I N ■ H A R E M ■
S M O R G A S B O R D ■ O B I
A M O S ■ T E A R S ■ U T E S
R O K ■ C O N T I N E N T A L
■ A P A R T ■ Z I P C O D E
C U B E R S ■ T O P O L ■ ■
U S U A L ■ T E N S P E E D S
F E R R Y B O A T ■ E S T E E
F U R L ■ R O S A ■ E A T E R
S P A S ■ O N E L ■ S M A R T
```

87

```
D E S K ■ A S H E ■ S H O U T
E T O N ■ S W A T ■ H O R S E
E C H O ■ H A L T ■ E M C E E
■ H O W D O Y O U P L E A D
■ S I R E ■ ■ I V Y ■ ■ ■
K A T ■ R E D T A P E ■ B A H
I C I N G ■ I M P ■ A L T O
W H E R E D O E S I T H U R T
I O T A ■ R I G ■ O A S I S
S O O ■ P I L S N E R ■ H A Y
■ P A L ■ O L A Y ■ ■
■ W H A T L L Y O U H A V E
B R U T E ■ S A N D ■ N A V Y
B E G I N ■ A L A E ■ K N E E
S N O O T ■ T E N D ■ S E N T
```

88

```
I S L A M ■ C H A W ■ V E E P
T H U D S ■ H A L O ■ L I V E
C O L D S H O W E R ■ A S I S
H O L E ■ A S K E D ■ S E C T
■ ■ D A L E ■ G O I N T O
B O W O U T ■ B R A N C H ■
B L A N D ■ S L O M O ■ O P A
L I L ■ I N P O W E R ■ W E B
S N L ■ B E A T S ■ D W E E B
■ F E L O N S ■ P E A R L Y
P O L L E N ■ P U R R ■ ■
A H O Y ■ S I R E N ■ Z E R O
T A W S ■ I V O R Y T O W E R
C R E E ■ G E T S ■ O N E A L
H A R E ■ N Y S E ■ M E R R Y
```

89

```
E L G A R ■ M A G N A ■ T B A
L E A S E ■ A P R I L ■ I O N
F I R S T S T R I K E ■ G L O
■ ■ I R E ■ T E E T H E R
C O N S O N A N T S ■ A T R A
U N I T ■ I S A Y ■ I T S O K
B I G S H O T S ■ L A I C ■
E T H ■ O R A C L E S ■ R O D
■ T A P S ■ E S T I M A T E
P A S S E ■ A N A S ■ E P I C
A R C H ■ B O T T L E N E C K
S C H E M E R ■ I T O ■ ■
T A O ■ C A T C H P H R A S E
O N O ■ I D A H O ■ O A S I S
R E L ■ I S L E T ■ S H A R P
```

90

```
S O R E ■ A T D A W N ■ T S P
E R A S ■ B E R T H A ■ O Y L
N A H S ■ A C E T I C ■ L S U
S C R E E C H I N G H A L T ■
O L A ■ L I I ■ ■ S O R R E L
R E H A B ■ E M O ■ S L O M O
■ ■ V O L ■ I R V ■ E A S T
■ H O W L I N G W I N D ■
I M A C ■ D O C ■ S H E
S A R A S ■ N E E ■ E S S E X
M E D D L E ■ G S A ■ E V E
■ W H O O P I N G C R A N E S
P E A ■ O C T A N E ■ M A N O
E S T ■ P O S T O N ■ E T T U
P T S ■ S T O O G E ■ N E S T
```

91

```
SNOW  OUIJABOARD
KONA  ANNABELLEE
ITTY  HEAVYMETAL
PROB  UNWISE  OLA
PAPAW  DOTS  COTY
ERICA  IRS  CANOE
DECKHAND  CANARD
  WONG  SORT
UPSHOT  ACTITOUT
NAPES  MIA  BORNE
SCAN  YELL  SPITE
TEN  NINEPM  TNUT
OLDOAKTREE  HONE
PLEASEHOLD  ACER
SIXTHSENSE  TOSS
```

92

```
TABU  KEELS  ASCH
AVES  AUDIE  ROLE
PATENTRITE  TRUE
ASTRAY  FESTERED
STEIN  CYR  AMY
  DADA  RISER
HISS  IMAM  ASIDE
ASH  TEETERS  TIE
SPITE  LENO  SEEK
HYPER  SECT
  WAR  SPA  HICKS
PERMEATE  CALLIT
ITIS  BACKUPLITE
ETTU  ALAIN  EVER
SEEP  BENNY  DERN
```

93

```
JABBA  NAVE  APBS
ABOIL  AMER  WARP
BUDGETCUTS  ELIA
  HAIL  TAP  ACT
UPCAST  PETROCKS
NOHITTER  ZONE
SLUR  ERIK  NAGAT
ELM  BROMIDE  UTA
ROPER  SATE  WASP
  CLAP  RESTAREA
MAHOGANY  PANDAS
ADA  SRO  PORT
MENU  FIRSTMATES
BUGS  USES  ADORE
AXES  MEAT  CSPAN
```

94

```
PACT  ITCH  CHOPS
ATOI  SOHO  HABIT
CONVENTIONALITY
  TOTO  PER
APR  STDS  ALPACA
TIA  MATS  OLIOS
TERM  OTOE  TARAS
ERIE  RARE  TIETO
SCAN  ASYMMETRIC
TENABLE  SIB
  TRITE  DRIVER
NITWIT  DEMOTAPE
ONIONY  IRONEDON
SCORE  TESTRIDE
HANKS  SITE  SEW
```

95

```
RAMONES  MAILBAG
EPISODE  ESTELLE
DONTROCKTHEBOAT
FLIED  ONEON  TMS
LOCO  SNERT  LOOM
AGA  WADES  GOUDA
GYMSHOES  TOUTED
  LANDLORDS
SPRITE  ANALYSTS
THATS  APTLY  HIE
ROWS  ALPHA  TYNE
IND  ALLEE  SUSHI
KEEPYOURSHIRTON
EMAILED  LAMBERT
RELEASE  YESORNO
```

96

```
ENAMORS  MOPPETS
RILESUP  AREAMAP
ONEMOMENTINTIME
TEX  CORONETED
IMA  MUSHINESS
CONLON
INDIVIDUALISTIC
STRAITOFMESSINA
THERESNOIINTEAM
  TOSSUP
  BATWEIGHT  ADO
REACHINTO  KIR
ASSTUPIDASCANBE
SPIELED  PIEHOLE
HOLDERS  ESTATES
```

97

LOYAL · CAPS · KISS
IRENE · ASHE · ACME
DELTA · MEAN · TOOT
SOLIDREASONING
· PER · ERIE ·
LIQUIDASSET · SAY
USURPS · HIS · YALE
CAINE · FIN · HOWLS
CATS · HIP · HOGTIE
ICE · GASSTATIONS
· POSH · IMP ·
WHATSTHEMATTER
JAIL · LAIR · NAIVE
IDEL · EIRE · TUNES
METS · SLED · START

98

RACE · GUILE · BOAS
ULAN · INDIA · APSE
DISCONTENTISTHE
ETHAN · EEK · RISEN
· PIES · UFOS ·
FIRSTSTEPIN · OPA
ESAU · SEQ · NICHES
TELLA · DUB · CHAOS
ORLESS · IAM · ARNE
REY · THEPROGRESS
· CHOU · COIL ·
MADAM · RAH · NORMA
OFAMANORANATION
TRIP · OPERA · TORT
TOSS · DEATH · ETES

99

ATSEA · PLOW · JOGS
SITAR · RAVI · ERIE
SMIRK · OMEN · SAVE
FLABBERGASTED
SPF · NEE · LEERS
HONEST · QTIPS ·
ELENA · BUON · ATO
DISENFRANCHISED
SOS · LARK · ALTHO
· FOUNT · ISSUER
TIARA · ERA · DES
INDEFATIGABLE
RUDE · XING · AUNTS
EROS · ELLE · LATER
DENT · DEAD · LUSTS

100

JAPE · VANYA · NUTS
EWAN · ESTER · ONCE
FORGETTHEPASTEL
FLA · DOA · WEILL
MADEBYHANDEL
CLORIS · OOZE ·
HAUTE · CLOUDNINE
AIRS · BAKER · OVEN
ITSYBITSY · SLANG
· ETTA · REINER
MOTLEYCREWEL
PEREC · EDU · ERA
FLASHINTHEPANEL
FELT · SPRAY · IDEA
TESS · TRIBE · LLDS

101

ANTESUP · WRAPPED
TERMINI · HITTUNE
TRIESTE · INRANGE
AVER · ATIT · ASCAP
CID · ICINESS · HRS
KNICKKNACK · DEDE
SETON · MAINIDEA
· CORRUPTED ·
LOCOWEED · TAPES
ELLA · PADDYWHACK
ADE · ROLLOUT · SHY
PLATA · TERP · STEM
FITINTO · SPATULA
ONESTAR · AIRDROP
REDHOTS · LESSENS

102

LIAR · DIPLO · UNTO
ISLE · ELIEL · POOR
PATSYCLINE · SONG
SKATER · EARWIGS
· URIS · KNEELS ·
SNAPBEAN · NAP ·
LIZ · ADMIRALBYRD
INON · EGO · TRIO
DAVIDSOUTER · HEN
· NIN · HOPALONG
STENOS · TOJO ·
COWTOWN · NAPALM
ODIE · JIMMYHOFFA
AONE · OPIUM · EXAM
XMEN · BEADS · ZETA

103

```
SAUL THIN CHANT
WINE ROSE OILER
AREA ALEE INLAY
ROADSIDEDINER
MUSSELS  CASINO
STY MET MEG GEN
  FIRESIDECHAT
ALSO AHS  OTTO
RINGSIDESEAT
TEA PRY TNN PBS
YUPPIE  HANGOUT
  BEDSIDEMANNER
CRETE LOCO ACNE
ONAIR SOUR SHOW
WANTS AMTS HOSS
```

104

```
CRAG GOAD  PAVED
LULU ERNE AGILE
ADOS TATS LEAFY
NEUTRALZONE
    AUG TORTOLA
REVERSEOSMOSIS
HEY DIAL  ONTOP
EWER PLEBE GENE
DOLOR  CAMS  AER
DRIVEUPTHEWALL
ADDEDTO  RAN
   PARKRANGERS
ATARI TEAL OKIE
LOGON ENID REST
BOOZE RODS ASKS
```

105

```
 RAT DAME JAMES
PARR ABED ALIST
LIMO MUNI MOLLY
ADAYINDUBLIN
NED ASH LINEAGE
BRAGG ATEN  SOL
  ARUBA DRESSY
 JUNESIXTEENTH
BUNGEE CONVY
ALL DROP EASEL
DEVIATE PER OVA
  LEOPOLDBLOOM
TAPIR ALII ATKA
ADLAI SENT CHER
JOYCE TOGS YES
```

106

```
SOLD WARM MOTES
EVER ALIA TOOTH
REVENGEON ALPHA
ARISEOUTOF ABEL
   SENT FEELILL
DETERS MITRAL
OCHS SORES LET
CHE GETLOST IDO
SOL ALEAN PNIN
  EASIER SERGEI
TEASHOP ACRE
ENDS THEMESSAGE
AVOID INONESWAY
MOUSE LYRE OOZE
SITIN LATS NLER
```

107

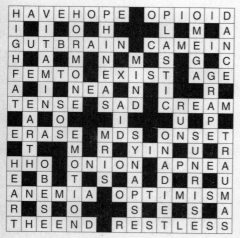

```
HAVEHOPE OPIOID
I I O H  L M A
GUTBRAIN CAMEIN
H A M N M S G C
FEMTO EXIST AGE
A I NEA N I R
TENSE SAD CREAM
A O I U P
ERASE MDS ONSET
T M R YIN U R
HHO ONION APNEA
E B T S A D R U
ANEMIA OPTIMISM
R S O S E S A
THEEND RESTLESS
```

108

```
JUMANJI LIONIZE
OPINION ACRONYM
GATELEG YANGTZE
GTO EYESORE EZR
ERSE SALVE KAYS
REINS RYE SERVO
SESAME ARKANSAN
   MINUSSIGN
STTERESA DEEPER
CHALK AFC STONE
REGS ATOLL HOLA
ERL EPOXIES RAD
AMISTAD MAESTRI
MINUTIA AVERAGE
SCENERY XEROXES
```

109

```
B I J O U   S E I K O   I R S
L O A M S   H A Z E L   V I E
U N M A N   A T O N E T I M E
  I E R   P R A D O   H E E D
M A S   C E E     R E D D Y
A N D   H A W G   F E R
I S A W E S A U H E S A W M E
D E L A W A R E P R O P H E T
S A Y S O N E S P R A Y E R S
    H U T   T R E K   E R E
E B E R T     I T S   L I Q
G A L A   A X O N S   J E N
B R A G A B O U T   J A D E D
D R T   M E U S E   A V I S O
F E E   P E T E R   M A N S E
```

110

```
T G I F   B R E W S   A S A N
A R L O   M A R I A   L E G O
P I L L O W T A L K   L O R I
S P O I L S     M I S C U E S
  G O D   S E A   A L L E Y
A S I S   P I N   A T E
B I C   S O F A   D E A C O N
B L A N K E T C O V E R A G E
A L L O Y S   T W I N   M R S
    F L Y   E E L   D E E T
L A U R A   A D D   S U R
E X H I B I T     S A L A D A
D I A L   S H E E T M U S I C
G A U L   L O R N A   T H E M
E L L S   E L E C T   H Y D E
```

111

```
U K E S   E M M E   C O M F Y
S E X Y   N E A L   A D O R E
E M I R   Z A G S   D E L I A
R O T A R Y D I A L   S T E T
    C U M E   A S S E S S
I N J U N E   B E M O A N
S E A S   S K E W E R   L I P
N A M E S   A G E   T R A D E
T R E   A R T U R O   A V O W
  S A L O O N   A P P A L S
C R I M E A     S K I S
R A V E   M U S C L E T O N E
O Z O N E   N O R A   A R C A
F O R D S   I S O N   R E A R
T R Y S T   T O D D   S O A P
```

112

```
P A C S   S L U R   D E F A T
I G O T   E I R E   A D E L E
T U B A   A L G A   N I N E S
H A B L A S I E D E U T S C H
    K N O T     A B S
A S H   I N H A S T E   A B E
S H A F T   R U E   E R A T
P A R L A T H E E N G L I S H
I N D Y   O U T     O S S I E
C A Y   S P E E D E R   E E R
    S P A   O D E S
P A R L E Z V O U S N O R S K
A L I E N   E R S E   D E A N
L O P E D   R E E L   A N T I
M E E T S   B O S S   S T E T
```

113

```
P A G O   A P E S   S U G A R
E R I K   P A V E   C N O T E
P A R A M E T E R   R S V P S
O L L Y O X E N F R E E
    S V E N   O A R I N G
Z S A   E S T   H M M   C A R
E P C O T   T E E   R I V A
S H E L O V E S Y O U Y E A H
T E T E   I T E   P A S H A
E R E   P A C   C R T   T O M
D E N T A L   L E O N
    I T S A M A D W O R L D
D O N D I   R A C O N T E U R
A V I A N   A N K A   E D N A
W A L L A   B A S K   S I N G
```

114

```
B L A T A N T   I N T A K E S
O I L Y G O O   C A I R E N E
W A L K I N A P A R T M E N T
L I K E N   T O N E S   P O T
I S I S   F E L T S   B A B E
N O D   A R E A S   B A S L E
E N D U R E   R E H A S H E S
    I D L E D   E A T S A
W A N D E R E D   T H I R S T
H A G E N   L I M E S   P O R
O M A R   O T T O S   D E S I
I I S   S M A S H   B U Y U P
S L I P P E R Y A S A N E E L
I N D I A N A   W E L C O M E
T E E N T S Y   K L E E N E X
```

115

```
M O V E S A S I D E ■ A L E S
I N E R T G A S E S ■ L O T T
D A N G E R L I N E ■ P A R E
S I T ■ L E A S T ■ R A N U P
T R I M M E R ■ ■ P A C E R S
■ ■ R O S Y S C E N A R I O
H O B S ■ C H O R D ■ ■ C A N
A H A ■ R E A U M U R ■ A N T
N I L ■ A P P L E ■ ■ O R S O
G O A C R O S S T O W N ■ ■
A R C H E S ■ ■ O V A T I O N
R I L E D ■ L E P E R ■ O N O
I V A N ■ C O V A R I A N C E
N E V E ■ T R I P L E B I L L
G R A Y ■ R E L A Y R A C E S
```

116

```
G R I D ■ D A T E ■ S T A L E
A E R O ■ O M A R ■ T I M E X
B L O C ■ R A V I ■ R E E V E
S Y N T H E T I C F A B R I C
■ ■ R A M ■ ■ O N A ■ ■
A R T I F I C I A L G R A S S
M O U N T ■ A N N I E ■ L E E
A R T E ■ O P T I C ■ M E N D
T E T ■ B U R R O ■ L O U S E
I M I T A T I O N B U T T E R
■ ■ A R R ■ ■ A S H ■ ■
C O U N T E R F E I T B I L L
H O R D E ■ E A R L ■ A L O E
U N S E R ■ E R I E ■ L I N T
M A A M S ■ L E N D ■ L A G S
```

117

```
A T B A T ■ G O L F S ■ I C E
M O O L A ■ A W E E K ■ S O D
B R A I N F R E E Z E ■ O L D
E S T ■ G I R D S ■ T O S A Y
R O S E L L E ■ A C D C ■ ■
■ ■ M E L T E D C H E E S E
W H A M S ■ A I R Y ■ L I D
R O B E ■ M A S S E ■ D E L I
A U S ■ S A L E ■ A I S L E
P R E T T Y P L E A S E ■ ■
■ N O R A ■ S C H M E A R
G O T T A ■ T O P I C ■ L S U
A P E ■ F L O R I D A K E Y S
Z E E ■ E A G L E ■ N O N E T
E L S ■ S T A Y S ■ S P A T S
```

118

```
M S N B C ■ R E I D ■ E W A N
U H A U L ■ E D N A ■ R A T E
C A N Y O U H E A R M E N O W
H M O ■ S P A N S ■ I N E P T
■ A E O N ■ E N T O ■ ■
T E S T I N G O N E T W O ■
A V I A N ■ I S A Y ■ R N A
M E N D ■ J A N E T ■ Z I O N
E R A ■ S O C K ■ B O N G O
■ I S T H I S T H I N G O N
■ T E N D ■ W A G E ■ ■
C H A I N ■ T A I L S ■ A F T
H E L L O H E L L O H E L L O
A R A L ■ A S T I ■ O N E A M
D O N S ■ S T A T ■ T E X T S
```

119

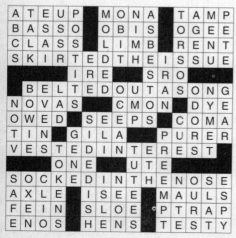

```
A T E U P ■ M O N A ■ T A M P
B A S S O ■ O B I S ■ O G E E
C L A S S ■ L I M B ■ R E N T
S K I R T E D T H E I S S U E
■ ■ I R E ■ S R O ■ ■
B E L T E D O U T A S O N G
N O V A S ■ C M O N ■ D Y E
O W E D ■ S E E P S ■ C O M A
T I N ■ G I L A ■ P U R E R
V E S T E D I N T E R E S T
■ ■ O N E ■ U T E ■ ■
S O C K E D I N T H E N O S E
A X L E ■ I S E E ■ M A U L S
F E I N ■ S L O E ■ P T R A P
E N O S ■ H E N S ■ T E S T Y
```

120

```
T R O T T E R ■ M A C H E T E
R I V I E R A ■ E S S A Y E R
I C E L A N D ■ S L A V I N G
C E R T ■ S I A M ■ E N T O
K A L ■ S T A G E F R I G H T
K R O N E ■ T U R R E T ■ ■
N O R E A S O N ■ E L M I R A
E N D O W E R ■ I D E A M E N
E I S N E R ■ S T A N D P A T
■ ■ L E V I E S ■ T E R S E
I N C I D E N T A L S ■ E S A
D O U G ■ L A M A ■ S C U T
T O S H I B A ■ E N S N A R E
A S H T R A Y ■ S C O O T E R
G E Y S E R S ■ S E A B E D S
```

Vocabulary Notes

PUZZLE #40

33-Across. Val Kilmer, a part-Cherokee actor who has played rockers Jim Morrison and Elvis Presley, took on the role of Batman in 1995. The part has also been played by Adam West (TV series in 1966), Michael Keaton (films in 1989 and 1992), George Clooney (1997) and Christian Bale (2005). For sheer length, this list of actors doesn't match the roster of James Bond portrayers, but it's worth trotting out as a trivial-factoid item among movie buffs.

37-Across. *Salad* is full of *salt*, etymologically speaking. When citizens of old Rome dined on vegetables in a briny dressing, they called it *herba salata*. The culinary use of salt is also reflected in *salami, sausage, salsa* and *sauce*. A Roman soldier's stipend allowed him to buy this precious commodity (in those days salt was a unique preserver and enhancer of foods); hence the word *salary*. Even in today's idiom, if you earn your pay you are *worth your salt*.

40-Across. A *coven* (pronounced to rhyme with "oven") is a group of witches— technically 13 of them, although we suppose that if 12 or 14 witches showed up for a meeting, it would still be a coven. The word comes from the Latin *convenire*, to agree. Ironically, it is a relative of *convent*.

30-Down. Monica Seles was the world's number-one female tennis player in 1993 before a deranged German fan stabbed her in the back. Her physical and emotional recovery took two years, and she was never again as dominant an athlete. But we lovers of wordplay will always regard her fondly, as she is the rare bearer of a palindromic surname. (A few others are musician Yoko *Ono*, former CIA director George *Tenet* and actress Daryl *Hannah*.)

PUZZLE #41

23-Across. *Taboo* (meaning "forbidden") was imported directly into the English language by Captain James Cook, who encountered it in 1777 in the Friendly Islands (now called Tonga, where the word is spelled *tabu*).

26-Across. *Atari* is the company that produced Pong, arguably the world's first video game. The company was founded in the United States in 1972 by Nolan Bushnell, who got the name *Atari* from the Japanese game go; it's a term used by an attacking player, equivalent to the word *check* in chess.

43-Across. A *vicar* is a deputy pastor taking a turn for the regular one (hence *vicarious*, "experienced secondhand") and he really ought to sit in *wicker*, which comes from the same stem (*weik*, "to bend or turn," as a willow twig does). In the same etymological vein, a *wicket* is literally a "door that turns"; a *weak* person is someone who's too pliable; and a *week* is the turning over of days.

46-Across. *Heckle* can mean a comb with long metal teeth for separating strands of flax. The word is related to *hackles*, the feathers on a rooster's back or the hairs on a dog's neck that stand up when the animal is riled. Hence, to heckle a guy is to tease him until his neck hairs rise.

PUZZLE #42
19-Across. Negation is frequently expressed through the root *ne-*, "not." In addition to simple cognates *nil, nothing, null, nix, neither* and *never* we have *naughty* (behaving in ways that add up to nothing), *annihilate* (to reduce to nothing), *negligee* (which covers almost nothing), *renegade* (one who *negates* or *reneges* on something or someone) and *nepenthe* (a remedy for pain, literally "no grief"). Even the word *nice*, which now usually means "pleasant," once meant "foolish" and is a disguised twin of *nescient* (ignorant, literally "not knowing").

27-Across. The *Amish* speak a form of German commonly called "Pennsylvania Dutch"—a misapprehension of *Deutsch*, the German-language word for "German."

27-Down. You can host some skull-cracking spelling bees with Aztec words like *Nahuatl* (their language), *Tenochtitlan* (their chief city), *Quetzalcoatl* and *Huitzilopochtli* (two of their gods), and *Cuauhtémoc* (their last emperor).

50-Down. One of our standard office dictionaries calls the color *ecru* "a grayish to pale yellow or light grayish-yellowish brown." How's that for wishy-washy? Another dictionary just calls it "beige." The word comes from Latin *crudus*—crude or unbleached, as linen.

PUZZLE #43
62-Across. *Sitars* and *guitars* are country cousins of the old-as-the-Greek-hills *kithara*, a stringed thing resembling a lyre. In India, the sitar is considered a classical instrument. It has something like 19 strings, some above a board of movable frets and some below for sympathetic resonance. One reference says of it dryly, "It is rather difficult to tune the instrument."

10-Down. *Kiln* may sound a bit exotic, but just like *cook* and *culinary* it goes back to the kitchen. In Italian the word for "kitchen" is the same as a word for "stove," *cucina*. However, no cooking of food is done in a kiln, whose traditional purpose is to dry, harden or burn things (e.g., wood into charcoal). You've heard about the careless potter who lost his job, right? He got fired.

29-Down. *Etui* (pronounced the way Elmer Fudd would say "a tree") is one of those words more common in crosswords than in everyday life. An ornamental case for keeping feminine valuables, it isn't often packed along by today's cellphone-toting go-getters. But once upon a time, a lady wore her *etui* at the waist upon her *chatelaine* (a set of chains for keys and accessories). The word is related to *study* and to *stir* in its meaning as "prison," because the box keeps its contents carefully under guard.

PUZZLE #44

64-Across. If you think *panic* might be connected to the Greek *Pan,* you're right. The goat-legged god of woods and fields was considered the source of mysterious, scary noises deep in the forest. Many a lone traveler felt spooked in the wild, suspecting Pan of playing tricks on the mind. To this day, when there's a case of mass hysteria, as in the face of financial collapse, we invoke the name of this hybrid deity.

5-Down. In Shakespeare's *The Taming of the Shrew,* the character Lucentio says at one point, "Basta, content thee," meaning "Enough already!" It's a common exclamation in both Spanish and Italian, where the verb *bastare* means "to be sufficient."

7-Down. The *Goths* and the *Vandals* were Germanic tribes responsible for the sacking and ruination of the Roman Empire; their names became synonymous with *barbarians.* This pejorative sense was retained by Renaissance artisans who viewed medieval architecture as dark and primitive. *Gothic* elements like gargoyles and demons contributed to a weird, supernatural mood that has prevailed in horror stories from Mary Shelley's *Frankenstein* to Stephen King's *Carrie.* A cultish preoccupation with death and violence has earned some postpunk rock music the appellation *gothic.* A lighter side of the macabre is represented by *The Addams Family.*

PUZZLE #45

16-Across. The sport of fencing involves three different weapons: *foil, épée* (French for "sword") and *saber.*

55-Across. Sometime, somewhere, lived a gossipy woman named *Yente* (connected to *gentle*) who unflatteringly became the eponym of a blabbermouth. Besides *buttinsky,* synonyms include *snoop, busybody, meddler* and *Nosy Parker.*

48-Down. *Stentor* was a Greek herald in the Trojan War whose voice, according to Homer, was as loud as those of fifty men. He was so proud of his forte that he challenged Hermes, the crier of the gods, to a shouting contest. He lost (and died in the process) but his name lives on. *Stentorian* means resonant and booming in oratory.

51-Down. Though called a mountain ash in the United States, the *rowan* is actually in the rose family, not the ash family. Its name relates to *red*, the color of its berries. The European rowan has a long tradition in magic and mythology. Credited with protective powers against witchcraft and misfortune, its wood was sometimes carried on ships to ward off storms and kept in houses to discourage lightning. Druids' staffs, magicians' wands and dowsers' rods have been made of its branches.

PUZZLE #46

14-Across. Imported from Africa and still practiced in parts of the West Indies and the southeastern United States, *obeah* is a religion involving witchcraft, sorcery, and animistic fetishes. *Voodoo* is a similar religion, and *hoodoo* is its magical power, which allows a believer to tap supernatural forces in everyday life. For example, a *mojo* is a small bag of herbs, powders and/or personal knickknacks worn under the clothes and believed to bring good luck.

16-Across. Moisés Alou is the son of big-leaguer Felipe Alou, who became a member of baseball's first all-brother outfield when on September 15, 1963, he and his younger siblings Jesús and Matty played side by side for the San Francisco Giants. (This didn't happen too often because the Giants had a regular center fielder by the name of Willie Mays.)

42-Down. *Bemuse* (to perplex) and *amuse* (to entertain) are not directly related to *muse* (divine inspiration). Oddly enough, the first two come from a word for *muzzle;* the old French verb *muser* means "to stand with one's nose in the air." Think of a dog having lost a scent, sniffing the breeze with a raised snout— that's literally *amusement.* The inspirational *muse* comes from Greek *mousa* and is connected to *music, memory* and *mind.* If you want your vocabulary to include the names of the nine Greek Muses, here they are: Calliope (epic poetry), Clio (history), Erato (love poetry), Euterpe (music), Melpomene (tragedy), Polymnia (hymns), Terpsichore (dance), Thalia (comedy) and Urania (astronomy).

PUZZLE #47

24-Across. An *ansa* is a curved handle, as on a vase. Among astronomers it can mean either of the projecting ends of a ring of Saturn. That *ansa* has this outer-space definition while being an anagram of *NASA* is—well, it's meaningless, but we had to point it out.

70-Across. On the subject of wordplay, when you take a term like *goon* and read it as *go on*, you're indulging in a *heteronym* (literally "different name"). A heteronym can be a single word with two different pronunciations, like *bow* (rhyming with *snow* when it means "looped knot," rhyming with *how* when it means "front of a ship"). More inventive heteronyms may employ multiple words and altered spacing, such as *amiable together* and *Am I able to get her?*

2-Down. An *augur* is a prophet and an *auger* is a bore. They're unrelated although homophonic. In ancient Rome the *augur* interpreted signs and omens in an official capacity. The root *aug-* means "increase," and an augur was expected to gain more favor from the gods; related words are *augment, auxiliary* and *auction*. As for the drill, *auger* really should be *nauger* (an old English word akin to *nave*), but people misheard "a nauger" as "an auger." The same faulty separation has brought us *apron*, which was originally *napron* (think of *napkin*), but people wrongly heard "a napron" as "an apron." In the formation of language, error plays a role.

PUZZLE #48
16-Across. These days your *rival*, if you have one, is liable to be a contestant in sports or affairs of the heart. But the conflict runs deeper. It was people sharing the same *river* and fighting over the water that brought this word into the language.

35-Across. Someone you can't stand is a *bête noire* (in French, literally "black beast"). Such a person is *anathema* to you. You find such an individual *odious* or *insufferable*.

6-Down. Continuing in the same vein, there's a British slang word, *lardy-dardy*, that implies excessive elegance, and some think *la-di-da* comes from that. Others believe *la-di-da* is an imitation of the affected speech of some stuck-up person or class. People putting on airs may seem *hoity-toity, grandiose* or *highfalutin*.

11-Down. A direct equivalent of *evildoer* is *malefactor*. When J. K. Rowling gave the name *Malfoy* to a character in the Harry Potter books, she was practically naming him "Bad Guy."

PUZZLE #49
15-Across. *Ague* is related to *acute* and means a fever in which periods of sweating and chills alternate—not much fun. The poet Byron used *ague* in his poem "Written After Swimming from Sestos to Abydos," rhyming the word with "plague you."

9-Down. If you lightly brush the leaves of a *mimosa*, they may contract and fold—a reaction that seems to imitate animal behavior. This plant is a *mime*. Its yellowish color inspired the name of a cocktail drink of champagne mixed with orange juice.

10-Down. An *adage* is a pithy saying that conveys a general truth, such as "Good things come in small packages." A *proverb* is similar and may involve an illustrative tale, such as the story of the tortoise and the hare, which culminates in the proverb "Slow and steady wins the race." A *maxim*, like a *motto*, usually has to do with codes of conduct—words to live by. Well-conceived and writerly maxims may be called *aphorisms*: "He that falls in love with himself will have no rivals" is an example from *Poor Richard's Almanack* by Benjamin Franklin. A particularly witty saying is an *epigram*, which borders on a *quip*, such as Oscar Wilde's "Seriousness is the only refuge of the shallow" and Dorothy Parker's "Brevity is the soul of lingerie." When a true saying gets overused, it becomes an *old saw*.

PUZZLE #50

37-Across. *Tepid* means *lukewarm*—but where did *luke* come from? It turns out that *luke* is simply a modern spelling of Middle English *leuke*, which means "barely warm." Therefore *lukewarm* means "barely-warm warm," and if that's not a repetitive redundancy, we'll have some *frozen gelato*.

60-Across. *Yen* comes from China where the original form of the word meant "a craving for opium." Hence a *yen* should be as powerful as an *addiction*, though it usually connotes a less intense *yearning*. A deep-down emotional longing may make you *pine*. An *itch* is more superficial and an *urge* more transitory. The etymology of *ache* suggests imitation of a groaning sound.

44-Down. Is there a person named Jean lurking behind the invention of *blue jeans*? No—but the story is interesting anyway. The material *denim* was developed in Nimes, France, and hence was *de Nimes*. The trousers made of this material were first created in Genoa, Italy, and hence were *genovese*. The pants were made specifically for the Genoese navy, whose sailors needed rough clothing that could be worn wet or dry. Their jeans were laundered by dragging them behind the ship in large nets; the seawater usually bleached them white. In the United States, jeans weren't much known until 1872 when they were popularized by entrepreneur Levi Strauss; hence *Levis*.

PUZZLE #51

28-Across. *Ankle* comes from an Indo-European root meaning "to bend" and is related to *angle*, which in turn was an Old English word for "fish hook." There's a hook-shaped area in Germany's Jutland peninsula called *Angeln*, and its old inhabitants were the *Angles* who crossed the North Sea and settled in Britain, donating their name to *England*. When you express yourself with *body English*, the most appropriate thing to twist around would be your *ankle*.

31-Across. *Enormous* literally means "out of the norm," and *norm* goes back through the Latin *norma* ("rule") to *gno* (the root for "to know"), which gives us *ignorance, diagnosis, cunning* and *ken*. So *enormous* originally applied to something strange, outlandish, extraordinary, never-seen-before, new to all knowledge—but not necessarily huge. The root meaning of the word is preserved in *enormity*, which can mean an outrageous extreme of immorality (as in "the *enormity* of your crimes"), although it can also be a simple synonym of *enormousness*, the quality of being immense.

PUZZLE #52

57-Across. A person *stunned* is one who's been *thunderstruck*—i.e., hit upside the head by that loud, lightning-bolt-throwing Norse god named *Thor*. In Latin, *tonare* meant "to thunder," and *extonare* "to leave thunderstruck," leading to our *astonishment*. You can hear the echo in *detonate* and *tornado*. The Swedish word for *thunder* is *tordon*, literally "Thor's din." The German word is *Donner*, like the reindeer teamed with Blitzen. As you may know, *Thursday* is *Thor's day*; in Italian that's *giovedi* (the Roman thunder god was Jupiter, or *Jove*).

10-Down and 11-Down. A serendipitous pairing. To *desire* is to want the stars—or at any rate, to hope for what they'll bring (from the phrase *de sidere*, "from the stars"). A good vocabulary word is *sidereal*, "pertaining to the stars." In the TV sci-fi cartoon *The Jetsons*, the family dog is *Astro*. An *asterisk* is, of course, a small printed star. A *disaster* occurs when the stars are against you—which certainly seemed to be true for *Stella* in the Tennessee Williams play *A Streetcar Named Desire*.

61-Down. In baseball *ERA* stands for *earned run average*. An earned run is scored without benefit of defensive errors. A pitcher's performance is measured by taking the total of earned runs scored against him, dividing that by the total of innings pitched, and multiplying by nine. So if a pitcher allows exactly one earned run per inning, his ERA is 9.0 (not considered good); if he allows three runs per nine innings, his ERA is 3.0 (pretty decent); if a pitcher's lifetime ERA is under 2.0, he's probably Hall-of-Fame material.

PUZZLE #53

6-Across. Your *thigh* got its name from being the thickest part of your leg. The Indo-European root *teu* means "to swell," and it's found in *tumor* and *tumult* (from a swelling up of sound). A *tumulus* is a mound, especially an ancient burial mound. A *tomb* was originally just a thick pile of earth.

44-Across. *Tater* is a word that's undergone *aphesis*—the gradual disappearance of an initial syllable or vowel. Other examples are *squire* shortened from *esquire, possum* from *opossum* and *skeeter* from *mosquito*.

58-Across. The root *skand-* ("to climb") gives us not only *ascend* and *descend* but *scan, scansion, transcend* and, oddly enough, *scandal*—from Greek *skandalon*, or "stumbling block." In other words, a *scandal* is something you have to climb over—to *scale*. The root also exists in *slander*, a maligning of one's character that can be hard to *transcend*.

1-Down. When *slander* occurs in print, it's *libel*. This word is from Latin *libellus*, "little book." In turn, *liber* is "book, paper, parchment" and originally meant "the inner bark of trees." It's probably a derivative of Indo-European *leub-*, "to strip, to peel," leading us to *leaf*.

PUZZLE #54
20-Across. *Claptrap* is phony, ingratiating speech (of a kind originally designed by actors to gain a cheap round of applause). Synonyms include *bombast, fustian, hokum* and *bunk*.

22-Across. *Capo* (pronounced KAH-po) means "head" in Italian, a language in which *capofamiglia* is the head of the family and *capoufficio* is the boss of the office. There's also *capotasto*, literally "head of the fingerboard" on a fretted instrument. Today a guitarist might use a *capo* (pronounced KAY-po), a sliding bar that can be moved to a desired fret and pinned down, changing the key.

44-Across. *Iris* is a colorful flower, a rainbow (and its goddess) and the colored part of the eye. The *pupil* of the eye, meanwhile, gets its name from Latin *pupilla* ("little girl, doll"), from the tiny image of oneself seen reflected in another person's eyeball.

1-Down. Why is a *cinch* something easy to do? It comes from *cingulum*, Latin for "girdle," and its primary meaning is still "a girth for a saddle or pack." Because it offers a sure hold, it represents something in life easy to grasp. *Precinct* and *succinct* are related—and so is *shingles*, the viral outbreak that typically wraps around the body's torso; *cincture* and *surcingle* are both encircling bands.

PUZZLE #55
1-Across. *Tiramisu* may have liquor in it, but it gets its name (the Italian phrase *tira mi su*, "pick me up") from its perky caffeine content. Typically the dessert is made with ladyfingers, espresso coffee, mascarpone cheese, eggs, cream, sugar, marsala wine and cocoa.

15-Down. When we say something is *true*, we mean it's just like a *tree*. Seriously—the word *true* goes back to an ancient Sanskrit root *dreu-*, meaning "wood." Long ago, when people wanted to say something was factual, they compared it to the firmness of a tree; think of the saying "solid as an oak." The same root (to make optimum use of the metaphor) is in *Druids*, the priestly Celts of ancient Britain who amassed great knowledge, professed magical powers and held certain groves to be sacred. The root is also found in *trust, tryst, durable, betrothed* and all words ending with -*dendron*.

27-Down. In *The Lone Ranger*, the radio serial that began in 1933, the title character, named Reid, was the last survivor of a team of Texas Rangers ambushed by a baddie named Butch Cavendish. Reid was rescued by the Indian *Tonto*, whose name was supposed to mean "wild one" in the tongue of his native *Potawatomi* tribe (never mind that the Potawatomi were not from the Southwest). Tonto called the Lone Ranger *kemo sabe* ("trusty scout," according to the scriptwriter; other theories abound). On TV, the Lone Ranger was played by Clayton Moore and Tonto by Jay Silverheels. The Lone Ranger's horse was *Silver*; Tonto's was *Scout*.

PUZZLE #56

29-Across. *Canter* is a contraction of *Canterbury gallop*, referring to the pace of pilgrims riding horses to Canterbury to visit the shrine of England's famous martyr Thomas à Becket. Among equestrians, four horse gaits are recognized; in increasing order of speed, they are *walk, trot, canter* and *gallop*. Only the walk and the gallop are natural to horses in the wild. The trot and the canter have been developed in horses through breeding and training.

26-Down. A *boon* is a good thing. As an adjective meaning "convivial" (usually in the phrase *boon companion*), it's connected to French *bon* ("good") and to words like *bonny, bonus, bonanza, debonair* and *bonhomie* ("a pleasant, affable disposition"). But as a noun meaning "a benefit or blessing," it stems from Old English *bannan* ("to summon, proclaim"), ultimately related to *ban* and *bandit*, not such good things.

29-Down. The Latin *caedere* ("to cut, to strike") gives us *scissors, chisel, excise, concise, decide, caesura* (a pause or break) and even *cement*, from the rough-cut stone rubble used to form mortar. (We could suggest that if you're having trouble with words like *he, she, we* and *us,* you need to firm them up with an application of *pronoun cement*—but that would make a joke of a *pronouncement.*)

40-Down. The *haj* (also *hajj* and *hadj*) is a Muslim's pilgrimage to Mecca. A pilgrim who has made the journey is a *hajji* (or *haji* or *hadji*). The novel referred to in the clue is by Leon Uris (himself a frequent visitor to crossword diagrams).

PUZZLE #57

9-Across. This word defined as "tricks" once meant "old stuff." *Antic* derives from Italian *antico* ("antique"). Ancient murals unearthed around Rome depicted weird and fantastic things that made people associate *antique* with *grotesque,* and eventually someone's wild and crazy behavior also got called *antic*. As a noun, the singular *antic* can mean "clown," such as the character of the fool in *King Lear*; the plural *antics* can mean "capers" or "monkeyshines."

8-Down. You might think the *sternum* (your breastbone) would have something to do with *stern* (your rear) but the word comes from the root *ster-* ("to spread") and is related to *strew, straw, structure* and *industry*. Anyhow, the breastbone's connected to the rib bones and comes in three parts named top-to-bottom the *manubrium,* the *gladiolus,* and the *xiphoid process*—which isn't the kind of active process you might think but just a blade-shaped projection (from Greek *xiphos,* "straight sword"). Folks, you can't get more valuable knowledge anywhere than you glean from these humble notes.

14-Down. A *serenade* (stereotypically sung by a lovestruck suitor under the window of his would-be sweetheart) may itself be *serene,* but the original allusion was to the calm, still condition of the open air in which the song was performed. Influenced over time by *sera* (Italian for "evening"), the sense of a twilight setting was enhanced. To be contrasted is the word *shivaree,* which is a noisy mock-serenade replete with the raucous banging of pots and pans, performed by revelers for the benefit of honeymooning newlyweds. *Shivaree* is Americanized from the French *charivari,* which is thought to come from a Late Latin word for "headache."

35-Down. *On the lam* is pure U.S. slang and nobody's sure where it originated. One guess is that it's connected to *lambaste,* evoking the term *beat it.* Not that anyone but an addicted anagrammatist would care, but *on the lam* can be rearranged to spell *methanol.*

PUZZLE #58

8-Down. Niccolo Machiavelli (1469–1527) was an Italian statesman and political philosopher whose book *Il Principe* ("The Prince") discussed at length the relationship between rulers and the ruled. Because he advocated a politics of expediency to unify the chaotic city-states of his time, he has become associated with an immoral ends-justifying-the-means mind-set. This is overly simplistic, but today the word *Machiavellian* suggests the use of cunning and deceit in the service of political gain.

24-Down. *Abracadabra* was a magic word in Latin, relating to *Abraxas,* a cabalistic name for a supreme god. The word was supposed to be written on an amulet with the letters in a pyramid and worn around the neck to ward off evil. Over time the word *abracadabra* came to mean "foolish or unintelligible talk," a synonym for *mumbo jumbo* (itself a corruption of a Mandingo word, now lost, for a certain idol).

45-Down. Russian-born author Vladimir Nabokov pretty much invented the word *nymphet* (a sexually precocious pubescent girl) in his 1955 novel *Lolita,* in which the barely teenaged Dolores Haze (nicknamed "Lolita") is seduced by an older man named Humbert Humbert.

PUZZLE #59

17-Across. There's no corn in *corned beef*, unless you count the salt. The Old English word *corn* originally meant grain of any kind. In America it now means only corn on the cob, but in England it has referred to wheat and in Scotland to oats. In any case, meats were often marinated in brine, and the coarse salt used in the pickling evidently had a grainy look, hence *corned*. The same root is in *kernel, grain, granule, granite, grenade* and *pomegranate*.

63-Across. A *picaro* may fairly be called a *vagabond* (a rambler and a rover) but not a *hobo* (a tramp or a bum). Specifically, he's a kind of adventurer who lives by his wits—often in a roguish way. In literature there's an entire genre for the *picaresque novel*—a satiric tale of a rascal's escapades in a society depicted as corrupt. This kind of novel originated in Spain, with *Lazarillo de Tormes* (1554, author anonymous) an early example. Le Sage's *Gil Blas* (1715) and Defoe's *Moll Flanders* (1722) were later developments. A *picaro,* sometimes rendered *picaroon,* may well have carried a *pike* and inspired fits of *pique*; all stem from a root meaning "to prick or pierce."

25-Down. Sculptor Alexander Calder is generally credited with inventing the *mobile* in 1931 (some say the name was suggested by Marcel Duchamp). Typically hanging and making use of principles of equilibrium, the art form is also called *kinetic sculpture*. The word root in *mobile* is also in *move*. But in case you're wondering, the city of *Mobile,* in Alabama, has nothing to do with any of this. The city's name refers to the *Mobile* Indians (sometimes spelled *Maubila*) living along the Gulf of Mexico when Europeans arrived and settled. The *Mobilian* language was spoken as a lingua franca from Florida to Texas, and European explorers like de Soto were obliged to hire Mobilian-speaking guides.

60-Down. *Gig* can mean a bouncy two-wheeled carriage, a ship captain's personal boat, a spear for catching fish or frogs, a spinning top, a three-digit selection in a numbers game, a military demerit and a professional job (especially a booking for musicians). For us, this *gig* as glossarists has been a veritable giggle.